Theatrical Consciousness

Theatrical Consciousness

The Actor's Mind in Russian Modernism

✦

Alisa Ballard Lin

NORTHWESTERN UNIVERSITY PRESS
EVANSTON, ILLINOIS

Northwestern University Press
www.nupress.northwestern.edu

Publication of this book was made possible, in part, by a grant from the First Book Subvention Program of the Association for Slavic, East European, and Eurasian Studies.

Printed in the United States of America

10 9 8 7 6 5 4 3 2 1

Library of Congress Cataloging-in-Publication Data

Names: Lin, Alisa Ballard, author.
Title: Theatrical consciousness : the actor's mind in Russian modernism / Alisa Ballard Lin.
Description: Evanston, Illinois : Northwestern University Press, 2025. | Includes bibliographical references and index.
Identifiers: LCCN 2024061491 | ISBN 9780810148437 (paperback) | ISBN 9780810148444 (cloth) | ISBN 9780810148451 (ebook)
Subjects: LCSH: Actors—Soviet Union—History. | Actors—Psychology. | Acting—Psychological aspects. | Theater—Soviet Union—History—20th century. | Modernism (Aesthetics)—Russia.
Classification: LCC PN2724 .L49 2025 | DDC 792.02/8094709041—dc23/eng/20250131
LC record available at https://lccn.loc.gov/2024061491

For Eden

CONTENTS

ILLUSTRATIONS

ACKNOWLEDGMENTS

I begin with my immense gratitude for Caryl Emerson, my graduate school advisor and continued mentor, who has read parts of this book dozens, if not hundreds, of times and has always given the most astute and encouraging of feedback. Caryl's expert intellectual guidance has been critical to my career in academia, and for that I am extremely grateful.

Boris Wolfson, Olga Peters Hasty, Michael Wachtel, and Kat Hill all gave useful and constructive criticism on an early version of this book. From my time at Princeton, I am also grateful to Devin Fore, Khristina Gonzalez, Amanda Irwin Wilkins, Genevieve Creedon, and the late Tim Vasen for shaping my intellectual (and theatrical!) journey.

To reach back even earlier in my career, Lynne deBenedette, Svetlana Evdokimova, Abbott (Tom) Gleason, Vladimir Golstein, Spencer Golub, Alexander Levitsky, and Michal Oklot of Brown University were all critical to my early development as a scholar and my choice of career. I am especially grateful for Spencer's guest lecture on the Russian theater for Volodya and Tom's class in my first semester at Brown, as this lecture—and the subsequent courses I took with Spencer—has sparked a lifetime of theatrical-philosophical inquiry.

I am so lucky to have ended up at the Ohio State University, where numerous wonderful colleagues have supported my journey. Many thanks to my two department chairs during the writing of this book, Yana Hashamova and Angela Brintlinger, who both oversaw institutional support of this project. Philip Gleissner is an especially prized colleague who has been an incredible source of friendship and support, both personal and intellectual.

This book has been developed and written over a number of years, and in that time, many excellent scholars have generously offered helpful comments and guidance. Maria Ignatieva, Anna Muza, Dassia N. Posner, Maria Shevtsova, Galin Tihanov, and Julia Vaingurt have all given feedback on portions of the manuscript. Tatiana Dzhurova, Nikolai Pesochinsky, Randall Poole, and Rose Whyman answered small but critical questions. I am especially grateful to Dassia for her mentorship and her role in bringing together communities of Russian theater scholars. In developing this book project, I also benefited from conversations with Harvey Young and Scott Magelssen at the Mid-America Theatre Conference Pitch Your Book session. I am grateful, too, for the wisdom of the writing sessions led by Debra Caplan at the Mellon School of Theater and Performance Research.

The Fulbright Program and the National Endowment for the Humanities both supported versions of this project, and I am thankful for their funding. The final stages of this project were made possible in part thanks to the Title VI National Resource Center grant from the US Department of Education held by the Center for Slavic, East European and Eurasian Studies at the Ohio State University. I was part of a wonderfully supportive small group in the National Center for Faculty Development and Diversity's Faculty Success Program in fall 2021, as well as incredible small groups on writing and productivity overseen by Laura Premack in 2022. The School of Russian and Asian Studies, specifically Renee Stillings and Andrei Nesterov, helped make some final archival research and procuring of images possible in post-2022 Russia. I am grateful to Princeton University Library Special Collections, the Harvard Theatre Collection, University of Notre Dame Rare Books and Special Collections, the Russian State Archive of Literature and Art, and the Bakhrushin Theatre Museum for permitting me to do research in their collections and obtain images for publication. I am also grateful to Faith Wilson Stein and the staff of Northwestern University Press for their magnificent efforts to publish this book.

I appreciate Luke Parker for reading the manuscript and for sharing many warm conversations and Molly Thomasy Blasing and Kat Hill for advising me on having a family in academia. I am so fortunate that Jessica Hinds-Bond has both edited and indexed this book; I am deeply grateful for her meticulous attention to detail, resourceful ideas for revision, and apt subject-matter expertise. I could not keep up a regular writing schedule without the incredible smarts and encouragement of my biweekly writing group: Lindsay Ceballos, Jinyi Chu, D. Brian Kim, and Emily Wang. This group proves that work friendships can really flourish. A number of other academic colleague-friends have been critical sources of personal support and intellectual feedback over the years, particularly in our wonderful dissertation colloquium in graduate school. This list includes Anna A. Berman, Geoff Cebula, David Hock, Victoria Juharyan, Natalia Plagmann, Cate I. Reilly, Elizabeth H. Stern, E. Susanna Weygandt, and Denis Zhernokleyev.

In thinking about the individuals and structures that made writing this book possible, I also want to thank my communities of academic mamas who appreciate the full difficulty of academic parenthood, who advise on everything from children's books to skincare to marriage and parenting to teaching and publishing. I am especially grateful to the mamas of 2018 babies, who are a truly special group and who brighten up the internet for me considerably.

I love my children—Harrison, Vivian, and Damian—so much. You three keep me going, even when our days start at 4 A.M. I am grateful to my mother and late father for truly everything, and to my in-laws for the extraordinary efforts they have put into helping us with childcare. And I am grateful to my husband, Eden, who believed in me and this book even though for a long time I didn't. This book is dedicated to you for supporting me through all those years when I was stressed and struggling. You knew I could do it. Here it is, and it's a testament to our love.

Part of chapter 1 appeared in *Slavic and East European Journal*, and I am grateful to the journal for the permission to reprint this material.

NOTE ON THE TEXT

Bibliographical references follow a modified Library of Congress transliteration system. Elsewhere, names are given in their standard English form when one exists.

In this text I use the singular "they" for persons of unspecified gender. Since all nouns in Russian have grammatical gender, however, I retain the corresponding gendered pronouns, such as "he" for "actor" (*akter*) in my English translation of quotations from Russian. Other English translations that I cite do this as well.

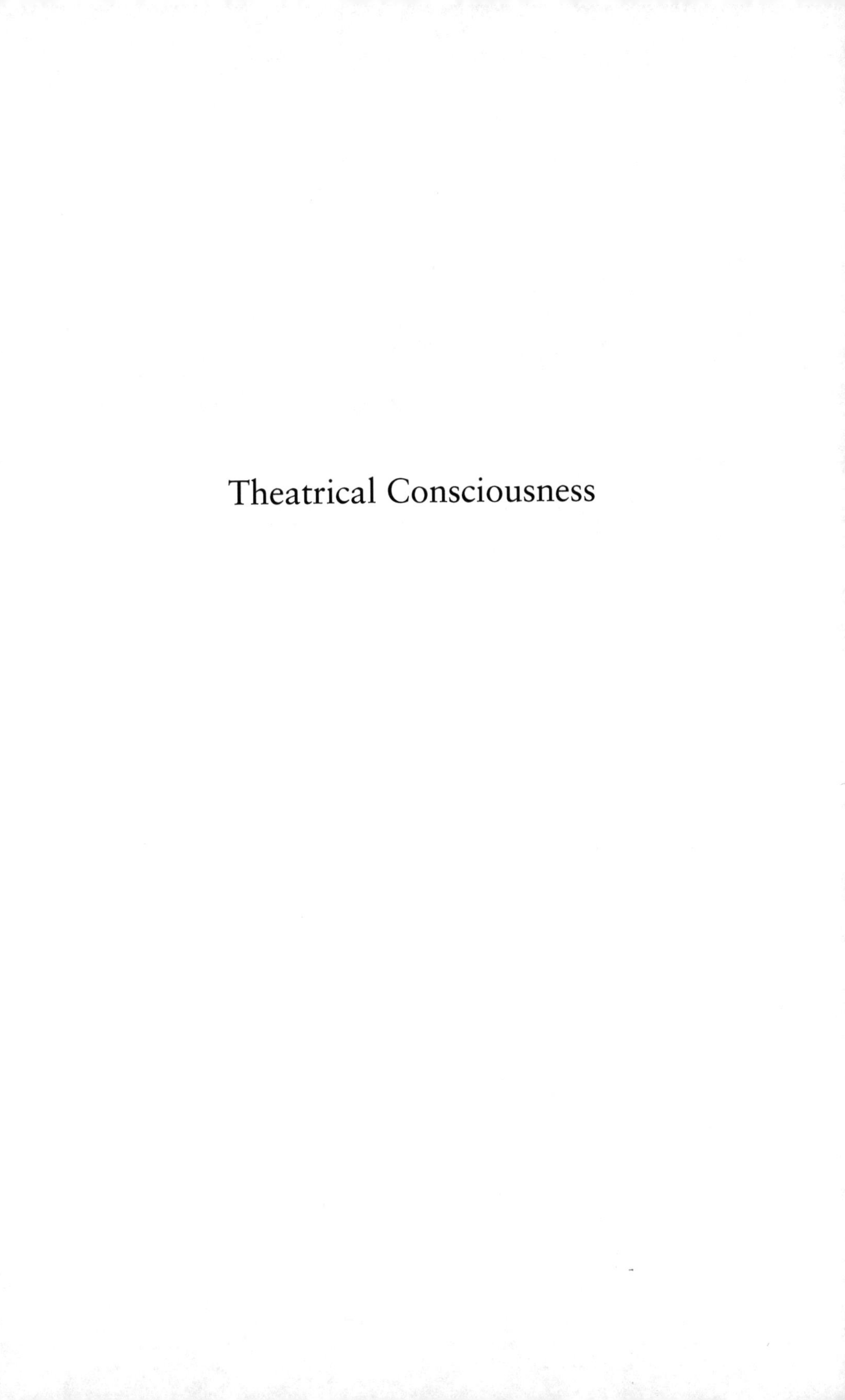

Theatrical Consciousness

Introduction

✦

Surveying the Soviet Actor

To what extent do actors sense as reality that which happens around them on the stage? Do actors experience a difference when performing a role before a full auditorium as opposed to an empty one? Does an actor's personal relationship to their partner influence their performance? Is there a difference between stage emotions and real-life ones? In other words, we might generalize, how do actors feel and experience the act of performance?

In 1923 critic and editor Liubov' Yakovlevna Gurevich posed these and other questions to some of Moscow's most celebrated theater actors on behalf of the Theater Section of the new State Academy of the Artistic Sciences (GAKhN).[1] Gurevich's survey of sixty-eight questions notably did not aim to document the implementation of acting methodologies deployed by Moscow's renowned theater companies, methodologies that at this time would have included Vsevolod Meyerhold's Biomechanics, Konstantin Stanislavsky's System, and Alexander Tairov's synthesized acting.[2] Instead, Gurevich and the Theater Section—whose members were Moscow's top theater directors, actors, artists, historians, critics, and patrons—sought to understand the *psychology* of the actor: how a particular actor thinks, feels, and behaves, irrespective of methodological practices. Their questions dissect the acting process from the moment of the actor's first acquaintance with a role to that of the actor's several-hundredth performance of it in order to continually foreground the subjective experience of acting: how the actor "sees" themself and their role. The survey seeks knowledge of acting as practiced, felt, and thought by individuals.[3]

The choice made by the GAKhN Theater Section to solicit these survey responses as one of its first institutional projects attests to a larger interest among the theater communities of the early Soviet Union in understanding the actor's individual experience as embodied, cognitive, and relational. Indeed, amid the early twentieth century's proliferation of new theaters, acting schools, and acting methodologies in Russia and the Soviet Union, we find numerous psychological and philosophical conceptualizations of the actor, conceptualizations that go beyond steps or exercises for improving acting technique and seek, instead, to understand the actor's fundamental essence and ways of being and experiencing performance. This phenomenon is the topic of this book, which examines efforts in the Russian and Soviet theater from around 1900 through the mid-1930s to stimulate, train, imagine, and ultimately understand the actor's mind—in fact, the human mind and self more broadly.

Gurevich's survey and the responses to it offer a preview of the scope of these matters. The survey understands subjective experience as both mental and embodied, as in such questions as: "During a performance how do the following reflect on your state of being [*samochustvi(e)*]: (a) the costume, (b) the makeup, (c) the set, (d) the props?" (Here Andrei Petrovsky gave a full narrative about the disastrous effects of unsatisfactory costuming and makeup on his craft.)[4] In answer to another question, Moscow Art Theater star Vasily Kachalov described maintaining awareness of his own self while performing a role, an issue of consciousness and identity: "Due to every actor's inherent ability to split their own consciousness [*soznanie*] onstage, I never forget myself onstage and don't imagine whether that is possible even for a second for an actor if he's normal, that is, a psychically healthy person. Sometimes I've noted that some actors (the majority of them old and past their prime) like to talk about how they forget themselves, don't remember themselves onstage. I'm certain they're not telling the truth."[5] The survey's inquiries into acting uncover themes of identity and selfhood in performance, revealing the psychological and philosophical complexity of acting and positioning an appreciation of the actor's mental and embodied experience as formative to a performance's success.

The vibrant GAKhN Theater Section, which lasted from 1922 until it was closed by the state in 1930, not only encapsulates a particularly tangible example of the inherent interdisciplinarity of theatrical discourse in this modernist era, but also is a physical site of connection and interaction for many of the individuals and ideas in this book. The Theater Section, which was dedicated to formulating the academic study of theater for the new Soviet state, featured frequent presentations on theatrical matters that were carefully discussed by attendees. In addition to theater folks, the presenters included such individuals from outside the theatrical profession as philosophers Gustav Shpet, Aleksei Losev, and Pavel Popov; psychologists Lev Vygotsky and Pavel Yakobson; and linguists Dmitry Ushakov and Nikolai Zhinkin.[6] In identifying their topics of study, the group explicitly prized psychological approaches to theater.

In fact, the Russian and Soviet theater's larger turn toward the mind in the early twentieth century owes much to the era's closeness among philosophy, psychology, science, and the arts. As the theater grasped for new psychological and philosophical approaches to acting and the stage, it in turn propelled developments in Russian and Soviet psychology and philosophy, as key thinkers from those fields—Lev Vygotsky and Gustav Shpet, in particular—discovered in it an instructive model of human perception and cognition.

Thus we will see that the exchanges between theater and other fields of knowledge in this interconnected period ran both ways, and as much as theater was theorized and practiced through psychological and philosophical lenses, it also contributed its own insights to psychological and philosophical knowledge.

This book unfolds the story of the mental turn in the modernist Russian and Soviet theater by examining a cross-medial range of sources, including theatrical theory, rehearsal stenography, production promptbooks, set and costume designs, dramatic criticism, plays, prose fiction, and philosophical and psychological treatises. Through case studies of the work of particular individuals, I demonstrate the era's manifold theatrical investigations into the unquantifiable, lived aspects of the mind. Where possible or productive, I trace the sources of theatrical thinkers' scientific or philosophical conceptualizations, but in none of the work considered here is the artistic a simple reflection of the scientific. Instead, theater functions as an experimental, philosophically fertile, knowledge-generating laboratory in its own right, seeking to discover on its own terms the workings and significance of the mind. In some cases, established scientists or philosophers served as reference points or inspiration for these theatrical experiments, but in most cases, modernist theater thinkers ventured into their own conceptual territory, even prefiguring the phenomenological turn in European and American theater of the midcentury, although the Russian and Soviet modernists lacked a codified vocabulary to identify the phenomenological emphasis in their work. Thus the aim of this book is to elucidate the philosophical implications of the early twentieth-century Russian and Soviet theater's inquiries into the mind: how and to what ends it understood the human actor against the backdrop of an increasingly technologized, industrialized, and politicized modernity that challenged the place of the human within it.

Revealed through this study, as well, is insight into theater's special use of minds—and of bodies. The thinkers in this book reflect on theater's presence and liveness, the relationship between actor and audience and between actor and character, the experience of acting and spectating, theater's powers and limitations, and the interfacing of theater and the real. As the art form capable of coming closest in appearance to real life, theater offers both "real" experience and a potent *something else*. The distinction between the two, or the erasure of it, will prove essential to the theatrical investigations of the mind in this book.

A Crisis of Consciousness

At the heart of this book are the actor's mind and subjective experience—the topic that unites the various thinkers, practitioners, methodologies, and performances discussed herein despite their stylistic diversity. The conceptualizations of the actor that I discuss in the book reflect and engage with larger intellectual trends in the era. In particular, both philosophy and psychology in the late nineteenth and early twentieth century in Russia were wrestling with concepts of consciousness (*soznanie*), a term that connoted resistance to positivism and empiricism, as well as a distinction between human and nonhuman animals. Consciousness raised questions around language and meaning, a transcendental ego, and the fact or not of the individual existence of consciousness in the self. In debates and journal polemics, the understanding of consciousness was framed as key to shoring up disciplinary boundaries, as questions turned not only on what consciousness *is* but on whether, how, and why philosophy and psychology should study it.

In broad terms, two sides emerged in these debates: a materialist side that sought to eliminate abstract concepts of the soul, mind, and consciousness from scientific study by explaining mental processes through physiology, and a more traditional side that defended the place of consciousness as an object of intellectual inquiry and that countered the incursion of Marxism. Theorists of Russian and Soviet modernity have emphasized the large cultural influence of the first side. As Ana Hedberg Olenina and Anna Toropova have shown with special reference to film, concepts from physiological psychology and its close neighbor, reflexology, saturated cultural life in the early Soviet years, with writers, critics, filmmakers, and even theater directors engaging with the artistic potential of precisely measuring and engineering bodily states.[7] In studies of the Soviet theater, Meyerhold's interest in physiological psychology has been well noted, particularly by Jonathan Pitches.[8] Physiological psychology is invoked, for example, in Meyerhold's 1922 public lecture on Biomechanics: "All psychological states are determined by specific physiological processes."[9] Other theater artists indeed used similar rhetoric, such as director Grigory Kozintsev at the Factory of the Eccentric Actor (FEKS), founded in 1921 in Petrograd, who instructed actors that year: "Forget about emotions and celebrate the machine, forget passion and turn to jest [gesture]."[10]

Less studied, however, is that second, non-Marxist side. This book mines the history of Russian and Soviet theater from the era to tell the understudied story of modernism's resistance to physiological and reflexological understandings of the human organism in favor of centering consciousness, mind, and soul, as well as other more qualitative and incalculable means of assessing the human, like narrative, memory, identity, spirit, and the construction of a community and sense of self. From the 1900s through the early 1930s, we find in Russian and Soviet culture opposition to reflexology-inspired modes of attending to corporeal movement. In their place is a more holistic, humanistic, and introspective exploration of the human organism, one that follows the lead of thinkers such as psychologist Georgy Chelpanov, who spearheaded the resistance to materialism in late imperial and early Soviet psychology. This cultural opposition takes various forms, from declaring the incalculability of the human to seeing the human mind and soul as ungraspable by machinery and empirical study. It is often—though not always—politicized as a means of opposition to Marxism and, by 1917, to the Soviet state. The protagonists in this book were wary of popular concepts of mechanization and depersonalization, of the notion that experiences can simply be mapped as cortical activity. Instead, they sought in the living, breathing art form of theater a more humanistic, more philosophically inflected investigation of individual psychosomatic experience—of the perceptions and sensations received by an embodied consciousness in the here and now.

Many Russian and Soviet artists and thinkers, including those I discuss, however, took complex and changing positions on physiological psychology and the nature of consciousness, particularly in the face of the political pressures of the early Soviet years. In her thorough investigation of these questions with regard to Stanislavsky, Rose Whyman has shown, for example, that Stanislavsky both appropriated and rejected the reflex theory of Ivan Pavlov and Ivan Sechenov.[11] Further, the era's focus on the mind diminished with the Soviet state's insistence on materialism by the mid-1930s, which steered the arts more firmly toward the principles of physiological psychology. And yet, even in the early Soviet years, theater offered moments for exploring the thinking, feeling consciousness. This spirit of seeking something particularly human in consciousness and the mind—as a form of resistance to both mechanistic conceptions of modernity and the dramatic political changes of the 1920s—pervades the Russian and Soviet theater.

The story of consciousness in theater is, for the thinkers in this book, closely tied to the story of phenomenology's influence in Russia and the Soviet Union. No one was more responsible for this phenomenological turn than leading Russian-language phenomenologist Gustav Shpet, who worked closely with Moscow theater life and the GAKhN Theater Section (as well as in Chelpanov's psychology institute), as I discuss in chapter 2. Scholarship on theater phenomenology in the West has steadily advanced since the 1980s, increasingly taking historical perspectives, as well as questioning the validity of the classical opposition between phenomenology and semiotics.[12] The Russian and Soviet strand of theater phenomenology, which we find both explicitly in Shpet's writings and implicitly in many of the theatrical theories and practices discussed here, emerges in part from the heavy influence of Orthodox Christianity on Russia's philosophical tradition. Less reactionary against mind-body dualism than its Western counterpart, Russian and Soviet theater phenomenology adds a valuable dimension missed by scholarship that is wholly situated in the philosophy of North America and western Europe.

Recent examinations of the psychophysical nature of acting by such practitioner-scholars as Dick McCaw and Phillip B. Zarrilli have been grounded in phenomenological insights and have tended to position Stanislavsky's practice as key to an accurate understanding of body and mind in performance.[13] But Stanislavsky is only one figure in a dynamic field of theatrical thinkers.

With this book, I demonstrate the breadth of early twentieth-century Russian and Soviet investment in a deeper, cognitive-corporeal understanding of the actor, both including and beyond Stanislavsky's contributions.

Mind and Consciousness in Theater

This book uses the term *mind* to refer to a range of cognitive processes and phenomena: human cognition, perception, consciousness, self-awareness, and self-conception. In this way, it is in line with Bruce McConachie's definition of *mind* in his short survey text *Theatre & Mind*: "the cognitive operations that underlie and constitute theatrical participation for human beings."[14] But *mind* is here an inexact term because of the boundaries it implies. More precisely, this book is interested in conceptions of the actor's craft and lived experience in performance that are not exclusively physical and physiological. *Mind* captures thought and perception but also the embodied cognition of feelings and emotions. As McConachie and McCaw have both pointed out, the term *mind*, just like the term *body*, plays into the tenets of Cartesian dualism because both words segment off portions of the human organism and enter this organism into a binary.[15] The Russian and Soviet thinkers and practitioners in this book largely reject Cartesianism, just as they reject a wholly physiological model of the human organism. The term *mind* in this book is also a deliberate counterweight to efforts by Soviet scientists to collapse concepts of the mind and consciousness into the movements of neural reflexes.

Theater in its essence, just like any other realm of human experience, deploys complex cognitive operations by all humans involved. The recently booming field of theater and cognitive science, which encompasses theater's manifold intersections with neuroscience, cognitive psychology, and evolutionary studies, often emphasizes the insights that the latest developments in the cognitive sciences can offer to the practice and understanding of performance, whether contemporary or historical. This field has been mapped out by numerous scholars, including McCaw, McConachie, Rhonda Blair, Rick Kemp, and Matthew Wilson Smith, among many others.[16] But such studies often deemphasize the value of taking a historical period's insights into the mind's workings on its own terms, preferring instead to approach theater history by using recent science to reveal the prescient insights of theater practitioners and thinkers of the past. While such discoveries are exciting and productive for the contemporary understanding and application of acting methods of the past, they are not the approach of this book, which examines the richness of Russian and Soviet modernist thought on its own terms, however imaginative, illogical, unscientific, or subsequently disproven. As Joseph R. Roach asserts in his classic study of acting in the context of the history of science: "In fact, each acting style and the theories that explain and justify it are right and natural for the historical period in which they are developed and during which they are accepted. In order to understand historical styles of acting in the context of their contemporary settings, we must therefore restore the meaning of outmoded terminology and explanatory principles."[17] At the same time, it is important to acknowledge that this task in its purest form is impossible: my own scholarly frameworks cannot be emptied of discourse on the mind of the past century.

I refer to *consciousness* here to capture the philosophically and psychologically inflected conceptualization of the acting and spectating experience that we encounter in these theatrical exemplars, as well as to explicitly situate Russian theatrical thought within philosophy's and psychology's turn-of-the-century polemics about human consciousness. Just as the mind is not detached from the body and world in which it is embedded, acting and spectating are not separate, distinctive acts, as we will see most clearly in the work of Nikolai Evreinov, for whom the two actions merge, or even in the thought of Lev Vygotsky and Sigizmund Krzhizhanovsky, who emphasize the mutual dependence of acting and spectating. Within these paradigms of mind in the theater, this book centers primarily on the *actor's* mind, rather than the *spectator's*, as the actor's mind is most tangibly thought by our personalities here. The spectator's mind would become a particular fascination of early Soviet filmmakers, such as Sergei Eisenstein and Lev Kuleshov, as Olenina details in her book.[18]

Notably, the term *consciousness* developed its own materialist currency in the lead up to the 1917 revolution and the early years of the Soviet Union. Vladimir Lenin's notion of "revolutionary consciousness" referenced the class and social awareness of the people as they navigated a changing political situation. In socialist discourse consciousness denoted not an abstract function of the mind but an individual's understanding of their own place in the social hierarchy. Theater's psychological and philosophical attention to the cognitive act of consciousness was not fortressed off from this socialist rhetoric but, in fact, engaged with it. The two concepts of consciousness would eventually intersect under Stalinism, as I show in the book's coda.

Modernism's Problem with the Human

The scientific developments of the early twentieth century occurred alongside the vibrant thrust of modernity, with all the excitement and anxiety of the era's new forms of mass culture, cinema, technology and automation, transportation, shifts in labor practices, worldwide war, and, in Russia, political upheaval. This book's focus on theater's interest in the mind challenges common scholarly pictures of the human in the modernist plastic arts as a limitation that must be overcome. That view takes several forms, latching onto several different but closely connected trends in the era. One trend is perhaps best characterized by one of England's central and most provocative modernist figures, beloved in the Russian theater at the turn of the century, Edward Gordon Craig. In his "Über-Marionette" manifesto of 1908, which proposed replacing actors with marionettes, Craig declared: "The whole nature of man tends toward freedom; he therefore carries the proof in his own person, that as *material* for the theatre he is useless."[19] Such views took the actor as theater's weakness, as the piece of a production that, due to interference from the automatic and unconscious processes in human biology and psychology, cannot be fully controlled or, indeed, fully abstracted from its natural human form.

Many theater artists were less adamant than Craig that humans make useless theatrical material but still, like him, sought to break away from direct expression of a character's personality and to otherwise push human actors to abstract themselves from any naturalistic tendencies. At the same time, scholarship on modernism's problem with the human and the body points to the body's resistance to total abstraction. Martin Puchner argues that modernism's drive for abstraction sought to eliminate mimesis, thus resulting in a peculiar problem for theater, the corporeality of which is inescapably mimetic.[20] Similarly, Olga Taxidou, who identifies an "anti-humanist strand in much of the art of the period," shows that the puppet becomes central to European modernism because it is better suited than the actor to abstraction: "In its quest for stylized modes of acting that do not rely on psychological expression but rather tend towards abstraction, modernist theatre finds in the puppet a highly appropriate model."[21] Both Puchner and Taxidou suggest that early twentieth-century Europe was frustrated with the problems posed by the human body.

The tension between mimesis and abstraction in modernist theater can be juxtaposed with an equally essential theatrical tension between mimesis and the real, a tension that opens up an avenue for what I identify as modernism's embrace of the human. Theater's human material (like its real objects that serve as stage properties) is both actually real *and* mimetic of the real: when Vasily Kachalov plays Hamlet, he is engaged in mimesis of various human behaviors that make up the character of Hamlet, *and* he is really the human Vasily Kachalov in real fabric clothes, really aging by the minute before our eyes. Modernism was particularly attuned to the relationship between the mimetic and the real, given that it was only half a century earlier that theater had begun deploying sets that were not mere painted backdrops but actually consisted of functional objects and three-dimensional representation. The naturalism of the end of the century, given prominence in Russia through the work of Stanislavsky and Vladimir Nemirovich-Danchenko (arguably far more poetic, expressive, and ethnographic than their critics give them credit for), was a particularly detailed version of mid-nineteenth-century realism.

Indeed, Russian and Soviet theater in the early twentieth century continually problematized its relationship to the real in ways that foregrounded, rather than diminished, the importance of the human to performance. In his study of theater and reality, Marvin Carlson writes of contemporary (2010s) theater: "The concern is rather to demonstrate that the real and the represented are not a set binary, but are the products of human consciousness and ways of seeing and encoding."[22] Carlson observes that our perception of where theater's blurred borders between illusion and reality lie is conditioned by our perspective and changes over time. Resonating with Carlson's argument about the contemporary theater, this book asserts that one way in which Russian and Soviet modernist theater in fact makes space for a kind of humanism, rather than trying to reduce the human's role onstage, is through framing performance as perceived and experienced (by humans) in all its complex and shifting relationships to reality. Through this line of thinking, the human actor is reconstituted as essential to bridging and blurring theater's relationship to the real, as well as vaulting it into larger questions in philosophy and psychology. The human actor is thus key to this theater's interrogation of consciousness.

The humanism that this book finds in the theory and practice of theater in early twentieth-century Russia and the Soviet Union requires that we reexamine how much the aesthetics of the era—by centering on how and what we perceive—in fact makes the unfragmented human essential to its enterprise. This is not to say that Russian and Soviet modernism did not seek to critique, break up, enhance, automate, depersonalize, and erase the human figure in its theatrical positioning of the human body as an object instrumentalized for scenographic or spectacular effect. Such trends are indeed prominent in the discourses of Meyerhold on Biomechanics, Eisenstein and Sergei Tretyakov on the theater of attractions, and Yulia Slonimskaya on marionette theater, all of which sought means to break away from conventional deployments of human actors. It is simply to say that this is not the full picture, and that such a restrictive view misses the complete vibrancy of the theatrical explorations of the era.

This is also not to suggest that depersonalization and automation are necessarily seen as restrictive in scholarship; scholars like Olenina and Julia Vaingurt demonstrate the breadth of artistic innovation and reimagining of the human that emerge from Soviet meetings of mechanism and mind.[23] Further, a spate of scholarship in the 1990s and early 2000s explored the rich intersections of body and technology within European modernism, often revealing the body to be positively enhanced and recuperated by machinery. Tim Armstrong writes that technological augmentation of the body made the body in itself seem both incomplete and insufficient: "Modernity, then, brings forth both a fragmentation and augmentation of the body in relation to technology; it offers the body as lack, at the same time as it offers technological compensation."[24] Such might be the case within Europe, but—as this book's chapters reveal—the machine thinking of Russian and Soviet modernism often bore a more spiritual and emotional tint that infuses it with traces of humanism. Whyman astutely characterizes the Russian theater's approach to machine thinking as a philosophically complex set of paradoxes, one that rejects a common opposition between Stanislavsky as bodily naturalist and Meyerhold as bodily instrumentalist.[25] Whyman writes:

> The modernist preoccupation with the machine extended to the way the human body was conceptualized, as a machine with a spiritual dimension. The influence of this on the views and theories of acting propounded by Stanislavsky, Chekhov, Meyerhold and others led to the conceptualization of the actor, as it were, as an emotional machine, a dualistic entity who could and should be trained to work to full capacity according to scientific laws of mechanics, while being required at the same time to be emotionally, even spiritually expressive—this being a more capricious capacity. This fascinating dichotomy pervades the thinking on acting of the epoch, with various solutions being explored in order to resolve it.[26]

The thinkers in this book do largely treat machinery as an impetus for identifying what is distinctively human rather than as a productive augmentation to the human, but the ever-shifting balance between mechanization and emotional expression that Whyman identifies in Russian theater makers is central to this book's view of the era as continually challenging and challenged by its larger philosophical and scientific landscape.[27] Machine possibilities and threats vis-à-vis the human loom large over the material in this book, for, like Whyman, Olenina, and Vaingurt, I see machinery in this era as permitting new ways of prioritizing and conceptualizing the human, including those aspects of the human that physiological psychology, in its precise transcripts of cortical activity, is unfit to capture.

Remapping Russian and Soviet Theatrical Modernism

Much has been written about acting methodologies in Russian and Soviet modernism—those prescriptions for the concrete steps that actors can take to optimally do their duty as actors. That approach has tended to portray the era as one of fierce polemics and opposing values; as Irina Shevelenko points out, studies of Russian modernism have historically taken for granted the truth of the polemics the factionalist modernist groups themselves espoused.[28] This book, however, follows in the mold of more recent scholarship, like that of Dassia N. Posner, that sees the key directors and thinkers in the Russian theater as forming an aesthetic "constellation," rather than a set of binaries.[29] By interrogating the beliefs underlying those theatrical theories, we can tell a story of connection and community, showing the deeper similarities and dialogues across differing practitioners' and theorists' approaches to acting.

Thus central to this book are the networks, communities, and collaborative enterprises like GAKhN, within which modernist figureheads like Stanislavsky, Meyerhold, and Tairov thought and worked.

I also seek to integrate into the narrative of the early twentieth-century Russian and Soviet theater key figures whose stories have remained on the margins of theater history, as this integration provides a more holistic and representative picture of the lived experience of modernist theatrical culture than do the traditional biography-centered studies of, for example, Stanislavsky or Meyerhold. The marginalized figures that this book takes as central include Liubov' Gurevich, Lev Vygotsky, Gustav Shpet, and Sigizmund Krzhizhanovsky, as well as Nikolai Evreinov, who has largely been branded an idiosyncratic director peripheral to Russian theater thought, even though his work has received significant scholarly attention. Here, I follow in the footsteps of Konstantin Rudnitsky, whose classic *Russian and Soviet Theatre: Tradition and the Avant-Garde* (1988) wrote into theater history a number of lesser-known directors, including directors from Georgia and Ukraine. As Rudnitsky writes: "Each of them—Stanislavsky, Meyerhold, Vakhtangov, Tairov, Eisenstein, Mikhail Chekhov—can only be fully understood in relation to the rest, keeping constantly in mind the intensity of their mutual attractions and repulsions, the clash and rapprochement of their ideas, the diversity of their activities and, of course, the general flow of the time that carried them along. . . . Some directors who were actively setting the tone in the early stages are now less well known."[30] Work at expanding the biographies that make up theater history of this era has also been done by Amy Skinner in her volume *Russian Theatre in Practice: The Director's Guide* (2019), which includes chapters on Nina Simonovich-Efimova, Alexandra Remizova, and Natalia Sats; by Stefan Aquilina, whose *Modern Theatre in Russia: Tradition Building and Transmission Processes* (2020) includes a discussion of Valentin Smyshlaev and of female voices in the theater, particularly Asja Lācis; and by others including Maria Ignatieva and Catherine Schuler, who have studied female actors of the period.[31]

It is only by continuing to expand and make more inclusive our picture of modernist culture, as in Leonid Livak's concept of "modernism as a cultural community" comprising a diversity of producers and publics, that we can comprehend the lived experience of thinking and making theater in this era.[32] Thus I reject the notion that we can understand thought on the actor in early twentieth-century Russia and the Soviet Union by centering just one or two key figures, be they the pillars of Russian theater Stanislavsky and Meyerhold or a figure like Krzhizhanovsky, who offers a tantalizingly rich and poetic theatrical phenomenology that opens up fresh angles on theater of the period but that is best understood alongside the theater practices and theater makers to whom he was responding.

At the same time, it must be acknowledged that a number of fascinating and significant figures whose stories intersect with this book's argument have been left out of it in favor of deeper study into the works of a smaller number of thinkers. Though some of these names are briefly mentioned in the chapters that follow, none are discussed at length. On the philosophical side, writings on theater by Fyodor Stepun, Pavel Florensky, and Aleksei Losev deserve more attention, as does the work of psychologist Alexander Zaporozhets, a student of both Vygotsky and Meyerhold. The number of influential, thoughtful theater critics from the era is large, including Yuly Aikhenval'd, Vsevolod Vsevolodsky-Gerngross, Adrian Piotrovsky, Boris Alpers, and Aleksei Gvozdev. And of theater practitioners and thinkers, there are dozens whose work falls under the purview of this book, including Prince Sergei Volkonsky, Evgeny Vakhtangov, Sergei Eisenstein, Sergei Radlov, Vasily Kandinsky, Fyodor Komissarzhevsky, Vera Komissarzhevskaya, Vasily Sakhnovsky (who studied philosophy at the University of Freiburg), Evgeny Bezpiatov (sometimes Bespiatov, author of a book on the psychology of theater), Nikolai Demidov (who practiced psychiatry before becoming one of Stanislavsky's closest assistants and a theater director in his own right), Maria Knebel', and Mikhail (Michael) Chekhov. Some of these figures' stories remain to be written into Russian or Soviet theater history. Absent from this book are also the many forms of puppet theater, popular theater, amateur theater, and proletarian theater that flourished both before and after the revolution. This omission, too, is intended to narrow the book's scope, not to suggest that these other theatrical forms are categorically at odds with the book's argument.

Coming Attractions

This book explores how Russian and Soviet theatrical thought and practice contributed to a wider pre- and postrevolutionary discourse on the mind, including concepts of consciousness, perception, identity, and the constitution of the subject. Each chapter addresses a central concept in the era's theories of the actor's mind as developed in the theatrical thought and/or practice of one or two individuals. Crucial to my engagement is that I examine many of these figures in dynamic pairings to map out the dialogues and conversations on the actor in which they were immersed. To demonstrate the symbiosis between theory and praxis in the era, each chapter highlights a play or production that theorizes through practice the issues at hand. In some cases these productions are rough experiments, or even flops, but in all cases they speak directly to the process of working out a practical understanding of some aspect of the actor's mind in theater.

The first chapter takes up the concept of actor as self—in which value is placed on the actor's mental conception of themself as a distinct individual. "Self" (*sebia*) is a term that comes up frequently in the theatrical theory of Nikolai Evreinov (1879–1953), who, I argue, offers discussions of acting focused almost exclusively on internal mental processing. Evreinov's concept of the self resists and builds on Russian symbolist beliefs about the actor, which I detail here. Further, Evreinov, perhaps more than any other theater thinker in Russia, saw the mind as constitutive of theater, an idea I trace through multiple theoretical concepts Evreinov developed prior to his emigration in 1925. The play analyzed closely in this chapter is Evreinov's *Samoe glavnoe* (*The Main Thing*, 1921), which astutely parodies his claims about endlessly transforming actor-selves before revealing the ultimate theatricality inherent in life.

While chapter 1 examines a wholly internal view of the actor, chapter 2 reckons with the external: the body. Russian and Soviet theater of the early twentieth century was enraptured with movement theory, and in discourse on theater, a rhetoric emerged around the concept of "actor as material." But how did thinkers and artists who emphasized the actor's mind understand the actor's bodily material? Vsevolod Meyerhold (1874–1940), often considered the paradigmatic case of reflexological understandings of the body in theater, made space for the mind and experiential understandings of bodily movement in his work at the Borodinskaya Street Studio (1913–17), which would develop into his acting program of Biomechanics after the revolution. Further, the cognitive implications of actor as material are directly theorized by philosopher Gustav Shpet (1879–1937), who argued in an influential 1922 essay that actorly bodies in performance possess a special intangible and invisible meaning that is both created and perceived phenomenologically. The chapter culminates by examining the intersection of these two approaches in Meyerhold and Shpet's collaboration on the production *Dama s kameliiami* (*The Lady of the Camellias*, 1934), directed by Meyerhold with a text translated and edited by Shpet. I use the production as a lens to examine and speculate on the implications of Shpet's philosophy for theatrical practice.

Chapter 3 takes on a deeper synthesis of body and mind, together with spirit, through the concept of the actor's personhood: how the actor is constituted as a person within the larger theatrical (and worldly) context. This question connects to choices about the style of staging, as I examine discussions of how these choices can permit personhood for the actor. Konstantin Stanislavsky (1863–1938) distinguished his approach to theater from Edward Gordon Craig's during their collaboration on *Hamlet* (1911) by the claim that the actor is a human being (*chelovek*), and Stanislavsky argued for costumes and acting that would foreground this point. The full implications of the statement that an actor is a human being are best understood through a reading of Stanislavsky's theories, where deep respect for the actor as a thinking, feeling, spiritual, and ethical human being emerges. The chapter then shows that Stanislavsky and Craig's debates over acting thought are echoed in debates over consciousness in Soviet psychology in the 1920s. In particular, Lev Vygotsky's efforts to enmesh the philosophical abstractness of consciousness within a Marxist psychological discourse employ Stanislavsky's term "experiencing" (*perezhivanie*). In articles and theater reviews, Vygotsky (1896–1934) takes from the stage, and especially from Stanislavsky, core intuitions about the mental contexts and environments that shape our perceptions.

These studies of actor as self, actor as material, and the actor's personhood within the theatrical context lead us to a more metaphysical topic in the final chapter: the actor's sense of personal identity. The mind as a perceptive and cognitive faculty plays a central role in Sigizmund Krzhizhanovsky's conception of theater, as does the mind's self-awareness, or sense of identity and place in the world. Philosophical resonances of this idea play out in short fiction by Krzhizhanovsky (1887–1950), which is studied here, but they are most richly developed in one of Krzhizhanovsky's only texts to reach the stage, his adaptation of G. K. Chesterton's novel *The Man Who Was Thursday* for the Kamerny Theater. This 1923 production, directed by Alexander Tairov (1885–1950), strove to distinguish the Kamerny's approach to theater and the actor through the Kamerny's appreciation of the actor's *humanness*, as manifested in the actor's search for personal identity in the theater world. The chapter ends on a somber note: the consequences of the actor's identity can be tragic, Krzhizhanovsky and Tairov show.

All these thinkers were forced to adapt to changing ideological conditions as the Soviet Union entered the 1930s (save Evreinov, who had emigrated to France). The coda of this book reflects on the legacy of the focus on the mind in Russian acting thought as it unfolded in the USSR under Stalinist censorship. For insight into the changing ideological expectations, I examine briefly here the little-known Soviet psychologist (and GAKhN Theater Section participant) Pavel Yakobson's book *Psikhologiia stsenicheskikh chuvstv aktera* (*The Psychology of the Actor's Stage Feelings*, 1936). With theoretical writings on theater dwindling in this decade due to the political climate, this text by Yakobson (1902–79) provides a sense of how psychology under Stalinism could think about the stage.

Chapter 1

✦

The Actor as Self

In 1921 Nikolai Nikolaevich Evreinov (1879–1953) published a children's book called *Chto takoe teatr* (*What Theater Is*). Its cover features a drawing approximating Petrograd's Alexandrinsky Theater, and its text is interleaved with black-and-white sketches of theater interiors and history's famous actors. In the book Evreinov cheerily invites the young reader into the theater hall for a performance of Nikolai Rimsky-Korsakov's opera *Sadko* (1897). We follow Evreinov's narrator through the doors of the theater building to the ticket counter, we learn how to purchase a ticket through the little window, and we get our program from the usher. Entering the auditorium, we learn the names of the seating levels and are given a peek backstage before the show starts, as the narrator patiently explains the social and artistic norms of theatrical institutions. And then, in the pages of this chatty introduction to attending the theater, addressed to "children who haven't yet been to the theater or who have been to it but don't really know anything about it," we find one of Evreinov's lengthiest explicit discussions of acting.[1] Upon our visit to the wig- and makeup-filled dressing rooms backstage, an actor named Platon Ivanovich speaks to us about the actor's "inner transformation":

> When you sense that *you've touched the audience's heart*, when you hear them crying under the influence of your art, when you know that after this they might start to relate differently to beggars, to all those wronged by fate, and, lastly, to the trials that fate sends to people—it's difficult even to relay to you all how joyful the soul of the actor is then!—he then realizes his own purpose—the purpose of awakening wonderful feelings in people, and he is right to be proud: his work, his talent, his art have not gone to waste!.. That is one of the actor's joys, and the other is—you yourselves know, children—the joy of *transformation*, the joy of knowing that thanks to play, you for a while have stopped being Platon Ivanovich, having become sick and tired of yourself in your own form, and have become Napoleon, a doctor, a monk, a chimney sweep, a cook, King of the Sea, or whoever else![2]

For the fictional Platon Ivanovich, as for Evreinov himself, the most natural form of theater is that of child's play: "you yourselves know, children" this joy that the actor experiences.[3] Thus although Evreinov's peculiar children's book points to a number of truths—the complexity of social customs around theatergoing, the theater's economic stratifying of the masses across its range of ticket prices, and the heavily Francophone vocabulary of the Russian theater hall—it is Evreinov's own childlike wonder at theatrical transformation (at "witchcraft," *koldovstvo*, as his Platon Ivanovich calls it with fondness) that shines most strongly.[4]

Platon Ivanovich's words about transformation in the theater echo a much broader sentiment Evreinov expressed a decade earlier, in 1912, at the end of his book *Teatr kak takovoi* (*Theater as Such*): "We love ourselves only theatricalized."[5] Both utopian and tragic, this statement tasks us with theatricality as a means of self-realization: only in costuming or role-playing do we find self-love. It also points to what this chapter argues is a larger theme in Evreinov's thought: namely, the centrality of the actor's or spectator's mind (as self-realization is ultimately a cognitive act) to the constitution of theater. In taking this position, Evreinov establishes in Russian theatrical thought a set of modes for understanding the actor as a being with inner experience and as a self, who has a sense of themself as a distinct person. While many other thinkers in Russian modernism would focus on the actor's interiority and articulate a sense of the actor's selfhood, none would do so as purely and exclusively as Evreinov, as only Evreinov would base his entire understanding of theater around actor as self.

The author of more than twenty-five plays and fifty books and articles beginning in 1906, Evreinov was known in his lifetime for expressing odd, outlandish ideas in rambling, rousing prose and for staging provocative performances, like his 1908 production of Oscar Wilde's *Salome*, which was censored by the Holy Synod after a well-attended dress rehearsal.[6] A foppish, coquettish trickster, Evreinov presented a dynamic personality both in life and on the page. He unfolded this performance of himself across the tomes of his numerous histories, theoretical treatises, popular writings, and plays, as well as his captivating public lectures (his future wife, Anna Kashina, found an early production of his confusing but a lecture he delivered enchanting).[7] A collection of portraits of him in his unusual book *Original o portretistakh (K probleme sub"ektivizisma v iskusstve)* (*The Original on the Portraitists [Toward the Problem of Subjectivism in Art]*, 1922), an exercise in introspection via other artists' illustrations of him, depicts him as stylized, angular, and expressive. As recalled by his brother Vladimir, he enjoyed dressing up as a woman for dramatic effect.[8] Evreinov's own elaborate performance of self—and his investment in the sort of public self-examination that *The Original on the Portraitists* engages in—might suggest that the theatricalization needed to "love ourselves" occurs in a putting-on that subverts social expectations and dispenses with ordinariness. But in his theoretical writings from the same period, Evreinov also identifies rather mundane actions as theater—things like looking out the window or combing one's hair. His thought both formulates and erases polarities between the ordinary and the outlandish and between the theater hall and the theater of everyday life. Meanwhile, through all his writings, Evreinov continually returns to an emphasis on the self—*sebia*—in theater. This self is sometimes an actor, like Platon Ivanovich, and sometimes a spectator; the distinction is ultimately often meaningless to him. What does matter to Evreinov's concept of the self is that the prized act of theatrical transformation is located within the mind. The consequence, then, of this mental manifestation of theatricality is the potential for therapy or healing by the mind through the act of theater.

In devoting this book's first chapter to Evreinov, I assert his role as an innovator and shaper of theatrical conceptions of mind in the era and a prime contributor to understandings of the actor's interiority. Nonetheless, Evreinov has often been treated as more anomalous than representative of the Russian theater. From the beginning, he earned curiosity and scorn for his provocative ideas. Some theatrical critics have seen the only consistency in his thought to be anarchic posturing. That Evreinov endorsed self-transformation as the task of theater was, to critic Yuly Aikhenval'd, evidence of theater's broader failure as an art form. In his lecture "Otritsanie teatra" ("A Denial of the Theater," delivered orally in Moscow on March 16, 1913, published in 1914), Aikhenval'd argued that "theater is a false and unlawful form of art," supporting this claim with Evreinov's line that "in the 'theater,' the main thing I want is to not be myself, but in 'art' it's just the opposite—to find myself."[9] Aikhenval'd's choice to position Evreinov's ideas as the ultimate proof of theater's degradation reveals the director to be not an eccentric on the periphery, however, but a central force in the Russian theater of the day. Aikhenval'd's language was then taken up by the Soviet scholar Boris Kazansky, who in 1925 called Evreinov's work a "denial of theater as a specific professional art," considering his innovations to be in the practice of theater in everyday life rather than in theater as a skilled art form.[10] But Kazansky, like the contemporaneous American critic Oliver M. Sayler, also named Evreinov as one of the most important Russian theater directors of the day.[11] Kazansky writes: "The whole ideology of the new theater goes back to [Evreinov], and even the new way of understanding the theater is connected to his name and, above all, strives to transcend his idea."[12] Such tension around the legitimacy of Evreinov's understanding of theater defined his work then as it continues to do now, when his theories are often read as anti-theatrical (and anti-theater).

This chapter traces how Evreinov's beliefs about the actor as self evolve through multiple interrelated theoretical concepts. I begin not with Evreinov's own writings but with the Russian symbolists, whose ideas defined the early modernist Russian theater. Evreinov's notion of the self both drew on and critiqued symbolist ideas, embracing symbolism's belief in theater's power to transform life, while rejecting its subordination of the actor. From there, I turn to Evreinov's theorizations of monodrama, in which all the characters, design, and happenings onstage are portrayed as though from the perspective of a single protagonist; "theater in life," in which theater exists in the performance-like practices that are part of everyday human activity; "theater for oneself" (*teatr dlia sebia*), which places special emphasis on the spectator's individual benefit from or enjoyment of the performance; and "theatrotherapy" (*teatroterapiia*), which denotes theater used for physiological or psychological benefit, whether for oneself or for another person. Finally, I analyze Evreinov's 1921 play *The Main Thing* as an instructive case study in synthesizing his beliefs about the actor as self. Through the many iterations of his theories, Evreinov shows that the actor's mental sense of self is integral to the creation of theater.

Symbolism's Depersonalization of the Actor

Although Evreinov is one of the most prolific writers among early twentieth-century Russian theater thinkers, he neither worked with an imperial or state-sponsored theater nor laid out an acting methodology.[13] Initially trained in law, Evreinov saw himself as something of a scholar. He wrote books on theater history, aesthetics, and corporal punishment in Russia. He was attracted to both the conventionality and ritual of classical theater and the popular entertainment of satirical cabaret and variety show performances, a diversity of interests that is evident not just in his writings but in his directing projects. At his own Ancient Theater (Starinnyi teatr) in Saint Petersburg (which produced two short theatrical seasons, in 1907–8 and 1911–12), he staged medieval and Spanish baroque plays with great attention to historical detail. There, he practiced a method of "artistic reconstruction," through which the director would harness the "spirit and minutiae of the historical era" as creative inspiration rather than dutifully replicating it.[14] Nearby, and somewhat concurrently, he intervened in the then-booming variety genre as a writer and director at Alexander Kugel' and Zinaida Kholmskaya's Crooked Mirror Theater (Krivoe zerkalo) in Saint Petersburg from 1910 through 1917.[15] In these two theaters, the breadth of Evreinov's theatrical engagement is revealed. If the latter theatrical work shares a common spirit with Vsevolod Meyerhold, who was similarly attracted to theaters of small forms, then the former better evinces the ideas of the symbolists.

In fact, while Evreinov's understanding of the theatricality of the self and mind was nurtured by many folks in the turn-of-the-century Petersburg theater scene, no one was more influential to him than the Russian symbolists, whose concept of *zhiznetvorchestvo*, the merging of life and art, is probably the closest approximation to a concept of theatricality prior to Evreinov in Russia. Evreinov staged plays by Leonid Andreev and Fyodor Sologub at the Crooked Mirror Theater and was well familiar with the symbolists' work.

The symbolist appreciation for theater's power to transform the soul of its participants, the symbolist embracing of artifice over naturalism, and the symbolist tendency toward provocation all would become cornerstones of Evreinov's work. At the same time, symbolist theatrical thought completely denies selfhood to actors in its radical depersonalization of them, a move that Evreinov would counter by heading to the opposite extreme.

The symbolists were a dynamic group of poets, active from roughly 1895 through 1910, who rapidly propelled the launch of Russian modernism. As Jonathan Stone has shown, symbolism took root in Russian culture through its prolific publishing institutions, which produced journals and books in close dialogue with their readership, shaping and in turn being shaped by the desires of those readers (who were often the same as the producers). The movement developed alongside the formulation of an engaged, though small, public audience that was eager for intellectual stimuli, debate over the new aesthetics of the modern age, and fresh forms of art.[16] It thus left its mark on Russian culture not merely in the specific artworks and ideas contributed by individual symbolists but in the larger cultural shifts that their activity precipitated. Evreinov's own compulsion to publish his many opinions and theories, often expressed in rhetoric rallying his readers to his views, builds on these symbolist precedents.

The symbolists' essays and lectures on theater (which account for but a portion of their many writings on literature and other arts) are often regarded as the foundation of modern Russian theatrical theory. The symbolists resisted the notion of theater as conceived by the nineteenth-century state and private theatrical institutions and proposed radical changes to theatrical norms. Valery Bryusov sparked this conversation with his provocative article "Nenuzhnaia pravda" ("The Unnecessary Truth," 1902, published in the journal *Mir iskusstva*, *World of Art*), which critiqued the efforts of Konstantin Stanislavsky and Vladimir Nemirovich-Danchenko at the Moscow Art Theater to achieve scenic naturalism. Although Stanislavsky would soon experiment with symbolism himself, the Moscow Art Theater of these early years filled the stage with real objects and naturalistic special effects, realia that Bryusov condemned as an "unnecessary truth." Instead Bryusov advocated "conventionalization" (*uslovnost'*). Conventionalization frees theater from the unachievable burden of precisely replicating life. It stipulates identifying and amplifying the artistic possibilities unique to theater, while dispensing with strictly imitative practices, just as, Bryusov notes, bronze and marble statues are by convention not painted, their bronze or marble state considered superior to imitative pigmentation.[17] As explained by Dassia N. Posner: "Conventionalization is a conscious, overt application of theatrical conventions that are defined by each individual director or production in an eternal quest for new ways of making meaning together with an audience. Rather than being a specific style, conventionalization is a structural philosophy of theater-making that generates expectation, surprise, and thought by rejuvenating and reapplying how theatrical conventions are used."[18] Bryusov's call for conventionalization thus laid out not merely a description of a theatrical style for the new modernist era, but rather a manifesto for theatrical self-consciousness that could give rise to a multiplicity of styles. Conventionalization breeds theater that feels fresh, new, and innovative.

Bryusov's essay provoking the symbolist conversation about theater was followed by lectures and journal articles by the symbolists and their critics, the highlights of which were collected in influential books, including *Teatr: Kniga o novom teatre* (*Theater: A Book about the New Theater*, 1908), *Krizis teatra* (*The Crisis of the Theater*, 1908), and *V sporakh o teatre* (*In Dispute about the Theater*, 1914). In their criticism the symbolists evaluated stylistic approaches to theater and envisioned bolder, more daring, conventionalized ways of practicing it. They sought to reinvigorate theater by recasting it as ecstatic or spiritual and anti-mimetic. Vyacheslav Ivanov (and, later, Andreev) imagined a theater that resembles a Dionysian dance from ancient Greece in order to goad the audience into a collective, spiritual act that forsakes their individual selves: "We wish to gather together in order to create—'to make'—communally, and not merely to contemplate," Ivanov declared in one of several essays on the subject.[19] Ivanov saw in theater a potential for transforming the audience—and, indeed, society—through the energy of ritual, which would draw its participants away from mundane reality and closer to divine truth. By turning actors and audience into "participants" with equal status in the performance, Ivanov envisioned both activating the spectator and homogenizing the actor. This was a move in line with other symbolist theorists throughout Europe, who, as Daniel Gerould writes, "called for the 'depersonalized actor'—rarefied, dematerialized, spiritualized—who could be a celebrant in the holy theatre" and thus "eliminate the mimetic weight of performers."[20] Symbolism as a whole thus turned away from the concrete fleshiness and temporality of the living actor, who bears the "mimetic weight" of ordinary humanness, in favor of constituting the actor through spiritual abstraction—and depersonalization. For the symbolists, uniting individuals through connection with the divine, universal self, a self that transcended the individual selves of mundane life, was the very purpose of art.

Indeed, actors posed a problem for the symbolists, who saw them as prone to egotistical swaggering and declaiming across the stage, disrupting the artistic and spiritual unity of the production. For art to reveal divine truth, it must be carefully measured, a task that could only be carried out by a single artistic vision—that of the playwright, in the symbolist view. Not only were actors depersonalized, but so too were characters, who were often denoted as generic character types, such as Mystics or a Young Girl, rather than named and delineated as individuals. Sologub, in the movement's most extensive and perhaps most extreme plan for a symbolist theater, would visualize the actors' task downsized to the illustration of a dramatic text that is read aloud onstage by another person, called a "reader": "There must be no acting. Only a level word-by-word delivery. The calm enactment of situations, scene by scene."[21] Curiously, in his denunciation of theater in 1913, Aikhenval'd faults theater for denying actors artistic agency. His language echoes Sologub's prescription, as though suggesting that the symbolist ideal had in fact been implemented: "[The actor's] hands are tied, his soul is commissioned; he heeds the prompter-author. . . . The actor's sensations are premade, his task is but to find for them corresponding physical expressions."[22] Sharon Marie Carnicke describes the symbolists as having dual antipathies: "antipathy to the actor" and "antipathy to the independence of character."[23] To her assessment we might add a third: antipathy to the active spectator. Just like the actor, the spectator of symbolist theater is deprived of individual processing and engagement with the performance. Sologub's imagined spectator sits quietly in the dark, impervious to their neighbors in the auditorium, absorbing the drama exactly as intended by its author.

Although Russian symbolism denied expressive agency to the actor, the movement invested the writer with a belief that life and art were not only intertwined but mutually informing—a concept known as *zhiznetvorchestvo*, which translates as something like "life-creation." As Michael Wachtel writes, "[*Zhiznetvorchestvo*] suggests both a synthesis of the two constituent elements (creation *and* life) as well as the creation *of* life (that is, divine creation)."[24] *Zhiznetvorchestvo* has theatrical implications that resonate with Evreinov's thought. Through *zhiznetvorchestvo*, the symbolists sought to live life artistically, and their personal biographies as stand-ins for the essence of human life in general become closely linked to the understanding of their poems, paintings, and other artworks. For them, a life lived artistically was the only true way to honor aesthetic and divine truth. This aestheticization of life manifested in artistic creations that merged the fictional and spiritual with the real and mundane, as well as in a broad philosophical stance, derived from the religious philosopher Vladimir Solovyov, that aesthetics was "a force capable of acting on and changing reality."[25] Believing in the spiritual renewal of society through art, the symbolists defined art's purpose for society not as a means of moral or political instruction or as an aesthetic end in itself but as a means for bringing the individual soul closer to its essence—a concept that Evreinov would drain of its mystical qualities and rework into his concept of a renewing and healing theatricality.

Perhaps the most instructively innovative example of the symbolist vision of theater as applied to the stage is found in Alexander Blok's commedia dell'arte play *Balaganchik* (*The Little Show Booth*, 1906), first produced by Meyerhold in a joint showing with Maurice Maeterlinck's play *The Miracle of Saint Anthony*. Simultaneously a parody of symbolism and an earnest exploration of the possibilities of symbolist theatricalism, Blok's text, whose layers of unexpectedness continue to challenge scholars, revels in bucking tradition, resisting naturalism, and revealing the constructedness of the stage world. In many ways it is a precursor to Evreinov's dramas, including *The Main*

Thing, which I discuss in this chapter. Central plot events happen offstage, the Clown delights in bleeding out cranberry juice, Harlequin leaps through a window that turns out to be made of paper, the set suddenly rolls up, the character of the Author protests that his "perfectly realistic play" is being mangled and mocked by the actors, and a character turns to cardboard—to name only a few of the short play's dramatic curiosities.[26] Pierrot, cast as such a stock figure that he has a face "common to all Pierrots," believes a woman in white to be his beloved Columbine, while the Mystics around him insist that she is Death, causing him much consternation that captures the plight of a character aware that he is trapped in an unstable, conventionalized world.[27] In its incisive exploration of symbolist theater, the play examines the experiences of the Author and his characters—characters that because of their generic roles, their existence outside of and beyond this particular play, behave almost like actors self-aware that they are here to perform. The symbolist blending of life and art is captured and critiqued in the Author, who is both part of "his" play and horrified by its unfolding. *The Little Show Booth* opened to critical reviews and confused, disinterested audiences, but Meyerhold saw these reactions as proof that he had created something truly new. The director called it "the first stimulus to lend definite direction to my art."[28]

Ultimately, however, the symbolist stage experiments in Russia were largely ineffective at translating theory into practice. The symbolists' efforts to subordinate the actor and resist mimesis could not overcome the inherent mimesis of the human body in performance. This tension between abstraction and mimesis in the theater, a tension that came to a head in modernism, is captured by Martin Puchner, who argues:

> As a performing art like music or ballet, the theater depends on the artistry of live human performers on stage. As a mimetic art like painting or cinema, however, it must utilize these human performers as signifying material in the service of a mimetic project. Once the nature of mimesis is subject to scrutiny and attacks, as it is in modernism, this double affiliation of the theater becomes a problem because, unlike painting or cinema, the theater remains tied to human performers, no matter how estranged their acting might be. The theater thus comes to be fundamentally at odds with a more widespread critique, or complication, of mimesis because this critique requires that the material used in the artwork be capable of abstraction and estrangement.[29]

Symbolism's efforts to transcend the prosaic, individualized human body were thus complicated by the fact that symbolist theater did not wholly reject the performing human. Symbolism's embracing of conventionalization as, in particular, an alternative to mimesis sent symbolist theorists in radical directions that seemed to be divisive and polemical rather than serious proposals. In the end Russian symbolism's influence on theater was greatest as a provocation to theater artists like Meyerhold, Evreinov, Alexander Tairov, Evgeny Vakhtangov, and Stanislavsky, all of whose innovations built on symbolist ideas. As Carnicke writes: "Symbolism's major role in theatrical history was not the production of a large body of texts; its role was rather that of intermediary between realistic production, which had lost its freshness, and non-representational theatre, which advanced significant stage reforms."[30]

Indeed, if symbolism fell short of fulfilling its theatrical ideals, Evreinov took them on, returning the theater to the human, mimetic self, while at the same time reimagining the relations between actor and spectator, actor and art. He drew from the symbolists a reconsideration of the role of the spectator and a sense that theater can offer us a kind of spiritual uplifting. Theater is for Evreinov a more concrete form of *zhiznetvorchestvo*, "principles of world-creation," as Vadim Maksimov writes, for Evreinov understands theatricalization as a means to both awaken our experience of life and connect us to our natural human essence.[31] When Evreinov writes of the "self" in the theater, this self is tinged with a symbolist sense of the ideal and divine, more so than with realism and baseness. But Evreinov's self in theater is the particular, individual, *selfish* self, rather than the symbolist aspiration to a universal transcendent self. Likewise, the actor in Evreinov's work is individualized, rather than depersonalized, and the actor becomes, in his theories, the instigator of theatrical art, rather than a pawn of it.

Monodrama: Staging One Mind

Evreinov heralded this fervent interest in individualization and (to quote Maksimov) an "extreme subjectivity" in theater when he developed his theory of monodrama, which he first presented in a 1908 lecture for the Literary-Artistic Circle in Moscow.[32] In a monodramatic production, all the characters, stage design, and happenings onstage are portrayed as though from the perspective of a single protagonist, in an externalization of the character's interior experience.

Evreinov advocates monodrama on the basis of beliefs about perception and emotional identification, stressing the spectator's need to feel individual ownership of a performance. An audience member in the theater wants to feel that the staged events are *their own* (*moi/svoi*), Evreinov explains:

> When some event unfolds before me on the theatrical boards that stand for the world, I regard it as drama in the highest sense of that word only when I myself become, as it were, a participant in what is transpiring on stage, when I myself share the illusion of becoming an active participant, and not a secondary one at that, ever since I became acquainted with the pleasure that resides in the most powerful, most profound emotional reactions of my responsive spirit. In

> other words, I accept as drama only such "action" as I can, without violence to my imagination, call "my drama."[33]

Theater's power for illusion, this statement suggests, is to be directed toward a private illusion experienced by each spectator: the spectator must feel that they are an "active participant" in the staged events. Within this paradigm the difference for Evreinov between the ideal performance that is "one's own" and a performance that is someone else's (*chuzhoi*) is the difference between a "drama" and a "spectacle" or "attraction." He continues: "The rest which I am unable to accept as my own drama I consider the spectacle of someone else's drama, no matter how beautiful, amusing or absurd it may be, only 'spectacle' and not drama."[34] In contrast to the private, emotional resonance of "drama" here, the term "spectacle" implies a degree of indifference and distance between audience member and performance.[35] In Russian, as in English, the word "spectacle" (*zrelishche*) shares a root with words related to seeing and vision (*zrenie*). While we merely *see* a spectacle, in Evreinov's classification, we *experience* a drama, mentally and emotionally, as though we were undergoing it ourselves: he terms it "a sympathetic emotional experiencing [*perezhivani(e)*] of what happens on stage."[36] The staging, then, must be attuned to how the person in the audience—one select *ideal* audience member—will mentally experience and react to the performance.

Evreinov's 1908 lecture on monodrama outlines a program for how a theater production could arouse in its audience members the kind of emotional experience that leads them to feel that what they are watching is "their" own drama. In writing this lecture, Evreinov was the first to directly theorize in Russian about this form of extreme individualization of the stage, but his concept was notably not new. Further, Evreinov claimed that his theory of monodrama derived from his idea for his monodramatic play *Predstavlenie liubvi* (*A Representation of Love*, 1909), rather than the other way around.[37] Although Evreinov's critic and colleague Alexander Kugel' recalls objections to Evreinov's concept from all sides, he also concedes that "Evreinov's idea was rich with implications."[38] Boris Geyer, who collaborated with Evreinov at the Crooked Mirror, would write several monodramas following Evreinov's principles.

In theorizing monodrama, Evreinov draws on psychological assumptions in symbolist ideas, most notably Sologub's argument in "Teatr odnoi voli" ("The Theater of the Single Will," 1908) that we can sensorially process but a small portion of our field of vision at once. According to Sologub, who also wrote several plays of his own (Evreinov would direct Sologub's *Nochnye pliaski* [*Night Dances*] and his *Van'ka-kliuchnik i pazh Zhean* [*Vanka the Servant and Jean the Page*] in 1909 for Vera Komissarzhevskaya), most productions overwhelm the spectator with sensory stimulation, making it difficult for the spectator to understand the production in the way the author (the playwright) intended. Because human consciousness cannot take in everything at one time, Sologub argued, theater should deploy lighting and other scenographic devices to focus the spectator's attention on a narrow portion of the stage space.[39] Evreinov concurs that we can only really grasp what we see when we focus on one specific thing: "A shift from unclear perception to clear apperception occurs only when the mind wholly yields to the power of one specific impression."[40] For Evreinov, though, the shift from perception to apperception is rooted not in a sensory narrowing but rather in a shift from what we might call indifferent or objective seeing to seeing from a particular psychosomatic perspective and with the full participation of one's own mind. That is, for him, our limited capacity for sympathy is what necessitates a drama of "one's own" (a drama of only one person—one character—at a time). His justification of this is simple: when seeing a man through the eyes of a painter, we cannot at the same time see him through the eyes of a sculptor. A production must thus choose which one character should receive the audience's sympathy.

Like Sologub, Evreinov stresses the importance of scenography here. But whereas the symbolist conceives of scenography as a set of devices that should replicate *the spectator's* cognitive process, darkening those portions of the stage that are outside the focus of the spectator's vision, Evreinov argues that scenography should elicit sympathy by visually replicating *the protagonist's* mental perception of their surroundings (or, in other words, by embodying the protagonist's state of mind), which should in turn provoke the desired emotions in the spectator. The production need not indirectly appeal to emotions; according to Evreinov, when the spectator is presented with the protagonist's emotionally colored visual experience of their world, the spectator will have the same emotional reaction to an experience as the protagonist does. Evreinov explains: "we are talking about an architectonics of drama based on the principle of the drama's stage coalescence with the way the active participant [the protagonist] is presented."[41] Monodrama portrays both the inner private experience and the exteriority of a single character at the expense of an objective view of all other characters or the stage world. Even physical objects (e.g., stage properties) appear differently depending on the protagonist's mental state: a gun the protagonist is about to use to murder someone will look different than a gun the protagonist displays proudly on his wall. Importantly, the protagonist's distorted perspective prevents us from seeing secondary characters through either an objective or a sympathetic lens. The sympathy that monodrama identifies as one of theater's goals is thus not collective: it is a lone, one-to-one identification between spectator and character (not spectator and actor). Further, from the spectator's perspective, the actor as an individual is erased and fused with the character, anticipating Evreinov's waxing on about self-transformation in *What Theater Is*.

As Evreinov emphasizes through his use of the term "participant" (*uchastnik*) to refer to the spectator, monodrama assumes a spectator that though seated and immobile is an active part of the performance. This concept recalls not only Ivanov's vision of theater as a Dionysian rite, which dates to 1906, but also Evreinov's own productions at his Ancient Theater in 1907–8 and 1911–12, where he often sat a set of actors in front of the real audience to portray an audience from the time period of the production. As Yu. B. Lisakova writes: "They showed . . . what the spectator of the corresponding epoch was like, how he watched the play and how he reacted to it. . . . The principle of 'a theater in a theater' separated the actor from the contemporary spectator, and the footlights played the role of museum glass."[42] Like the spectator in the Ancient Theater, who is encouraged to mimic the reaction of the performed audience before them, the spectator in monodrama is allowed little room for interpretative freedom.

With monodrama, Evreinov outlines an artistically radical and phenomenological understanding of the theatrical event, one that explores the externalization of mental phenomena. It is, quite literally, an attempt to portray the mind through the stage. Monodrama operates on assumptions about psychology, perception, and identification in equating what a character *sees* with what that character *experiences*, suggesting that experience is wholly sensory and immediate: "if [the dramatist] wants to represent the life of the mind, he must operate not on extrinsic realities, but on intrinsic reflections of actual objects. For what is important to the psychology of a given character is his subjective vision of the actual object and not the object itself in a relation irrelevant to him."[43] Underlying the theory of monodrama, then, is a belief in the nonobjectivity of space and the intentionality of the spectator's perception. Space and what is in it do not exist independently of how they are perceived by a consciousness. This is true for how the production's protagonist perceives his world, as well as for how the audience member perceives the production's world. Evreinov would exercise control: he aims to deny the audience member the freedom of perceiving the production's world from *any* perspective but his chosen one, in the service of granting that audience member a kind of vital identification with the protagonist's experience, conferred through the sympathy for it that the staging is designed to elicit.

Staging monodrama as Evreinov envisioned poses practical challenges. Expressionist and symbolist plays are most conducive to monodramatic staging, as are plays that convey a dream, since dreams are by nature the nonobjective projections of a single mind. Evreinov himself only wrote one full-length monodrama, *A Representation of Love*, and one short dramatic parody of monodrama, *V kulisakh dushi* (*Backstage at the Soul*, 1911). These plays explore the ramifications of subjectivity by staging the flexibility of time according to how we experience it, the shifts in how we perceive and relate to others, and our attachment of emotions to properties and things.

In *A Representation of Love*, the story of a young male known by the first-person I who is in love with a young woman, She, is told by two old men gazing out at sea, the Catarrhal Subject and the Hemorrhoidal Type.

The stage directions are relayed from the first-person perspective, and they describe the dramatic lighting and sound accompaniment that help convey the emotional tenor of each scene. They also provide information about the subjective experience of I. The fact that *only* the perspective of I is supplemented by this additional information stresses that his subjectivity is the play's center. For example:

> SHE: I didn't think that you . . .
> I [*wanting to ask "Do you like me?"*]: What?
> SHE: That you're so . . .
> I [*the same*]: So what?
> SHE: So strange.
> I [*intoning the phrase "I'm more interesting than I seem"*]: What does strange mean?[44]

As the part of She is not supplemented with stage directions about the character's interiority, Evreinov implies that She must be acted in a way that does not convey psychological independence from I. The play was not performed in Russia (only in Vienna and Budapest).[45] Certainly, how it *could* be performed in a way that would center not just the words but the unspoken perspective of I is difficult to imagine, perhaps reliant on textual information conveyed in the playbill combined with a perceptive audience.

The popular *Backstage at the Soul*, by contrast, is a far more self-conscious, double-voiced, and ambivalently didactic parody of monodrama. Such good-natured parody is consistent with Evreinov's continual efforts to make his points with surprise, shock, and humor, rather than sober conviction. It also follows in the symbolist paradigm of self-parody exhibited in *The Little Show Booth*; this parody pokes fun at theoretical stances and critiques them but does not, ultimately, undermine them, instead using its self-consciousness constructively. In *Backstage* a "professor" lectures to us at a chalkboard, citing the psychologists Wilhelm Wundt, Sigmund Freud, and Théodule-Armand Ribot about the three components of the self: the rational self, the emotional self, and the subconscious or eternal self.[46] The scene then changes to replicate the professor's diagram of the soul, where these selves reside, with the heart above and the diaphragm below. We witness an internal conflict among the selves of an adulterous husband: should he run off with a café singer or stay with his wife and child? The turmoil ends in its subject's suicide. In Evreinov's original production at his Crooked Mirror, the giant, animate heart—which hung above the actors, pulsating at a feverish rate of 125 beats per minute, according to Liudmila Tikhvinskaya—went still.[47]

Evreinov's early career is notably tinted with the biological: the undulating and partially nude bodies of his censored *Salome* in 1908, the characters known as the Catarrhal Subject and Hemorrhoidal Type in *A Representation of Love*, and the thumping heart and heaving diaphragm of *Backstage at the Soul*. The references to anatomy and illness that structure these works reveal in Evreinov a fascination with the human body as a setting for theatrical art. Given this interest in the biological and monodrama's focus on mental perception, it is little surprise that in the coming decade Evreinov's thought would shift even further toward the mind as a source of theater and as a stage.

Perception in/as "Theater in Life"

Many of Evreinov's plays and directorial projects were metatheatrical, commenting explicitly on both the essential nature of theater and the practice of theater by others around him. His *Revizor* (*The Inspector General*, 1912) and *Chetvertaia stena* (*The Fourth Wall*, 1916), satirical sketches performed at the Crooked Mirror, both parodied Russian theatrical trends, such as Moscow Art Theater naturalism. As these plays show, although he wrote stand-alone theatrical theory prolifically, Evreinov also consistently thought *through* theater, making theory central to his directorial and playwriting practice. In general, his productions in Russia (prior to emigration to Paris in 1925) were bold and vibrant, often exaggerated and comedic, frequently deploying spectacular tropes of theater traditions past, such as commedia dell'arte or the medieval mystery play, with a flair of self-consciousness. Thus, when in the 1910s he developed a theory of theater in everyday life, rather than in the theater hall, it was less a negation of his practice than an extension of it because Evreinov's productions had always centered the wonders of self-transformation, rather than elements more suited to the conventions of the stage, such as narrative or physical movement.

In the opening to the 1912 *Theater as Such*, Evreinov calls out to the reader: "Tra-ta-ta! I loudly sound a call to the *presentation* of your very own life."[48] Evreinov's concept of "theater for oneself," first advanced in 1915 and later reformulated as "theater in life," builds on multiple ideas that he had tested in the theory of monodrama a few years earlier, expanding on the notion of "one's own" theater and not only *permitting* the subject's individual desires but springing from them: one of its principal aims is pleasure. The word *theater* usually references a place, Evreinov writes in *Teatr dlia sebia* (*The Theater for Oneself*, 1915–17): whether an auditorium in which dramatic productions are presented, a "theater of war," or an anatomical theater. But theater is not specific to these places, and its potential is constrained by them. Productions in a theater hall are obedient to social and economic demands, he argues, and the spectator there is denied agency and choice: the same production is presented to an audience of any size at a fixed time and place.

Although, as discussed above, Evreinov's Ancient Theater and concept of monodrama deny the spectator agency in *how* they view a performance, the concern he indicates here is that theater denies the spectator agency in *what* they view. Commercial mass theater does not account for the fact that we do not all want to see the same thing. "Mass culture," as Louise McReynolds explains in her study of leisure practices in tsarist Russia, "is not a spontaneous expression by a group but rather a constructed product that represents the interests of the producer before it does those of the consumer."[49] It is not driven by the individual spectator's desires. In contrast to the non-individualized theater in the theater house, Evreinov proposes a "theater for oneself" in the spaces of everyday life, thus implicitly acknowledging monodrama's inability to *fully* shape the individual spectator's theatrical experience.

Whereas the theater hall fixes a spectator in a particular seat at a particular time, the spectator in everyday life is free to move about and watch *or* not watch. Watching becomes itself a form of "creating" theater: for Evreinov voyeurism is a key element of theater for oneself, or the creation of theater outside of traditional theatrical structures and institutions. This decoupling of theater from the stage is further emphasized in his later term "theater in life," which he used as the title of a 1927 English-language volume that combined and condensed many of his theoretical writings.[50] Theater in life, as Evreinov envisioned it, was intensely personal—which is why much of his theater in life fits under the more specific concept of theater for oneself, or theater in life enacted for oneself.

Evreinov identifies with the term "theater in life" the performance-like practices that are part of everyday human activity, such as child's play, ritual, and apparel and self-presentation, an idea for which Evreinov is often cited as an early theorist of performance studies.[51] Like the discipline of performance studies, Evreinov finds theater (performance) in ordinary activities and believes that theater is essential to human nature. Unlike performance studies, Evreinov alludes to but does not emphasize the social and cultural significance of performance, attending instead to its significance for the individual. Social constructions of identity, such as gender, race, sexuality, and class, as well as the power structures they reinforce, do not come up in his writings on theater in life, but at the same time, he suggests that through theater an individual has a great ability to fundamentally change, a point that implies theater's essential role in formulating identity.

These concepts of theater for oneself and theater in life show that for Evreinov all theater is born in an individual's natural drive and not from a theater building, text, costume, or other element. As Josette Féral writes: "One must conclude that for Evreinov, man is central to the process; he is the fundamental cause of the emergence and manifestation of theatricality."[52] This is the human-centered drive for self-transformation that Evreinov's Platon Ivanovich extols in the children's book. But taking the theater out of the theater hall radically overturns the relationships between the agents involved. The spectator—already integral to the creation of theater (theater is typically *for* the watching)—is brought further into the process, no longer free to sit passively. Extemporaneity is required of both actor and spectator.

In a voyeuristic scenario (theater for oneself), the event is "created" by the spectator, and the "actors" are unaware that they are being watched. Even the professional actor is an "actor for themself" and is driven by self-interest and self-pleasure, according to Evreinov, who tells of legendary Shakespearean actor Edmund Kean (1787–1833) being discovered disguising himself in his dressing room for no purpose other than personal entertainment.[53] As in monodrama, emotional "participation" can replace physical acting as the *activator* of the theater event. Evreinov felt that there was something more genuine in the humanness of untrained or spontaneous theater than in the careful calculations of the professional theater.

Theater for oneself does not often announce itself as a performance. Like voyeurism, it is private, even unnoticed by others: dressing up alone in front of a mirror, gazing out at the street, peeking through a window at an unsuspecting occupant. While the conventions of the stage demarcate the theatrical illusions taking place on it, theater for oneself can lack such an indicating frame. What, then, delineates and constitutes a performance of theater for oneself? Evreinov's understanding of the performance site or environment "in life" develops from the nonobjective conceptualization of performance space that he earlier articulated in the theory of monodrama. Both monodrama and theater for oneself engage in a psychological and emotional constitution of the performance site, refiguring relationships among actor, spectator, and role.

By posing spectating or seeing as a means of creating scenes, theater for oneself does not merely identify theatricality as inherent in ordinary life; it implicates the subject that experiences this theatricality. Several scenarios Evreinov gives for performing *for oneself* are telling:

> Lying on a windowsill to observe the street "mass scene" or "everyday scenes" in the courtyard. . . .
>
> Attending so-called "society" and playing there a "tsarina of the ball," "society lion," "important dignitary," "daredevil personality." . . .
>
> Spying under the windows or through the chink in a bathhouse.
>
> The hoaxing dramatization of an apparition.[54]

Evreinov's word choice in these scenarios suggests that the subject plays an integral role in the event. Perhaps the "theater" here is not, for example, *what is happening* in the courtyard as viewed from the windowsill, but rather the *act* of "lying on a windowsill to observe." In these brief theater for oneself prompts, Evreinov does not imply that everyday happenings *are* theater. Instead, he uses the nouns *lezhan'e*, *poseshchen'e*, *raygryvan'e*, and *podsmatrivanie* (in English, the gerunds *lying*, *visiting/attending*, *playing/putting on*, and *spying*, respectively) to emphasize that a subject is *doing* something in relation to the everyday happenings in their environment, regardless of whether the subject is only looking at those happenings or is actually physically interacting with them. Evreinov continues with other examples of theater for oneself: disguising oneself as a driver to drive one's aristocratic friends around incognito (an example that certainly suggests only an aristocratic subject) and riding around town just to look out at life as though the view were a "living cinematograph."[55] Again, the subject's actions and perspective vis-à-vis their environment appear for Evreinov to be closely intertwined with the significance of that environment itself.

Each of these prompts or "plays" describes in prose an existing location or situation into which the actor enters either to intervene in some way through transforming themself or to position themself as a spectator.[56] For Evreinov, intentionality must radiate from the actor-spectator, who must activate the ground and perform in response to it. These situations are supposed to be intrinsically enjoyable and *pure*: "theater for the sake of theater. Only. But it was shameful to confess it."[57] As his examples show, Evreinov seems to feel that one can insert theater into everyday life because that is where theater occurs naturally, without the commercialization or professionalization that characterize the theater hall. Evreinov presents us with different examples to show the *prevalence* of theater for oneself, including for various kinds of pleasure. He does not deny the more perverse possibilities of secretly watching others for personal entertainment, and in fact he compares the theatrical instinct to Freud's theory of the sexual instinct, an innate drive to mate and satisfy one's needs through sexual activity.

Not only actions and voyeurism can make up the perceptual content of theater for oneself. The performance space can be constituted in the actor's mind, as well, through the "viewing" of memories as its own kind of performance. When we remember, Evreinov writes, our present self brings to life the past one, staging the past self in the mind such that we triumph over the force of time.[58] He suggests that one can set up an entire array of scents, objects, clothing, music, and ambient temperatures to help give life to a memory, but the memory is only internal. We are our own theater or, more specifically, gods of our own theater. Evreinov uses archaic religious language to declare that he is staging a memory of a dead friend: "But I am I [*esm' az*]! I [*Az*], who wisely knows that the other, most importantly *for me*, is none other than one of the performances of *my* consciousness [*odno iz predstavlenii* moego *soznaniia*]."[59]

Skepticism toward Evreinov's concept of theater for oneself has persisted. Carnicke has concluded that it is "at the most basic level . . . simply an exalted form of self-dramatization."[60] Other scholars have preferred to describe theater for oneself as a form of "theatricality," citing Evreinov's key term *teatral'nost'*, while carefully avoiding the implications carried by the word "theater," although Evreinov himself intended such a link.[61] Puchner refers to Evreinov's *teatral'nost'* as something "directed against the dramatic text and thus [against] literature at large," highlighting what he considers to be a modernist distinction between theatricality (as a reaction *against* dramatic texts) and theater (which may be neutral toward these texts).[62] Féral also draws a line between theater and theatricality with respect to Evreinov, on the basis that for him the inherence of theatricality in life has no connection to the stage: "Evreinov's view of theatricality concerns anthropology and ethnology more than theater. Because he has inscribed theatricality in the quotidian, Evreinov has caused the specificity of stage-related theatricality to disappear."[63] Evreinov does claim that our natural instinct for theatricality is "pre-aesthetic": biologically natural, without aesthetic purpose, and independent of traditional auditorium-based theater. But this instinct for theatricality is also the source of this theater, and the theater of "theater for oneself"—from a director who staged performances in traditional theaters throughout his adult life—merits more careful consideration.

A common understanding of theatricality in the modernist period opposes it to realism. Thomas Postlewait and Tracy C. Davis write: "The concepts of realism and theatricality set up a binary configuration in modernism, with realism aligning itself with the idea of 'artless' art and the many alternatives to realism embracing and celebrating the explicit theatrical conditions of the stage, its genres, and its traditions. . . . This new antinomy allowed the concept of theatricality to achieve a positive definition."[64] And yet, for all Evreinov's outlandishness, his examples of theater for oneself, like staring out the window, are terribly ordinary because of the way that theater elides into everyday life for him. In a way, the theater for oneself scenarios achieve *both* ends of the realism-theatricality binary, for they are so real that they may be unnoticeable, and thus "artless," but they are simultaneously the very height of theatricalism, celebrating the theatrical conditions of life. Evreinov does also write about theater as a means of becoming "other than oneself," but in fact both extremes of ordinariness and outlandishness make up the content of theater for him.

Theatrotherapy and the Mind-Cure Movement

One of the more elaborate scenarios that Evreinov lays out in his *Theater for Oneself* makes particularly vivid the medicinal properties of theater—not merely within the art of the stage (as in Harlequin's resurrection from the dead by the curtain call in Evreinov's *Veselia smert'* (*A Merry Death*, 1909), but on the real bodies of real life. In this scenario, the subject, or actor-spectator, is instructed to open his veins for bloodletting. With a nod to responsibility, Evreinov advises that a doctor approve the procedure and be present to monitor the subject's pulse, and he also suggests a luxurious and dramatic setting: a warm bath in a marble tub, a white sheet wrapped around the doctor, and a friend performing background music off to the side.[65]

The purpose of these theatrics is for "trying on deaths" (*primerka smertei*): deliberately and temporarily bringing a healthy body closer to death to provoke a deeper appreciation of life.[66] An awareness of physiological mortality is summoned through the intensification of the subject's experience of their own body: the physical sensation of pain and weaknesses, as well as (we can imagine, though Evreinov does not describe it) the visibility of one's own blood, uselessly and detrimentally dripping out of one's body. As Evreinov concludes more explicitly in the revised and abridged English-language version of his writings in 1927: "It isn't for nothing that our great-grandmothers were so fond of blood-letting: I assure you that this excellent tradition was based on theatrically psychological, rather than medical, foundations."[67]

In this bloodletting scenario, medical intervention into a healthy body structures the performance, which ends if the body's pulse approaches the danger zone. Notably, the bloodletting scenario establishes an elaborate mise-en-scène and deploys a historical medical procedure on the body for the purposes of *mental* therapeutics. Moreover, it is not the physical procedure itself that treats the mind in need of better appreciating the value of life, as Evreinov acknowledges when he refers to bloodletting's therapeutic function as "theatrically psychological, rather than medical."[68] Instead, the mind is treated by the larger *phenomenology* of the performance of that physical procedure. It is not so much the bloodletting in itself that is therapeutic, but the particular psycho-physiological experience the bloodletting induces when carried out in Evreinov's prescribed setting.

Evreinov posits that a particular setting and set of actions can have healing power, as he outlines in the bloodletting scenario and other performance scenarios in his *Theater for Oneself*. He develops this concept explicitly under the label of theatrotherapy in an article in the Petrograd journal *Zhizn' iskusstva* (*The Life of Art*) in 1920. He suggests multiple forms of theatrotherapy; indeed, as is typical of his splashy and verbose writing, he explains the concept through examples rather than through rigorous definitions. One might cure oneself of an illness by *pretending* to be cured. Or one might implicate an ill person in a situation that prods them to act *as though* they are cured—and to therein *be* cured. Sylvia Sasse makes a key point that in theatrotherapy's act of playing healthy, "it's not about deceiving oneself, but about experiencing for oneself the spell [*chary*] of healing."[69] In other words theatrotherapy is less about tricking oneself than it is about strategically utilizing performance to *transform* oneself.

In one example Evreinov asks us to imagine that we are fatigued and depressed (perhaps the common turn-of-the-century diagnosis of neurasthenia, though he does not use the term). A doctor sends us on a vacation abroad to rejuvenate. We go, and it works. Why? Evreinov explains: "You have been removed from your familiar place, from which, due to accommodation to it and a multitude of affairs that distracted you from a contemplative relationship to your surroundings, you ceased to look at these surroundings as at some sort of show that is interesting in its own right, regardless of your role in it. You have been removed and thrust into the conditions of a real theatrical spectator!"[70] In Evreinov's theatrically, rather than medically, informed diagnosis, our failure to look at our habitual environment as we look at a theatrical performance is the real cause of our illness. The vacation restores our health because we see unfamiliar streets, buildings, and monuments, and we look at these things, as Evreinov writes, "as at an array of stage scenery that excites with its novelty, awakening and arousing in you your sleeping and frozen instinct for transformation."[71] This example might recall Viktor Shklovsky's device of estrangement (*ostranenie*), the belief that art makes us look at familiar things in a new way. But the point here is not the defamiliarization that familiar objects undergo when they become stage properties. When we take a vacation, we see new things, not familiar ones, and it is these new things that induce us to *see* differently, to see with a "contemplative relationship to our surroundings." By seeing new sights, we acquire a new mode of perception (much like that achieved by the subject of the bloodletting scenario), and we are thereby, according to Evreinov, healed of our mental and physical troubles.

Treatment by vacation—or rest cures, often in unfamiliar environments—was frequently advised to patients at the turn of the century. It was widely thought that fresh air and rest allowed the body to heal. Evreinov, however, identifies the vacation's success in its particular effect on the patient's mind, namely on the patient's perceptive faculties—the patient's ways of perceiving and mentally relating to their surroundings. This changed perception, according to Evreinov, then leads to healing in the body. This view is inverted from traditional understandings at this time. As Eric Caplan explains of American medicine's use of the rest cure in this period: "Any changes in a patient's mental condition that resulted from prolonged bed rest were interpreted by most physicians as deriving from some overriding physical transformation."[72] Angela Brintlinger writes similarly that late nineteenth-century psychiatry in Russia, "was intricately intertwined with the body. When medical doctors began to claim authority over the mentally ill, they emphasized physical rather than psychic causes. . . . Russian doctors sought answers in neurological processes rather than psychological ones, in physical treatments rather than 'talking cures.' "[73]

The transition to treating mental illnesses more directly in Russia can be located around the turn of the century. Mental health care for mild psychiatric disorders in the 1900s and 1910s was principally based at institutions for "nervous" patients, who might have such illnesses as epilepsy, hysteria, and neurasthenia, as Irina Sirotkina explains, with a number of nervous sanatoriums founded in Russia between 1908 and 1914.[74] At these sanatoriums, patients underwent various physiotherapeutic procedures along with more psychically focused "moral treatment," which involved establishing positive relationships with the doctors and caretakers at the institution and basking in its isolated, rural atmosphere.[75] Meanwhile, in the early 1910s, the intellectuals of the capital cities were caught up in the faddish fervor of psychoanalysis, though, as Alexander Etkind points out, early psychoanalysis in Russia was more often applied to cultural phenomena at large, rather than to individual patients.[76] But while Evreinov was clearly in touch with the psychoanalytic trend and the works of Freud, as demonstrated by numerous references throughout his writings, the mechanisms of psychoanalysis seem fairly distant from Evreinov's above example of the therapeutics of spectating at a vacation site just as one spectates in the theater. Psychoanalysis instead functions through conversation with a trained analyst who attempts to elicit, understand, and reshape the patient's narrations. Sasse has addressed this distinction already, noting that in theatrotherapy, unlike psychoanalysis, "the therapeutic effect is directed not at the understanding of and repetition of an unresolved problem, but at the unsatisfied desire to play a different role or find oneself in a particular situation."[77] Theatrotherapy operates, unsurprisingly, far closer to the mechanisms of *theater*.

A different psychiatric spark for Evreinov's understanding of mental—and physical—healing is suggested by his reference, in his theatrotherapy article, to the journalist, humorist, and essayist Prentice Mulford (1834–91). Mulford was a prominent figure in the American movement known as New Thought, a religious-philosophical movement that had a hold on America's popular imagination throughout the nineteenth century and into the twentieth. (The branches extending from New Thought even reach to the present day, in such contemporary concepts as the law of attraction.) New Thought sought to allow people to recuperate agency and power in their experiences of their bodies by seeking healing within. Though New Thought was a fairly diverse and disjointed movement, one of its core components was what William James termed the "mind-cure movement," which held that our mental states are manifested in our physical reality, including both the biological behavior of our own body and the things that happen to us in the external world.[78] It is a belief in the power to heal—and even cure—ourselves through our minds. This movement was thus premised on a belief in the mind-body connection, insisting that healing oneself, whether of psychic or somatic illnesses, requires the full participation of the mind. Its founder, clockmaker Phineas Quimby (1802–66), was sickly, with diseased kidneys, lungs, and liver, his body weakened by a poison (calomel) doctors had prescribed to him as medicine. One day, Quimby set out in a carriage, urged the horse to go faster and faster, and felt better again by the time he returned home.[79] He saw this experience as evidence that the cure for illness lay not in medical intervention but in one's self-perceptions and mental state. In fact, he would go on to preach opposition to professional medicine. Quimby "opined that doctors were a major cause of illness because they convinced people of the reality of disease," writes Wakoh Shannon Hickey.[80]

Although Quimby founded New Thought, Prentice Mulford was responsible for a number of its most popular and influential texts. Evreinov likely encountered Mulford's writings after they were published in Russian translation in Odesa in 1912 or in Petrograd in 1915.[81] In his 1888 essay "The Doctor Within," referenced by Evreinov, Mulford writes the following potently theatrical lines:

> What you think or hold most in mind or imagination, that you have most faith in. If you imagine a bugbear, much of the time you will make a reality of such imagining. The "confirmed invalid" sees himself in his "mind's eye" only as sick. He puts out, or imagines, the wrong image, or imagination. He is unconsciously working the same law. The invalid who always sees himself as sick, is in reality constructing a sick body. . . .
>
> The imagining of a fresh, sound, vigorous body, is in actual substance, though unseen, a fresh, sound, healthy, and vigorous body. It is a spiritual reality. The material body must grow to be like the spiritual reality. If your body is weak, do not see it in your mind's eye as weak. See yourself as full of life and playful vigor. Don't see yourself as an invalid propped up in a chair, or confined to the house, though for the time being your body is in such conditions. You are healing yourself when you see yourself running foot-races. You are keeping yourself an invalid when you see yourself ever as one.[82]

Mulford states that our mental perceptions, the way we "see" ourselves within the world, are constitutive of our experiences. This view comes remarkably close to Evreinov's notion that when the patient's perceptions are positively altered, the patient's health and embodied experiences will improve. Evreinov merely prescribes far more elaborate means of inducing one's change in perceptions than Mulford does: Evreinov's scenarios involve a full mise-en-scène, while Mulford relies on no external stimuli. (Quimby's carriage ride, however, would count as utilizing external stimuli.) Like Mulford, Evreinov is not solely focused on psychic problems, though he somewhat demurs on how far theatrotherapy can go in treating physical illness. At times, Evreinov suggests that theatrotherapy can directly affect the physical body by changing the mind, very much in alignment with Mulford: "Verify with doctors the colossal significance of will to live for a victim of tuberculosis," Evreinov writes.[83] He also identifies certain limits, with the caveat that the medical profession is limited, too: "Naturally, if it's a matter of a broken leg or a catarrh of the renal pelvis, then theatrotherapy won't help, but after all neither will hydrotherapy or helio- or electro- or radio- or many other methods of therapy, the significance and use of which, when appropriately applied, no one will dispute."[84] In fact, the principal difference between Mulford and Evreinov seems to be that Evreinov casts the process of positively changing one's perceptions as a theatrical one—a performance. What Mulford sees as a mental, even spiritual, process of imagining oneself to be healthy, Evreinov sees as an act of theater.[85]

Theater's association with therapeutic intent dates, as Evreinov himself points out, to Aristotle's concept of catharsis, and it develops particular steam in Freud's copious mapping of human psychology onto classics of drama, such as Greek and Shakespearean tragedies.[86] Evreinov may not have been the only one to experiment with theater's healing powers in early twentieth-century Russia. Philosopher and critic Vladimir Il'in (1891–1974, often spelled Iljine) is said to have worked with mentally ill patients in hospitals using what he termed "therapeutic theater," which consisted in training patients in improvisation over the course of dozens of sessions with therapists.[87] Unfortunately, evidence for Il'in's work with theater and therapy is remarkably scant.[88] But across Europe and America in the early 1900s, we do find a number of applications of theater to therapeutic contexts. Psychiatrist Jacob Levy Moreno (1889–1974) founded "psychodrama," a structured method of patient reenactment under the direction of a therapist, while psychoanalyst Sándor Ferenczi (1873–1933) asked patients to act in therapy sessions. Moreno may have even been familiar with Evreinov's writings on theatrotherapy prior to founding his first psychodrama theater in New York in 1936.[89]

And yet, even here, Evreinov's theatrotherapy is unique in that it is rooted in theatrical experience, unlike the work of Moreno and Ferenczi, which stems from clinical experience. Evreinov claims to have observed many times in his directorial career that a sick actor who nonetheless goes onstage regains their health as they perform their role.[90] The actor's self-perception changes as they play a different—healthy—individual. With this comment Evreinov again underscores his investment in the full phenomenology of performance: the experience of a *particular* person in a *particular* mental-physical state playing a *particular* role. That is, theater for Evreinov is not independent of how it is experienced by the individual enacting (or spectating) it. The positive theatrical effects on our perceptions that facilitate our healing are in themselves constitutive of theater in Evreinov's descriptions. His thought echoes with the (albeit never explicitly stated) notion that theatricality is a biological instinct that is—in its essence—curative.

The rampant popularity of the mind-cure movement changed the course of professionalized mental health treatment by pushing institutional medicine to recognize the mind's integration in overall human health and to, as Caplan writes, "consider seriously the role that mental factors played in the etiology, pathology, and treatment of certain functional nervous diseases."[91] Theatrotherapy is thus not so much an intriguing thought experiment by an eccentric, if philosophically interesting, director as it is part of a larger medical and cultural movement to understand the mind and its role in human health. This connection suggests provocative questions about the potential of aesthetic works as media for scientific knowledge discovery, rather than merely as reflectors of existing scientific knowledge.

Already in his early works, Evreinov suggests a powerful unity between the biological and the theatrical, as in the heart and lungs set of *Backstage at the Soul*, which falls silent when the protagonist dies. Further, scholars such as Carnicke have identified in Evreinov's work a continual deferral of the self through endless layers of masks and play.[92] But theatrotherapy attests to the opposite: a kind of self-becoming through theater and through consciousness of one's own body. "Theatre, like therapy, can lead us into a richer understanding of ourselves and our worldly relationships," writes Fintan Walsh in his overview of the multiple ways in which theater and therapy have intersected.[93] Theatrotherapy assumes that our experiences are shaped by our minds and our environment, permitting theater, that embodied, mimetic art form, to change who we are—and for the better. "We," here, are of course ordinary people as actors, as for Evreinov the actor's mind-body is a performance site.

The Main Thing, a Parody-Experiment

Despite his prolific writings, Evreinov seems never to have written out a traditional acting theory in the mold of Stanislavsky's or Meyerhold's. Little research has been done on his work with actors, though he does appear to have taught in Saint Petersburg from 1908 to 1911 at the Dramatic Studio of M. A. Rigler-Voronkova, which trained actors in gymnastics and other plastic exercises, and at the Factory of the Eccentric Actor, founded in Petrograd in 1921, which emphasized physical, machine-inspired movement akin to circus stunts over psychologizing and emotion.[94]

Evreinov's concepts of theatrotherapy and theater for oneself, as well as his love of commedia and hints of his beliefs about the actor, converge, however, in his acclaimed play *The Main Thing*, the first of his trilogy of plays devoted to theater in life.[95] *The Main Thing*, which premiered in February 1921 at the Free Comedy in Petrograd under the direction of Nikolai Petrov, was soon produced all over Europe and the United States, including in Rome by Luigi Pirandello. The 1926 Broadway production (as *The Chief Thing*) featured such actors as Henry Travers, Estelle Winwood, Lee Strasberg, and Edward G. Robinson. Even with this notable cast, however, American audiences generally found the play dull and difficult to follow, in contrast with European audiences, who tended to better appreciate the humor of the play and respond more favorably. *The Main Thing* bears many stylistic resemblances to Pirandello's metatheatrical *Six Characters in Search of an Author* (also 1921), though neither playwright was aware of the other's work at the time of their respective writing. Both plays interrogate the distinction between theater and life. *The Main Thing* also taps into the history of Russian metatheater, including not just Blok's *The Little Show Booth* but also Alexander Ostrovsky's *Les* (*The Forest*, 1871), whose protagonists are the provincial actors Neschastlivtsev and Schastlivtsev. The primary setting of Evreinov's play, a boardinghouse, echoes Maxim Gorky's proto-socialist-realist play *Na*

Figure 1.1. Set design by Yury Annenkov for *The Main Thing*, by Nikolai Evreinov, directed by Nikolai Petrov at the Free Comedy Theater, Petrograd, 1921. Act 1, a fortune teller's room. Copyright © Bakhrushin Theatre Museum, Moscow.

dne (*The Lower Depths*, 1902), a play much lauded by the Bolsheviks for depicting the stories of the unfortunate and impoverished.

The Main Thing portrays a set of provincial theater actors who are recruited to the "theater of life" by the mysterious director Dr. Fregoli (named after the famous Italian quick-change artist Leopoldo Fregoli). He sends three theater actors to take up temporary residence in a boardinghouse and bring love and joy to its most unhappy lodgers. Dr. Fregoli's real name is Paraclete, a traditionally Christian term referring to a counselor or advocate, usually the Holy Spirit.[96] He begins the play as a fortune teller. While photographs of the original 1921 production do not appear to have survived, we can tell from a painting by set designer Yury Annenkov that the set was luscious and colorful (see fig. 1.1). Paraclete disguises himself as five different personas throughout the play, including, in the Shrovetide harlequinade of the final scene, as Harlequin. In typical Evreinov fashion, the characters of the theater actors are referred to by character type rather than name: the Romantic Lead, the Barefoot Dancer, and the Comic. At the boardinghouse, the Barefoot Dancer plays the role of a coquettish servant girl who chases

Figure 1.2. Set design by Yury Annenkov for *The Main Thing*, by Nikolai Evreinov, directed by Nikolai Petrov at the Free Comedy Theater, Petrograd, 1921. Act 3, a furnished room. Copyright © Bakhrushin Theatre Museum, Moscow.

after a depressed lodger called the Student (another archetype), the Romantic Lead falls in love with the unhappy daughter of the boardinghouse mistress, and the Comic is a retired army doctor who tells jokes at dinner each night to lighten the atmosphere for all the lodgers. Dr. Fregoli joins the crew as Mr. Schmidt, a record salesman.

Yet the boardinghouse to which Dr. Fregoli sends the actors seems tightly tied to theater architecture and convention. Evreinov provides a detailed figure of the stage set for the boardinghouse, including six doors to residents' rooms, with the entire set clearly optimized for viewing from the audience seats of a proscenium theater. Most of the doors run along a narrow corridor that runs upstage directly perpendicular to the proscenium line. The set for the 1921 production did not arrange the doors so strictly, but it still presented a number of doors for audience viewing (see fig. 1.2). That is, this set of the boardinghouse in the theater of life is very much designed for the theater hall, and likewise the boardinghouse becomes a place of theatrical events. Indeed, in line with Dr. Fregoli's instruction, the boardinghouse undergoes different modes of transformation: first its residents are made happier, then its interior is transformed for carnival festivities. Furthermore, the resemblance of the boardinghouse to that of the proto-socialist-realist (and thoroughly miserable) *The Lower Depths* deepens the metatheatricalism of the setting. Though it is presented to us as a theater of life, it is heavily and deliberately staged.

Dr. Fregoli's task for the actors comes under the heading of Evreinov's concept of theater as therapy. And yet, the multiple, overlapping situations of theater for oneself or theatrotherapy in *The Main Thing* reveal Dr. Fregoli's speeches about theatrotherapy to be other than what they seem. Dr. Fregoli—a persona of Paraclete's invention—is of course himself acting "in life" when he recruits these actors in the theater hall where they work, meaning that the walls of that theater hall cannot keep out the theatricality hidden in everyday life. The illusion Dr. Fregoli creates may be as necessary to these actors as their adopted personas "in life" are to the people with whom they interact. Dr. Fregoli's speeches become quaint as we learn of the pretending or acting that is already happening outside this theater. Not only is Paraclete a master of disguises, but we learn from even before Dr. Fregoli's speeches that the actor known as the Romantic Lead has been pretending to be a detective to help two women track down their trigamist husband (who turns out to be Paraclete). More tragically, the Student at the boardinghouse has been going to elaborate lengths to pretend that his recently deceased brother is still alive for the sake of his ailing father's health, even driving himself to attempt suicide from the emotional toll of covering up his grief.

Whether we are—or are not—in a theater becomes completely confused. Are we debased and enfeebled by this universal theatricality, or are we elevated and empowered? Evreinov's understanding of the consequences of theatricality is prefigured by Ostrovsky's two provincial acters in the play *The Forest*, who are—like Tom Stoppard's Rosencrantz and Guildenstern—the only sources of genuineness in their metatheatrical world. *The Main Thing* presents the move from the theater hall to the outside world (the boarding house) as a move from one constructed and fictionalized space to another, both of them ultimately performance stages. At the end of the play, we are left with the commedia characters Harlequin (Paraclete), Pierrot (the Romantic Lead), Columbine (the Barefoot Dancer, see fig. 1.3), and the Doctor (the Comic), all of whom traditionally represent a kind of pure and whole theatricality, for which falsity or inauthenticity are not an obverse. This revelation that our characters are in truth stock figures from the commedia dell'arte is peculiar: rather than baring the trappings of the theater hall (as at the end of Blok's *The Little Show Booth*) or negating the conventions of the theater piece by revealing the characters to be actors (as at the end of Pierre Corneille's *L'Illusion comique*, 1636), Evreinov offers a world in which classically theatrical figures are also real, of reality. In the final moments, we are reminded that the theater—*our* theater—must concede to the demands of the world outside it, even if the outside world is only a stage, too. The Director exclaims: "The main thing is to finish the play on time. . . . The hour is late, the audience is anxious to get home, lots of them have to go to work early tomorrow! . . . What's more, the trolleys only run up to a certain time!"[97]

In the play, ultimately, the theater—and even the Theater (high art, aesthetic)—is everything. Or, at least, its constructs are everywhere in "real"

Figure 1.3. Female costume design for Columbine by Yury Annenkov for *The Main Thing*, by Nikolai Evreinov, directed by Nikolai Petrov at the Free Comedy Theater, Petrograd, 1921. Copyright © Bakhrushin Theatre Museum, Moscow.

life. The confusion of what is and is not "theatrical" in the play, who is and is not "putting on" at any given time, is not actually problematic in the end. The unraveling of the plot is not concerned with binaries between playing and not playing. Theatricalism is not opposed to realism; acting is not demarcated from not acting. The theatrical experience is individualized; to each character a different set of things are or are not theatrical. Despite its parody, the play undergirds the concept of theatrotherapy, especially through the Student, whose sobering role-playing is not revealed to the audience until the end. In order for theatrotherapy to work—much like monodrama—each person must have an individual experience of what is theatrical. These multiple individual experiences always for Evreinov bear some relation to theater.

Evreinov's interest is not so much in the recognition of inherent theatricality in life, but in the *apprehension* of it. It is the difference between the performance as an objective event and the performance as something experienced and internalized by the spectator (or actor-spectator). For him the act of observation confers theatrical status. Thus Evreinov's understanding of theater is phenomenological rather than metaphysical: he defines theater as a certain kind of subjective *experience* rather than as a certain kind of *thing*. His idea of theatricality goes against the dramatic text but not against the Theater, as there is no real difference for him between apprehending theatricality *in* a theater hall and doing so *outside* of one. But the Theater is always his model of the relationship between spectator and environment.

To return to where we started: Evreinov, the only major Russian modernist director to never form his own acting studio or acting methodology, is today not uncommonly viewed as both anti-theatrical and anti-theater. But is that accurate? Part of understanding whether Evreinov's ideas have anything to do with actors entails understanding whether his ideas about theater in life really have anything to do with the theater. That is, are the subjects in theater in life the same as the subjects in theater? Are professional actors different from actors in life? While other thinkers in this book emphasize the professionalizing of actors (especially Stanislavsky and Tairov), Evreinov asks us to consider what an actor is in a more basic sense. In the same way that we cannot ultimately tell what is and is not the theater space in *The Main Thing*, he brings closer together the actor of the theater and we actors in everyday life.

Even theatricality for Evreinov is underlined by the vocabulary of the theater, as he writes: "Under 'theatricality' as a term I mean an aesthetic showing of a clearly tendentious character, which, even far from a theater building, with one captivating gesture, one beautifully intoned word, creates scaffolding, scenery, and frees us from the eyes of reality."[98] Creating that scaffolding and scenery for the purpose of self-healing and self-realization is the task of each of us as actors in our interactions with the world.

Chapter 2

✦

The Actor as Material

"A living human, flesh and blood, transforms into art!" exclaimed Prince Sergei Volkonsky to roomfuls of listeners in 1911, in a talk that he delivered across Moscow and Saint Petersburg.[1] Speaking on the topic of "Chelovek kak material iskusstva" ("The Human Being as the Material of Art"), Volkonsky outlined the special advantages that the art of the actor offers, for such an art is neither exclusively visual nor aural but moves through space and time. Capable of rhythm, dance, and music, the human body makes for richly multidimensional artistic material, he claimed, and the actor's highest aim lies in the merging of body and spirit. At the time of his talk, Volkonsky had only just returned from Europe, where he had studied eurhythmics with Émile Jaques-Dalcroze, and he was eager to share this system of movement and music with Russia. He was even more enthused to share a related system, the gestural exercises of François Delsarte, which facilitate the body's expression of the spirit. His evangelizing was successful: many Russian theater workers would learn about emotion and physical expression through Volkonsky's Saint Petersburg courses in rhythmic gymnastics and his series of books on Delsarte's system (1912–13).

That the material of theater is the actor—and specifically, the actor's body, "flesh and blood"—was a point of fascination in the early twentieth-century Russian performing arts, a fascination that developed in tandem with the impact of Volkonsky's dissemination of Jaques-Dalcroze's and Delsarte's ideas, to be picked up by Konstantin Stanislavsky, Vsevolod Meyerhold, Evgeny Vakhtangov, Mikhail Chekhov, and many others who sought to train actors in movement. Alexander Tairov, whose actors at the Moscow Kamerny Theater studied Swedish gymnastics, among other movement forms, listed the components of the actor's corporeal material in his book of 1921: "You are an actor. You (your 'I') is a creative personality, conceiving and bringing to life the work of your art; you, your body (that is, your hands, feet, torso, head, eyes, voice, speech) also presents that material from which you must create; you, your muscles, joints, ligaments—serve as the instrument you need; and you, that is, your individual whole that is embodied in a stage figure, is as a result that work of art that is born from the entire creative process."[2] Discourse on the actor as material accompanied both a widespread devotion to actor training in the period and a rigorous new investigation of the signification of the actor—in particular as a body—onstage. While Nikolai Evreinov's approach to acting as articulated in his theories is almost exclusively focused on the actor's mind, rather than on movement or the body (see chapter 1), Volkonsky and the larger trend of movement training he launched remind us that the actor is a body and that this body makes up the material or perceptual content of theatrical art. Thus while Evreinov's concentration on the mind is much more moderate when echoed in his colleagues' work, movement theory and attention to the actor's body or the actor as material represent a broader concern in the era, one that crossed the disciplines of theater, dance, opera, and even the popular eurhythmics.

But this is not to say that the mind is disregarded for a focus on the body. Within the diverse new approaches to the physical training of actors in this period, we find nuanced attention to and implications for the role of the actor's mind. Rarely is the actor as material wholly divorced from the mind; instead, we find within programs for physical training beliefs about selfhood, identity, and mental processing that enrich our understanding of actor training overall in the early twentieth century in Russia and the Soviet Union. Physical exercises provided practical solutions—in the form of expanded movement repertoires and enhanced strength and ranges of motion—to essentially philosophical problems about how and what the body represents in performance. These problems include the turn-of-the-century symbolist friction between mimetic body and abstracted representation discussed in chapter 1. Furthermore, the era's efforts to train the body often centered questions of consciousness, awareness, and perception—in other words, channels of exchange between mind and body.

This chapter addresses the mind within understandings of the actor as material from two different but ultimately intersecting directions: the work of director Vsevolod Emilevich Meyerhold (1874–1940) and the work of philosopher Gustav Gustavovich Shpet (1879–1937). Meyerhold is often perceived as the paradigmatic figurehead for actor training focused on the body and on a reflexological understanding of psychology, wherein emotions are aroused exclusively by movements. His work at the Borodinskaya Street Studio, where he developed what he would later package in ideological terms as Biomechanics, however, is more nuanced and phenomenological than his later presentations of Biomechanics would suggest, and we find in this work interest in and space for the actor's mind. In the same year in which Meyerhold would premiere Biomechanics, Shpet presented his own philosophical investigation of actor as material in a journal published by Tairov, Meyerhold's competitor. In this essay Shpet picks up Volkonsky's and Tairov's vocabulary in writing that the actor "possess[es] in his own person the material out of which he creates the artistic image."[3] But Shpet would take the concept in a more hermeneutically and phenomenologically informed direction. Years later, in 1934, the director and the philosopher would work together on an actor-centered production of *Dama s kameliiami* (*The Lady of the Camellias*) at the Meyerhold State Theater, a production that suggests some practical implications of Shpet's theories.

Mind and Material at Meyerhold's Borodinskaya Street Studio

From early on, Meyerhold was drawn to the corporeal aspects of theater. In 1906, long before formulating his own system of movement, he criticized the Moscow Art Theater for neglecting actors' physical training: "[The naturalistic theater] fails to realize the fascination of plastic movement, and never insists on the actor training his body; it establishes a theatre school, yet fails to understand that physical culture must be a basic subject if one has any hope of staging plays like *Antigone* or *Julius Caesar*, plays which by virtue of their inherent music belong to a different kind of theatre."[4] Meyerhold's devotion to physical culture thus preceded its fashion in the Russian and Soviet theater under the influence of Volkonsky's teachings, dating back at least to his time at Vera Komissarzhevskaya's theater in Saint Petersburg. Later, in a 1922 lecture on his own Biomechanics, which requires fluid and dramatic physical movement by well-conditioned bodies, Meyerhold similarly emphasized corporeal plasticity: "Since the art of the actor is the art of plastic forms in space, he must study the mechanics of his body."[5] The movement of the body would continue to be a focus point of his work. Writing to the composer Vissarion Shebalin in 1933 about his production plan for *The Lady of the Camellias*, Meyerhold stressed the dances that were appropriate to the changing rhythms of the production: "we choose a period when the can-can was in full bloom. And the valse—the smooth, limpid, modest, naïve valse of Lanner, Glinka, Weber merges into the voluptuous, spicy, flamboyant valse of Johann Strauss."[6] Meyerhold's reverence for the physical and bodily in theater thus is evident throughout his career, from his early work with Komissarzhevskaya, through his development of Biomechanics, and finally in his Moscow productions of the Stalin era, when he was forced to pay close attention to the ideology that those bodies represented.

In defending the importance of the physical onstage, Meyerhold often in the same breath critiques either naturalism or psychologizing, two jabs at Stanislavsky and the Moscow Art Theater. His 1922 lecture continues: "There is a whole range of questions to which psychology is incapable of supplying the answers. A theatre built on psychological foundations is as certain to collapse as a house built on sand. On the other hand, a theatre which relies on *physical elements* is at very least assured of clarity."[7] Meyerhold suggests that a focus on movement is an antidote to both the naturalistic style and a psychological approach to acting and character (he elsewhere declares "the death of psychologism").[8] With this comment, he plays into a sustained opposition between himself and Stanislavsky that persuaded theatrical thinkers of their day as it has continued to persuade more recent scholars. Robert Leach, for example, contrasts Stanislavsky's prioritizing of the internal with Meyerhold's focus on the external: "For Stanislavsky, *action* was motivated from inside, and became powerful because it seemed spontaneous. For Meyerhold, *movement* was the result of an external stimulus, and became expressive because it seemed choreographed."[9] The implication, in the words of Meyerhold himself, as well as of others, is not only that he attended to movement and not to the mind, but also that the two are incompatible in theatrical work.

Meyerhold's emphasis on movement, however, is not genuinely opposed to psychology—or to the mind. This is, first, because his discourse around Biomechanics references the psychological research of Ivan Pavlov and reflexology, which were in vogue in the early Soviet Union and which convey a reflex-based understanding of mind.[10] Additionally, Meyerhold's bodily theory and practice are embedded in a larger theatrical context and heritage that stress cognitive engagement and the faculties of perception. Stage material for Meyerhold—whether bodies or properties—is enriched by the actor's and spectator's minds: in his work the imagination transforms bodies and objects onstage. If for Evreinov theater is constituted in the perception of it (chapter 1), for Meyerhold theatrical *transformation*, more specifically, is constituted through perception: perception is the mechanism of his use of conventionalization as a theatrical style, whereby simple objects and bodies onstage are perceived as other than they actually are. Meyerhold's deployment of the imagination in union with the sensuous material of the stage merges the mental and the physical while revealing the role of perspective and the positionality of the perceiver. This aspect of Meyerhold's theory and practice intersects with the thought of Shpet the phenomenologist on the actor as material, as well as with the theorizing of other figures in this book.

The theatrical roots of Biomechanics are most legible in the documentation of Meyerhold's work at his playful and generative Borodinskaya Street Studio (1913–17) in Saint Petersburg, where his actors took courses in the musical speaking of drama, commedia dell'arte, and stage movement technique. Although Meyerhold would present Biomechanics after the 1917 revolution in terms ideologically aligned with the new regime, this early work at Borodinskaya suggests a larger scope of vocabularies and fields of influence. As Dassia N. Posner writes: "Yet while new scientific discoveries, reflexology, and the time-motion studies of Frederick Winslow Taylor and Henry Ford provided Biomechanics with a contemporary vocabulary and up-to-the-minute relevance, the larger philosophy that gave the exercises their practical meaning is fundamentally theatrical in its origins, derived from theatre history in Meyerhold's pre-Revolutionary studio years."[11] Commedia, with its emphasis on improvisation within prescribed character types and scenarios, as well as its careful attention to physical movement and disinterest in psychological motivation, was the primary historical theatrical source at Borodinskaya.[12] The nature of this improvisation, in which the actor's imagination worked actively through their body, is of special interest here.

In his course on stage movement, set exercises emerged in Meyerhold's work with the students. They developed these exercises into short études and then extended them into full pantomimes. Students were often asked to manipulate objects as part of these exercises. Meyerhold's seasoned actor Alexander Mgebrov writes in his memoirs: "According to Meyerhold, the actor must make the audience believe that the most insignificant object can be significant and fascinating in his hands. Meyerhold has thousands of variations for this: he is able to invent an infinite number of varying combinations of play with anything you like, with what would seem to be the most trifling object—be it a simple handkerchief, a flower, a little ring, a bit of paper, a stick—whatever."[13] As the center of focus, the object would provoke the actor's spontaneity and improvisation, facilitating imaginative play and drawing the spectator's attention to the here and now, the present moment in which the actor creates the theatrical event. Such interactions with objects, which were also often sartorial accessories, such as hats, cloaks, and swords, appear to have been fundamental to the Borodinskaya work. In the great range of play provoked by these objects, Meyerhold grounds the imagination in the material: the transformed objects represent the meeting of mind (imagination, emotion, perception) and stage material. In a lecture to his students printed in the studio's journal, Meyerhold describes the centrality of objects to their work as receptacles for the actor's art: "If in film an object appears on screen for utilitarian reasons, then in the Studio (for pantomime) an object is provided to give the actor the opportunity to apply artistry to the act of performing with the object, with the goal of either delighting or saddening the viewer."[14] Stage objects are not merely useful; they are artistic material that provokes a reaction in the audience. Properly wielded, stage objects, in their power for transformation, inspire what Meyerhold calls "living *theatrically*."[15] He elaborates: "to take a bow with a beggar's cap as if it is strewn with pearls, to don a tattered coat with a hidalgo's flair, to strike a tattered tambourine with one's hand, not to make noise, but to convey the full brilliance of one's sophistication and experience with a wave of the hand, and to do so in such a way that the spectator forgets the tambourine is missing its skin."[16] "Living *theatrically*" involves acting with and on these stage objects to transform the audience's (and actor's) perception of them.

Meyerhold continued work with objects in Biomechanics, where the prop is often a stick or wand, which Jonathan Pitches calls the "prop of all props" for its inherent simplicity and potency for transformation: "It is an object that carries all the associations of [sport, circus, commedia, silent comedy] but none of the baggage, an object that speaks to the performer as much as it does to the audience, an object which, in terms of the development of biomechanics, increasingly speaks for all other objects."[17] That is, objects in the Biomechanical exercises, as at Borodinskaya, signify onstage not for their inherent nature but for what they evoke and how they are perceived, by both actor and spectator. Also for both actor and spectator, they are rich sites of imagination, emotion, and meaning.

Meyerhold's complex concept of the mask, developed before his work at Borodinskaya, is an especially potent object in all it signifies, with perspective an important component. In his 1912 article "Balagan" ("The Fairground Booth"), he makes clear that the mask is a perceptive meeting point for theatrical convention. The mask represents conventionalization and transformation, as well as the tangibility of character and archetype, including a preference for archetype over individualized character. As Pitches points out, the mask is a meeting point of contrasts: it signifies theatrical history and draws attention to the given moment, and it both constrains actors and liberates them.[18]

Not only do objects transform through the imagination, but so too can the actor's body. The actor Mgebrov describes the way in which such transformation could occur, creating striking effects: "The most wonderful quality of Meyerhold's talent was the ability to transform anything into grand, forever memorable impressions. If Meyerhold falls in love with hands, for instance, then under the influence of his love, they will eclipse everything else in the world for you; he will manage to fully capture your will and imagination in the most varied and fascinating ways, and, for the rest of your life, you will suddenly understand the significance of hands and fall in love with them."[19] As with stage properties at Borodinskaya, we see not only the importance of the corporeal in Meyerhold's theater but also the fact that the body is not inert but is infused with the "will and imagination."

In stressing the importance of play and the imagination, Meyerhold reveals the actor's mental involvement in creation, both intellectual and emotional, in addition to the actor's pure physical agility. Hints of this mental involvement appear in other contexts in the Borodinskaya studio notes, as well. Discussing the importance of theater history for all aspects of his practice, Meyerhold presents the actor's artistry as informed by conscious awareness: "Knowing why all the surroundings are this way and no other, knowing how the entire theatre piece came to be, the actor who enters the stage self-transforms, becoming a work of art. The new master of the stage—the actor—asserts his joyful soul, musical speech, and body, as supple as wax."[20] In this comment Meyerhold unites the actor's soul, speech, body, and intellect, showing each one to be essential to acting. The emotional component of the "joyful soul," a term (*anima allegra*) that came from Carlo Gozzi's fairy-tale commedia play *The Love of Three Oranges*, arose multiple times at Borodinskaya.[21] Meyerhold also claimed: "Joy becomes the realm without which the actor cannot live, even when he must come onstage to die."[22] This sense of joy invokes the freedom and play of Meyerhold's actor and provides an interesting parallel to Stanislavsky's more religious use of the term "soul" (chapter 3).

Although Meyerhold rejects the mind as a psychologizing force (as in Stanislavsky's concept of emotional memory), his use of stage material suggests an interest in phenomenological perspective, or perspective that emphasizes the subjectivity and experience of the perceiver. As in Bert O. States's concept of "binocular vision," in which one eye sees phenomenologically, while the other sees semiotically, or significatively, Meyerhold captures the dual perceptions of both the meaning of stage material and the properties of its materiality.[23] Posner identifies this aspect of Meyerhold's work when she describes his "fascination with plural perspective," or his efforts to draw attention to the many dimensions of realness and fictionality in performance and his explorations of the contingency of staged characters and events.[24] Not only is perception the means of theatrical transformation, but also the intersecting of perspectives matters. In a 1907 article, Meyerhold writes: "the theatre must employ every means to assist the actor to blend his soul with that of the playwright and reveal it through the soul of the director."[25] As Nikolai Pesochinsky points out, this is not the soul of the character but the actor's own soul.[26] The actor as an individual—at the character's expense—comes to the fore here. The notions of the actor's soul and the joyful soul imply individualization and personalization in Meyerhold's sense of the will and imagination that transform stage material: they suggest the importance of subjective experience to the creation of theatrical art.

Meyerhold's sense of imaginative transformation as facilitated through stage material resonates with the theories of Tairov, a prime rival to Meyerhold who also had much in common with him. Like Borodinskaya, Tairov's Kamerny Theater school, the Experimental Theater Workshops (EKTEMAS), prized a diversity of physical training, but Meyerhold asked students to pursue the physical base training on their own, while Tairov had all training taught in house, leading to a more comprehensive system.[27] In his single book of theatrical theory, Tairov emphasizes not only that each actor's approach is individualized but that inspiration comes through improvisatory interaction with something else, whether internal or external to the actor: "Even the same actor in search of different images often proceeds by diametrically opposite paths, and if in one case he may be led to the sought-after image by, let us say, a pantomimic approach, in another he may with great success depart from the sense of sound, and in a third from some internal emotion which suddenly catches fire, etc., etc."[28] He further addresses the actor's perspective. The naturalistic theater focuses the actor on an object onstage, whether another actor, something internal, or a stage property, while in the stylized theater, the actor attends exclusively to the spectator. In Tairov's synthesized theater, by contrast:

> When communicating with his partner, the actor must at the same time sense that before him is the audience hall and not the fourth wall of naturalism.
>
> Improvisation in the synthesized theater must lead the actor to a mastery of this dual object.[29]

Tairov's actor is consciously aware of both the stage world and its larger context (the reality of the audience), engaging actively with both. Notably, Tairov actually means to contrast himself with Meyerhold here (Meyerhold is the main representative of what Tairov calls the stylized theater in the book), but in fact, at Borodinskaya we see the complicated perspective of Meyerhold's actor.

By the time Meyerhold presents Biomechanics to Soviet audiences in a 1922 public lecture titled "Akter budushchego i biomekhanika" (The Actor of the Future and Biomechanics"), we see a different discourse around acting, one that would only change further in his work on *The Lady of the Camellias*, more than a decade later. In this lecture Meyerhold articulates his ideas wholly within a dualist framework and in the terms of efficient labor organization. No longer referring to creation *through* the actor's body, Meyerhold speaks of a separation of actor and body: "the actor must train his material (the body), so that it is capable of executing instantaneously those tasks which are dictated externally (by the actor, the director)."[30] Vadim Shcherbakov identifies the distinction here between *actor* and *his material*: "Meyerhold asserted that the actor's body is a machine organized by a fully aware mind. This meant, first, that the mind-machine needs to understand the machine's principles of construction and laws of functioning and, second, that it uses this knowledge to obtain maximally efficient labor from the body, that is, to create the most effective—in the sense of aesthetic impact on the spectator—spatial physical forms with the least expenditure of psychophysical energy."[31] Julia Vaingurt also notes a splitting of mind and body in the theory of Biomechanics as Meyerhold presented it in 1922: "The actor divides himself into body and mind, or more specifically, compartmentalizes that part of himself which is completely objectified (the body as raw material) separate from that part that imbues him with agency (mind). Instead of having its place in a holistic approach to personality, the body is stripped away, cast out so as to be transformed into an object for use."[32] Meyerhold's separation of actor and body replicates his 1912 discussion of a separation between actor and mask: the mask is creative and generative material that works with the actor's gesture and movement but is not one with the actor. Furthermore, Meyerhold articulates a distinction between body and mind only when he couches Biomechanics in the language of Soviet ideology, implying once again that the thread of theatrical thought and practice that resisted political pressure was that associated with an integrated body and mind, a point that will become clearer in the discussion of Stanislavsky and censorship in chapter 3.

Suggesting further that political pressures intersect with aesthetic concerns, Meyerhold's 1922 rhetoric about Biomechanics also presents a more depersonalized and wholly physical view of the actor, in its lack of reference to the actor's soul, imagination, or even emotion. (In fact, Meyerhold criticizes the actor who is overwhelmed by emotion, a far cry from his Borodinskaya emphasis on pervasive joy.)[33] The Biomechanical actor, he states, "must possess: (1) *the innate capacity for reflex excitability*, which will enable him to cope with any employ [or "emploi," character type] within the limits of his physical characteristics; (2) 'physical competence,' consisting of a true eye, a sense of balance, and the ability to sense at any given moment the location of his centre of gravity."[34] This list of qualifications constrains the actor's contribution to the physical, whether on the micro-level (reflexes) or the macro-level ("physical competence").

With time, Meyerhold's Biomechanical work would shed its dualist language. In contrast with Meyerhold's initial descriptions of Biomechanics, British actor and director André van Gyseghem describes a more ambiguous, nonetheless harmonious, relationship between mind and body in his observation of a 1930s Biomechanics session: "The actor must be able to use his whole body as an instrument to play upon. His mind and body must be in complete harmony. What he understands with his mind he must be able to express with the movement or non-movement of his body."[35] (Mental) understanding and (bodily) expression were united in the Borodinskaya work, as well.

Gustav Shpet, Phenomenologist Turned Theater Theorist

Meyerhold was an anomaly in his use of the trendy discourses of Aleksei Gastev, Taylor, Pavlov, and Vladimir Bekhterev to formulate his ideas about Biomechanical acting as a model for proletarian theaters in the early 1920s. Most others in the Soviet theater were not so quick to adopt ideological rhetoric but instead trod more cautiously. In 1922—the same year in which Meyerhold presented Biomechanics in his stunt-filled *Velikolepnyi rogonosets* (*The Magnanimous Cuckold*)—Gustav Shpet published his landmark essay on actor as material, "Teatr kak iskusstvo" ("Theater as Art"), in the journal of Meyerhold's principal rival, Tairov. Here Shpet interrogates our very definition of theatrical art to give a phenomenological understanding of actor as material. Although Shpet's essay invigorated theatrical discussions in early Soviet Moscow, spawning responses by Liubov' Gurevich and Sigizmund Krzhizhanovsky, in particular, it has received scant attention by scholars of the Soviet theater, aside from recent studies by Caryl Emerson, Frederick Matern, and Galin Tihanov.[36]

Shpet's ties to theater merit explanation, as these biographical details represent a particularly potent intersection of theater and philosophy in the era. But first, given that he is likely to be largely unknown to many readers of this book, his philosophical credentials: Gustav Shpet was Russia's foremost phenomenologist, a student and translator of Edmund Husserl, a psychologist, and a hermeneutist. He has emerged as a towering figure in twentieth-century Russian philosophy, and his philosophical writings stand at the forefront of the range of topics central to Russian thought of his day—namely, phenomenology and hermeneutics, but also aesthetics, cultural and literary theory, the history of philosophy and philosophy of history, metaphysics, and the philosophy of language. In his hometown of Kyiv, he studied in the psychological seminars of Georgy Chelpanov, introduced here previously as a leader of the defense of the study of consciousness in early Soviet psychology. After moving to Moscow in 1907, he was appointed privatdozent and taught philosophy at the University of Moscow and the Higher Women's Courses. He subsequently took courses in Scotland, France, and Germany, where he studied phenomenology under Husserl in 1912–13; his generation of pre-Soviet intellectuals would be the last to enjoy this privilege of a Western education. Shpet's first major work, *Iavlenie i smysl* (*Appearance and Meaning*, 1914), largely presents Husserl's treatise in phenomenology, *Ideas I* (1913), for a Russian audience. He took leadership positions at the Institute of Scientific Philosophy and at the State Academy of the Artistic Sciences (GAKhN), a body that centralized the study of philosophy, in addition to playing an integral role in the development of the academic study of theater in Russia (see the introduction). At GAKhN Shpet was a vice president and leader of the Philosophical Department, though he occasionally participated in and presented to the Theater Section, of which he eventually became a member. But Shpet was removed from his post as vice president at GAKhN in 1929 as part of a "purge" of the organization (it would be closed entirely the next year). Under the Soviet repression of non-Marxist philosophy, Shpet was forced to work primarily as a translator and editor, while constantly facing the pressures of financial insecurity.[37] "My mood is one of depression, because I am powerless," he stated in his remarks at the sham of a GAKhN purge trial.[38]

Although his fame comes from philosophy, Shpet had a special, lifelong interest in theater. This interest began as early as his twenties, when he would discuss acting and recent theatrical innovations with his friend and fellow Kyiv native Tairov, who credited discussions with Shpet for influencing his first steps as an actor and his attitude toward theater.[39] Shpet's friendships with theater artists would continue in the high-profile theatrical culture of modernist Moscow, where he was close not only with Tairov but also with Stanislavsky, Meyerhold, Vladimir Nemirovich-Danchenko, the Kamerny Theater actor (and Tairov's wife) Alisa Koonen, the Moscow Art Theater actors Olga Knipper-Chekhova and Vasily Kachalov, Gurevich, and many others. Shpet's daughter Marina Shtorkh even wonders whether her father might have had an affair with Koonen, given the closeness of their relationship.[40] Shpet never missed a premiere at Moscow's major stages.[41] After the 1917 revolution, Shpet was named as one of the three members of the theater theory section of the Theater Department (Teatral'nyi otdel', TEO) established within the People's Commissariat of Enlightenment (Narkompros), a post where he would have crossed paths with Meyerhold, the department's deputy.[42] In the next few years, while still working in philosophy, he published two theoretical essays on the theater: "Differentsiatsiia postanovki teatral'nogo predstavleniia" ("The Differentiation of the Staging of the Theatrical Presentation," 1921) and "Theater as Art."[43] The first essay examined the differentiation over time of the tasks required to create a work of theater. The second essay constitutes Shpet's fullest elaboration of his phenomenology of theater. These essays were followed by a December 1923 presentation at the Theater Section of GAKhN entitled "Soderzhanie i vyrazhenie v teatral'nom predstavlenii" ("Content and Expression in a Theatrical Presentation").[44] His work at the GAKhN Theater Section included collaborating on developing the volume *Istoriia teatral'noi Moskvy* (*A History of Theatrical Moscow*), which was developed in Theater Section meetings in 1929–30 but remained unpublished when the academy closed.[45] During the 1930s, when Shpet was forced by political circumstances to turn from philosophy to translation, he also moved further into theater practice and pedagogy: a reader of over a dozen languages, he translated *The Lady of the Camellias* for Meyerhold and *Julius Caesar* for the Maly Theater (apparently never staged), headed a small working group tasked with commenting on Stanislavsky's manuscript for *The Actor Prepares* (to be published in English translation), organized a nationwide discussion of Stanislavsky's memoirs in 1933, and devised a curriculum for a Moscow Art Theater Academy of Supreme Actorly Mastery (Akademiia vysshego akterskogo masterstva) that never materialized.[46] Shpet developed an especially close connection to the Moscow Art Theater. By the mid-1930s he was at work on a nine-volume history of Stanislavsky's theater, and the director wrote to his wife that he hoped Shpet might take charge of the literary aspects of the Moscow Art Theater's work.[47]

In exile in the Siberian cities of Yeniseysk and Tomsk beginning in 1935 for his involvement in leading GAKhN in the previous decade, Shpet renewed acquaintance with the playwright Nikolai Erdman, his fellow exile, and through Erdman he began advising on a performance of *Othello* at a Tomsk theater.[48] In Shakespeare, Shpet wishfully imagined hope for his bleak future, telling his daughter Marina in Eniseisk: "I want to write the same sort of detailed Shakespeare commentary that I did for Dickens's *Pickwick*. And when I finish Shakespeare, I'll receive awards over many years for the publications. Then finally I will be able to do philosophy again and finish those things of mine that are still unfinished. I'll then even be able to buy a house outside the city and live there and work on philosophy."[49]

Unfortunately, Shpet was arrested again in Tomsk in October 1937 and, after a rushed trial, was executed by firing squad on November 16, barely two years before Meyerhold would face the same fate. Like many victims of Stalin's regime, Shpet faced false charges: participation in a counterrevolutionary monarchical organization during his time at GAKhN. His family would not learn of his death until 1956.[50] The actor Vasily Kachalov, on behalf of the Moscow Art Theater, wrote a letter to Stalin in 1938 asking for Shpet's rehabilitation (unknowingly too late). He praised Shpet's theater work: "G. G. Shpet is one of the best Shakespeare specialists, knows nineteen languages, was a candidate in the Academy of Sciences, and is a great and astute expert in the theatrical art—we ourselves and the late K. S. Stanislavsky many times sought his advice."[51] Though Shpet may have always seen himself as a philosopher, the theater work to which he devoted the final years of his life was of the highest caliber.

Shpet's larger philosophical project fatally maintained independence from Soviet Marxism (unlike Lev Vygotsky's work in psychology, which took a compromising position toward the nation's mandated ideology; see chapter 3). This larger project, as we might call it, spanned philosophical subdisciplines, but it united around what Randall A. Poole calls:

> an effort to understand what it means to be human: to understand human being (or the human mode of being) as a distinct level of being. For Shpet, that distinctiveness consists in our existence as self-conscious persons, an existence that depends on the word and develops in society and history. His conception entails deep respect for individual human freedom, creativity, and dignity. The common source of the human level of being, of individual human personhood, and of human knowledge is "rational spirit," communicated and understood through signs.[52]

That is, Shpet, who matured in the human-centered philosophical environment of Russian neo-Idealism, sought in his work the underlying principles for understanding the human, across disciplinary divisions. His work investigates human consciousness as a specific object for understanding, one that is molded by history, culture, and language. Language serves as a primary shaper of consciousness, and thus of the distinctively human, for him. In his turn toward the linguistic, historical, cultural, and aesthetic as a grounding of selfhood, Shpet departs from Husserlian phenomenology and formulates a hermeneutical revision of it, in which social context secures the model of the self. In an approach complementary to Vygotsky's, Shpet sought meaning in the relations, contexts, and histories that make the human a social being.[53] The theatrical art would serve his work in this endeavor.

The Body Detached

Theater has long held a special attraction for phenomenologists, beginning with Husserl's own little-known writings on theater from the early twentieth century.[54] Just as phenomenology, in attending to phenomena as presented to consciousness, characteristically "brackets" the question of the existence of the natural world (this is Husserl's *epoché*), so too in the theater do we accept what is onstage as real even though we may at the same time recognize that it is fictional and constructed. A chair onstage is a real chair but also a fictional chair, an ambiguity that the phenomenological perspective finds especially intriguing. We as an audience accept that in a performance we see *what* is made by the stage artists but not *how* it is made; moreover, we see those events that, in the fiction of the show, take place onstage but not those that "take place" offstage. As States calls it, the theater's reality is "frontal."[55] Because the audience experiences only what passes before their senses, the theater is always aware of the presence of the audience, and of the audience's viewpoint, even in the sort of theater that rushes to lay bare its own devices. In the words of the editors of a volume on theater phenomenology: "Both performance and phenomenology engage with experience, perception, and with making sense as processes that are embodied, situated, and relational."[56]

As a theoretical framework for studying performance, the phenomenological approach, which has enjoyed a vogue in theater scholarship over the past few decades, lends to a focus on the sensuous and material aspects of a performance (including sounds, textures, smells, tastes)—not just the spectator's subjective perception and reception of a performance, but also a sense of temporality and of theater's delicate layering of the real and the fictional. Meanwhile, coming from the phenomenological tradition, Shpet's work examines the presentation of the world to the subject and the subject's apprehension of the world through sensuous experience of it. The world we perceive is, for phenomenology, all that we can know. For this reason the world as posited by a phenomenologist will challenge identification: it can be understood only in relation to a consciousness, and this relationship is constantly changing. The world is real only insofar as it is sensory and lived.

Examining theater through this more abstract phenomenological lens, Shpet is invested, like Husserl, in understanding consciousness, perception, and the relational processes of making sense. Shpet saw in theater a special challenge for an aesthetic philosophy concerned with the relationship between the real world and the creative, or created, one. Theater is unique among the arts for using the materials of everyday life to create something that looks very much like everyday life but that is, in certain ways, very different. A chair onstage is not only both real and fictional: it may look just like one in a spectator's living room. Likewise, a woman actor can comb her hair onstage and look just like a woman combing her hair after getting out of bed in the morning. Shpet considered the difference between the real and the aesthetic in these kinds of examples critical for understanding what theater does and how it relates to reality, and for devising a set of principles to guide theater practitioners. For him, the phenomenological allure of the theater was not in the analogous structure between the spectator's experience of theater and the phenomenological reduction, but rather in the special instance of perception and meaning that theater creates when everyday objects and organisms onstage bear an aesthetic character.

Shpet's brief 1921 article "The Differentiation of the Staging of the Theatrical Presentation" was published in *Kul'tura teatra* (*Theater Culture*), the short-lived biweekly journal of a group of Moscow theaters, where it was nestled among writings on theater history and memorial pieces to Alexander Blok. The article argues for the importance of interpretation to a theatrical production. Written during his appointment to the theater theory section of the Theater Department within the People's Commissariat of Enlightenment, it asserts that an outside interpreter who is distinct from the author, actor, and director is necessary in order to identify the "idea-based, *intellectual* meaning" (*ideinyi*, razumnyi *smysl*) of a production.[57] This is only natural, Shpet suggests, given that over time the roles associated with the creation of a theatrical production have become more specialized and numerous: first, the roles of playwright and actor were distinguished from each other, then later the roles of director and even stage designer were born. Playwrights, actors, directors, and stage designers have limited capacities for interpretation due to their focus on fulfilling their specific tasks, he proposes, and thus a skilled professional interpreter (critic) is needed in order to return to the stage not only idea-based meaning but also "the meaningful *word*, which, alas, certain contemporary performances treat with contempt."[58] He concludes by critiquing recent theatrical trends, likely the sort seen in productions by Meyerhold or the Factory of the Eccentric Actor: "Efforts to redeem the eradication of meaning through amplified rhythm, melodeclamation, gesticulation, and bodily contortions have brought automatons and marionettes to the stage, that is, parodies of meaningful [*osmyslennye*] dramatis personae, rather than animate and rational beings."[59] Shpet champions the human actor who behaves rationally and subtly onstage on the grounds that such an actor, unlike more exaggerated counterparts, expresses and amplifies meaning. Notably, along with this actor, he champions the *word* in theater—language and its meaning-making functions. The language revered here need not be a dramatic text, but it is language given meaning in its oral expression by an actor (and its reception by a spectator). Language, which preoccupied Shpet's work throughout the 1920s—he was a member of the Moscow Linguistic Circle, founded by Roman Jakobson—for him is enmeshed in a social and cultural context, like that of the complementary set of roles in a theatrical production that he designates here. Thus language serves, alongside the sensible actor, as a symbol of meaning-making theater, and language's eradication is linked to meaninglessness.

Ultimately, though, it was Shpet's 1922 essay "Theater as Art" that established his philosophy of theater and the actor, sparking debates among theater scholars in Moscow that would continue for years to come.[60] Shpet framed the essay in provocative, polemical terms. Even its title, "Theater as Art," is a polemical act, placing Shpet in opposition to thinkers of his day such as Evreinov, Yuly Aikhenval'd, and Vsevolod Vsevolodsky-Gerngross, who variously claimed that theater is *not* art or that life and art must merge.[61]

Further stirring polemics, Shpet argues that theater is an independent art form, one that is not secondary to any other. Shpet's concern was not that theater should wholly rid itself of music, dance, and literature but that theater must be understood and practiced as a specific art form in itself, composed of its own forms, rather than as a mere combination of other forms. Shpet boldly first presented the essay in a lecture at Tairov's Kamerny Theater, then published it in the first issue of *Masterstvo teatra* (*The Craft of Theater*), the Kamerny's short-lived journal. This seems a counterintuitive choice, as the Kamerny proclaimed itself "synthesized" and blended dance, pantomime, acrobatics, and music in its productions. The Kamerny's *Princess Brambilla* (1920) and *Romeo and Juliet* (1921), both of which included long physical interludes, had already earned Shpet's disdain.[62] In the journal Shpet's essay was preceded by an article by Tairov criticizing Meyerhold's recent presentation of Biomechanics—a fact that illustrates the fierce sparring of Russian theatrical opinions in the early 1920s.[63]

In "Theater as Art," Shpet argues apophatically for theater's independence as an art form. Theater is not secondary to and derivative of literature: it is not limited to executing the directives of the playwright. Theater is not uniquely a synthesis of all other arts: *all* arts, Shpet claims, synthesize features like rhythm, plasticity, and the poetic.[64] Instead, he writes, theater has its own distinguishing qualities that must be given precedence when understanding and classifying theatrical productions. Theater is an independent art by virtue of (1) its specific material, the body of the actor; and (2) its specific form of presenting this material, the *act* (*akt*) of the actor.[65] These two conditions depend on a concept of the actor performing in the stage environment in contrast to an ordinary person going about their life. There is something, Shpet suggests, specific about the fact that the body onstage is that of an *actor*. Shpet asks: How does the *act* of an actor differ from an act in the real world? And how do those two parallel acts relate to each other? Is the act of the actor the same act that is carried out by the character? Understanding the actor and their act in a way that accounts for these questions is the central problem of the stage, he writes:

> A dramatic action is invariably a kind of conventional, symbolic action, it is a sign of something; it is not itself something real, produced, just as it is not a simple copy—an artless, technically and photographically accurate copy reproducing reality. The problem of this *conventionality* is in fact, strictly speaking, the problem of the theater. The theater as such seeks its practical resolution, and any theory of the theater as art is a quest for its theoretical justification.[66]

That is, theater seeks to resolve the puzzling relationship between the aesthetic and the real through practice, namely through its use (or not) of conventionality, while theory seeks to explain it—as Shpet himself will do in this essay.

Further, Shpet clarifies that dramatic actions take on meaning through their sensual presentation to a consciousness: "we must proceed from the 'act on the stage,' which is directly given, and analyze it as it is given, i.e., in all its fullness, specificity, and concreteness: first in its actual material composition and its own intrinsic form and contours, and second in regard to its specific status as an artistic and aesthetic entity, as a product of art, within the general structure of the consciousness apperceiving it."[67] Here Shpet attends to the phenomenology of the stage act, emphasizing that it exists (and makes meaning) only in relation to the spectator, or the consciousness, apprehending it. Further, it functions on two planes of being: the philosopher of theater must analyze a stage act both as the ordinary act it appears to be, with all its material, sensual properties, and as an act embedded in a specific aesthetic whole. The act of an actor is not merely a human act but an aesthetic one, just as the actor's body is not merely the body of an organism or a human being but an aesthetic, actor's body.

Shpet characterizes the relationship between the aesthetic and the real as "detached" (*otreshennyi*). Theater's aesthetic world is "detached" from the real world: "A principle that is fundamental and common to all arts stipulates that the 'reality' that art creates is not the reality around us, the reality of our practical life experience, it is not the 'empirical' reality that the natural and historical sciences study, but it is a reality of special properties and a *special* perception—it is a *detached* reality."[68] This detachedness is for Shpet what separates the parallel actions—or "homonyms" (*omonymy*)—of the stage and of real life.[69] Extending Shpet's claims, we can imagine that we respond differently to a sobbing woman in a drama onstage than we do to a woman sobbing before us in our ordinary experience. While the woman onstage may elicit a range of emotions from the spectator, the spectator regards her with a certain distance—a lack of urgency and no impulse to intervene. But the woman in ordinary life may spark action on the part of her witnesses, who cannot trust that her experience will unfold on its own in a predetermined manner. Shpet suggests that the theatrical action elicits a greater amount of contemplation (or "*special* perception") than does ordinary experience.

Shpet had introduced detachedness in his "Germenevtika i ee problemy" ("Hermeneutics and Its Problems," completed in 1918, first published in 1989). It appears throughout his writings on aesthetic topics, including his book *Esteticheskie fragmenty* (*Aesthetic Fragments*, 1922–23) and his essay "Problemy sovremennoi estetiki" ("Problems of Contemporary Aesthetics," 1922), works that together with his "Theater as Art" cap an intense period he devoted to aesthetic questions. In these texts Shpet presents detachedness in art as twofold. In the first instance of detachedness, reality presents itself as content for our understanding. Here something in our experience is not purely instrumental but becomes available for critical analysis. In the second instance of detachedness, that understanding is shaped into an aesthetic object, an artwork. With this additional step, the aesthetic object suspends or modifies the natural givenness of the world. Not only is it an object of understanding, but it takes on form and becomes meaningful. This meaningfulness comes from art's inherent expressiveness. As Robert Bird writes: "Alongside the broader detached sphere that Shpet calls concrete reality, art is distinguished by the precise manner in which its expressions are fully 'externalized' and therefore rendered transparent for interpretation."[70] We can infer that the recognition of aesthetic detachedness is most vivid in the theater, where actions and objects are analogous to those in ordinary life. Our character sobbing onstage undergoes the first detachedness when we as a spectator distinguish her as a woman crying from the cacophony of sensory material surrounding her. She undergoes the second detachedness when we identify her emotive expressions as a performance that is structured and intentional and we see in that performance aesthetic meaning.

Detachedness creates a self-sustaining sensuous impression, a "reality" that is informed by the real but not bound to it. Like the Formalist "estrangement" or "defamiliarization" (*ostranenie*), detachedness describes a partial identity between something as it appears in art and as it appears in life, and requires a certain perceptual posture by the spectator. But the difference is significant. Estrangement presents a common thing (object, word, gesture) to the reader/spectator in an unfamiliar way so as to make the reader notice and appreciate it, to make the "sun sunnier and the stone stonier," in Viktor Shklovsky's famous formulation. The estranging move thus draws attention to how things are perceived, and to perception itself, asking the reader to see something for how it presents itself in a given moment rather than for how it is commonly already known, or often merely recognized in passing. This device always keeps in play, and reflects back on, the real-life instantiation of the estranged thing. Detachedness, in contrast, is not invested in this reflection back on the real so as to see life anew. While estrangement makes a thing look *different from* (though recognizable as) its analogous thing in life, detachedness—again—might make a thing look exactly like its parallel but real form, just as a chair onstage looks identical to a chair in life. Detachedness instead facilitates aesthetic form—the role of the chair with all its material and functional properties within the structure and aesthetic purpose of the production as a whole.

The idea that theater conditions a particular way of seeing, and that this way of seeing is somehow integral to making something theatrical, is of course not unique to Shpet. This view is important to theater theory generally and, in particular, central to other theater phenomenologies that we explore in this book. Evreinov favors a solipsistic conception of theater "for oneself" (*dlia sebia*), in which a person or actor-spectator creates theater that is tailored to their personal desires and needs. The person often does this not by orchestrating a physical performance but by identifying what they desire within the experiences of everyday life and *spectating* it in a particular way, thereby conferring on the experience the status of theater. Similarly,

Krzhizhanovsky imagines the stage actor as nonexistent without a spectator's eye looking back at the actor, therein confirming the actor's reality. In Krzhizhanovsky's short stories, the theatrical actor's contingent existence is refigured into imagined worlds that exist so long as the stories' protagonists *see* the existence of those worlds. But whereas these two theorists arrive at their focus on spectating through a belief that seeing is generative, such that they bestow creative power on the spectator, Shpet is more subtle. For him perception's crucial role is to make sense of theatrical presentations. At the same time, Shpet's definition of the aesthetic as doubly detached, and as a reality of a special perception, suggests that theater exists *in* our perception of it as theater: its forms and content are *perceived* forms and content. As Bird writes: "human understanding changes the status of reality itself by creating a separate realm of meaning."[71]

For Shpet the distinction between seeing in ordinary experience and seeing the doubly detached aesthetic form is conceived as a difference between sensing what is and sensing what could be—a possibility rather than an actuality. Detached reality is for him a possible but also an ideal reality, a concept echoed in Krzhizhanovsky's idea of the theater as an "As-if" (*by*) space, full of potential (chapter 4).

Motor-Sympathetic Forms and the Material Body

The range of artists contributing to a theater production do not hold equal control over the act of detachment. Detachedness in the theater, for Shpet, is enacted specifically by the actor's body. This body creates "motor-sympathetic forms" (*motorno-simpaticheskie formy*)—both the external actions and the internal senses with which the actor invests the role—to evoke in the spectator the sensuous impression of a particular character. Shpet's claim that a sense of a character is presented to the spectator's consciousness *through the actor's body* is a core phenomenological component of his philosophy of theater. When the actor leaves her real self in the stage wings so she can create an unreal persona onstage, she brings the reality of the detached aesthetic world (at once unreal and nonactual) into being.[72] The aesthetic meaning of all else in the theater—the set, the properties, the music—depends on the actor and the "material" of the human body.

Motor-sympathetic forms are visual, aural, and sensual; crucially, each form is particular to the capacities of a specific body. They are not the result of pure movement but spring from an integration of mind and body, the cognitive and the physical. Shpet explains that the actor, like any artist, is grounded in the possibilities and limitations of their material: "the actor starts out from the forms of intonation, gesticulation, and body movement in general that he has at his disposal, and combines them into new complex forms; but also, as an actor he remains within their bounds."[73] Shpet's emphasis on the individualization of the actor speaks to his attention to the spectator's perception of the actor's particular, material body moving in its unique ways. That is, Shpet draws us to the presence of the actor's body before us onstage and to its physicality—its "tension of forces, its density, its resistance, its mass, weight, trajectory, etc." in this precise moment.[74] Motor-sympathetic forms take as their content the actor's "expressiveness" (*ekspressivnost'*), which, for Shpet, is close to the concept of the actor's *sense* of the character, or the actor's creative imagination.[75]

Shpet reasons further that if we treat a theatrical presentation as the presentation of sensuous forms specific to performance, rather than as the presentation of a text or an idea, then theater productions should be broadly classified by these forms, much like the term "emploi," which Meyerhold used to designate character types. Genre labels like "tragedy" and "comedy" are wedded to an understanding of performance as the presentation of a literary text.[76] In contrast, Shpet suggests terms such as "comic," "moralizer," and "lover" to categorize performances. Such classification deprivileges theater's basis in dramatic texts, instead emphasizing those bodily forms that Shpet values as unique to the theatrical art. This suggestion also, crucially, refigures the vocabulary of the theater as those individual perceptions of meaning-making forms that the spectator experiences, rendering, in essence, a phenomenological and hermeneutic classification of performance.

In Shpet's conceptualization of theater, the actor's work is conventionalized (stylized), not imitative: "[The actor] *conventionally* portrays a character in a play; he does not copy any real subject. He himself creates imaginary personages *through himself*."[77] This suggests that actors create from within (their own imagination, cognition, physical and emotional capacities), rather than from without (imitation of external forms). Further, characters are not *embodied* by an actor: the character need only have the semblance of a body offered up for phenomenological perception by the spectator. Likewise, the actor does not in any way share in the *mind* of the character. Actors experience themselves creating the character, but the character is "detached" from them: "Herein lies the aesthetic *compositional* aspect in the actor's creativity, his art: namely, to grasp an idea, to place it in the center, to weave a 'character' around it, and to develop from this center a sequence of manifestations and actions of the portrayed 'personage' in unity with the compositional, external and internal, motor-sympathetic forms of expression."[78] The actors' personifications—and art in general—are governed by a unified, meaningful sense (*smysl*) that the actor derives largely from themself; the dramatic text serves only as a starting point: "only a 'spirit,' an idea, a tendency, a direction, a task!"[79] Here, too, Shpet moves the artistic center of a performance away from the dramatic text, and even from the director, such that the actor is—mentally and physically—the central creator.

This perspective allows Shpet to implicitly level criticism against naturalism, and in part against Stanislavsky's early work at the Moscow Art Theater, though the director would become Shpet's friend and employer in the coming decade.[80] By imitating life, a naturalist staging confines the actor to *one* portrayal of a character, that portrayal endorsed by the author of the dramatic text and shaped by the actor in their own "natural" body. Since Shpet saw an actor's portrayal of a character as closely linked to the possibilities of the actor's unique body, not merely to lived experience, he disapproved of the reduction of theater to *one* portrayal that ignores the specificity of each actor's physical material. He also criticizes the technique of drawing on one's own real experiences to portray a character. Actors may draw on their own moods, but that is all. To draw on their own personal experiences would be to limit actors' creativity and make the character more imitative and real than expressive and potential. Further, a character is not a real person but a possible persona, as detached forms are possibilities, rather than actualities. Just as the character does not share in the actor's personal experiences, the actor does not and should not share in the character's. Shpet writes: "the actor as such just as little 'experiences' Tartuffe, Iago, or Cain as a violin experiences the piece being played upon it."[81] For Shpet, because characters are merely a conveyance of a sense of a possible person, they do not require interior psychologies, and thus they have no interior mind or body for the actor to "experience." Stanislavsky's System would ultimately take a similar approach, as Matern notes: *both* Stanislavsky and Shpet believed that a stage act must "look right" rather than "be," with Shpet and Stanislavsky thus approaching similar ideas from different directions.[82]

The most distinctive contribution Shpet makes to theater phenomenology lies in his analysis of how the actor's body becomes perceptible as art onstage. This process is viewed both in terms of its perception (whether by the spectator or the actor) and in terms of its formation: the detached way in which the actor uses expressiveness to offer motor-sympathetic forms up for perception. For Shpet the actor's body is central, but he understands it differently than European phenomenologists would in the decades to come. Unlike Maurice Merleau-Ponty, who examines the ways in which our perception of the world is mediated through our bodies, Shpet does not perceive the actor themself as experiencing or gazing onto the audience: the actor-audience relationship is not a mutual dialogue. The actor's body enters into his philosophy as a means of structuring sensual artistic content and not as an experiential medium or a filter of consciousness in itself.

What might Shpet's theater look and feel like? We would not expect theatrical spectacle, illusions, or excessive use of acrobatics, dance, or music, which might distract from the actor's task. Defending theater as an independent art, Shpet opposed any dilutions of it, and he directly attacked avant-garde experiments that muddied the boundaries between the theater and other performing arts, and between the theater and life. Cabaret shows, popular at the beginning of the century, featured pastiches of one-act plays, musical numbers, burlesques, and pantomime. Futurist street performances by Vladimir Mayakovsky and David Burliuk brought eccentric, theatrical costumes into the domain of everyday life. Evreinov had proposed in 1912 that the theater is properly defined as a natural biological instinct that manifests in the human tendency toward preening, deceit, and child's play, just as it manifests in performances on a proscenium stage.[83] Not so, claimed Shpet, without directly accusing anyone by name.

Puppets and marionettes, favorites of Meyerhold, do not satisfy Shpet.[84] Movement and actions in the theater are properly brought about through actors' use of their *expressiveness* to create with their *own* body. Merely putting an externally animated body onstage is insufficient. Naturalism is also at fault for being imitative (too enslaved by the real): it is beholden to imitation of reality and thus cannot serve a created artistic unity. Just as Shpet dislikes the fact that puppets are not animated by a consciousness *from the inside*, an implicit critique of a psychology-based naturalism here is that one cannot really *be* another from the inside, nor can one's own self be the psychological basis for a character. And thus Shpet leaves us with human bodies that express movements and concepts that *are not* but *could be* real. This theater he proposes is sensuous: in watching it, we can imagine how it feels and tastes. We hear and smell it. Shpet brings alive the materiality of the theater world, its presence and contingency that emerge from its detached motor-sympathetic forms.

For Shpet, these material bodies that convey the possible are the definition of realism, a term that governs his beliefs about how theater should be. Realism, he feels, is dependent on the audience's sense that the actor's portrayal of a character *could be* possible in life, rather than on a realistic visual style or a necessarily realistic set of events. Such potentials are as "real" as actualities. Art that is successfully realistic is "indifferent" to the real world and "unrelated" to it, in the sense that this art, unlike the real world, is shaped into aesthetic form.[85] Shpet concludes: "The realism of the theater lies in the sensuous embodiment of lawfully possible being, not of a 'happenstance' or a 'confluence of circumstances.' It is the realism of the internal forms of the character portrayed, not of the circumstances surrounding an action."[86] That is, realism occurs in the creation of sensuous forms that convey a seemingly authentic persona. A spectator must *feel* a role to perceive the "internal" aspects of its realism. At the same time, we can recall that for Shpet an actor's body is like a musical instrument, one that is played by the actor themself; the instrument does not feel or experience the art it produces. It is precisely the actor's psychological distance from the role that preserves the role's potentialities, as well as its capacity to make use of non-naturalistic theatrical conventions. This returns us to Shpet's starting point: that theater's proximity to and yet distance from reality, captured in theatrical conventionality, constitute the central problem of the theater and of a theatrical philosophy.

Actor as Human

Shpet's essay on theater as art offers several arguments useful for understanding the central polemics underlying the Russian modernist theater. First, he recognizes that the spectator attends to the sensory aspects of theater as they present themselves, rather than to theater's "backside"—that is, the efforts to create it. Characters, then, are not full and real "people," but only sensory impressions. The audience perceives the created character-persona as an embodied potential that *has not yet lived*. In making this argument, Shpet relies on the fact that we perceive happenings onstage in a special way, such that we can make sense of mere impressions. Questions of how the audience perceives and responds to a performance galvanized many theatrical experiments in this era, from Evreinov's concept of monodrama, which facilitated the spectator's emotional identification with one character, to Sergei Eisenstein and Sergei Tretyakov's theater of attractions, which sought to shock and startle the viewer. These experiments indicate the implications of beliefs about spectating for theatrical practice.

Second, Shpet defends the uniqueness of the individual, human actor, claiming further that *both* naturalism and an overly conventional puppet theater suppress the material and present actor in favor of an ideal and nongenerative one. (Evreinov, Stanislavsky, Meyerhold, and Tairov would all agree: they avoided these extremes in their practice, seeking creativity instead in more complex deployments of the actor.) For Shpet the actor might work within the aesthetic unity prescribed by the director of the production, but it is the actor who activates the stage reality and brings it into being. The conviction that the actor is a unique individual with particular capacities and abilities that shape his creative efforts drives the belief this book traces in this era that actors engage their unified body and mind in performance.

The actor's body for Shpet is, further, not reflexological. Shpet's essay protests implicitly against efforts rampant in the early 1920s to use corporeal movements and gestures to inspire the semblance of an emotion in the actor, as in Meyerhold's program of Biomechanics. Shpet's actor thinks, feels, and imagines, *in addition to* moving. In the expressiveness that Shpet considers the content of the actor's motor-sympathetic forms, the mental, perhaps even spiritual, aspects of the actor coincide with their physical movements. By attending to the role of the actor's mind in performance, Shpet resists his era's wholly physiological and empirical models of the human.

In defending his conviction that the actor is a unique individual, Shpet implicitly insists on the peculiarly human and individualized faculties of the actor. As participants in theatrical meaning, or the meaning of the doubly detached reality that is theater, the actor and spectator are rendered human because for Shpet the social realm of making meaning is specifically human. In the essay "Soznanie i ego sobstvennik" ("Consciousness and Its Owner," 1916), Shpet details the coexistence of individual consciousness and collective consciousness, which is formed within social relations and has no "owner." Made into a sign, or a motor-sympathetic form, the actor's body is arguably for Shpet a site for collective consciousness, much like language is. Insofar as theater consists of these forms and their meanings, theater both requires and expresses collective consciousness.

Furthermore, theater provides a venue for self-consciousness—the recognition of the self. Shpet describes the actor coming to self-consciousness through performance: "the actor hears and discriminates the echo, the resonance, of his own soul in what he is portraying. This is the timbre of *his* acting, the overtones of his expressiveness, which always, in fact, are individual, like the timbre of his voice, and derive from the individual properties of the instrument himself."[87] This experience of self-recognition, he claims, is more significant than the actor's imaginary experiences of the adventures and exploits they portray. Acting is thus a means for recognizing ourselves in our objectification of ourselves. As Poole writes of Shpet's overall project, "Being that is thus suspended, objectified, and made available for understanding (and for self-understanding) is the human level of being."[88] Acting is a means of self-objectification because it highlights, rather than covers up, the individual qualities of the actor. Theater seems most apt to this self-understanding of all the arts for the fact that its material is the actor themself.

A Focus on the Actor: *The Lady of the Camellias*

Meyerhold and Shpet trod wildly different, even opposing paths in theater, but they would come together in 1934 for a single production, the French comedy of manners *The Lady of the Camellias* at the Meyerhold State Theater (GosTIM). Reviewers called this choice of production on Meyerhold's part "surprising," but perhaps more surprising is that these men (one as director, the other as translator) came together at all at this stage in their respective careers. Shpet was largely sympathetic toward Stanislavsky's projects at this time, as evidenced by his work for the Moscow Art Theater and likely inspired by his own preference for theater that presents convincingly "real" (developing, potential, not-yet-lived) characters. Meyerhold, by contrast, was largely opposed to Shpet's belief in the necessity of aesthetic unity via the actor and the primacy of individualized character in the theater. Meyerhold's directorial work had embraced a more aggressive aesthetic of rupture, disharmony, circus, puppetry, provocation, and ideology.

Although Meyerhold had garnered great popular and critical success with his radical stagings in the 1920s, by the beginning of the next decade Stanislavsky and the Moscow Art Theater were, in watered-down form, showcased as the ideal model for a Soviet theater, one that could be replicated across the nation (indeed, the world), while Meyerhold, waiting eagerly for his long-promised theater building, came under increasing scrutiny for the experimentalism and "formalism" of his work, as well as his seeming alignment with a Trotskyist notion of "permanent revolution." Meyerhold's choice of repertoire in the 1930s indicates his ultimately futile attempts to regain his status in the tightly regulated art world. At the time of *The Lady of the Camellias* in 1934, his recent productions had included the politically risky choices of Yury Olesha's *Spisok blagodeianii* (*A List of Blessings*) in 1931 and Alexander Sukhovo-Kobylin's *Svad'ba Krechinskogo* (*Krechinsky's Wedding*) in 1933. His attempts to stage further Soviet plays were blocked by censors. All of Meyerhold's productions following *The Lady of the Camellias*—until 1938, when his theater was closed—were nineteenth-century Russian classics: dramatic texts by Alexander Pushkin, Anton Chekhov, Alexander Griboedov, and Mikhail Lermontov.[89] This period was marked by a steep decline from Meyerhold's October in the Theater campaign of 1920, in which he had attempted to dissolve all Moscow state academic theaters and require the others to produce avant-garde and pro-Bolshevik works. Edward Braun calls the choice of *The Lady of the Camellias* "an admission of weariness after years of struggling to extract something of worth from the contemporary Soviet repertoire."[90]

Katerina Clark argues that the dominant theatrical mode in the Soviet midthirties was a kind of melodrama that resonated both on the stage (especially in Stanislavsky) and in the transcripts of the show trials. This mode rejected the surface form, semblance, and "false" mask in favor of the inner form, the seemingly "real," and the "authentic." As this "melodramatic rhetoric" of authenticity increased in the 1930s, Meyerhold, whose work had epitomized for the Russian stage a theatricality of mask and illusion and the standardization of bodily *forms*, was an inevitable target.[91] Such was the charged environment in which he chose *The Lady of the Camellias*, a text with melodramatic sensibilities.[92] Presenting his conception within party-minded guidelines, Meyerhold (at least publicly) expressed hope that the play's show of licentiousness in the bourgeois epoch would provoke the spectator into rallying behind communist morals.[93] He almost certainly sought, as well, to feature his wife, the great actress Zinaida Raikh, in one of dramatic literature's most famous and sensual female roles.[94]

Shpet was one of Moscow's best translators and someone embedded in the Moscow theater community. By 1934 Shpet's desperation to earn a living would have been matched by Meyerhold's need to revamp his theater to fall closer to the party line. And thus the philosopher more sympathetic to the Moscow Art Theater found himself at Meyerhold's side. Shpet's Russian translation closely follows Alexandre Dumas fils's 1852 melodramatic play about the beautiful courtesan Marguerite, who falls in love with the bourgeois Armand Duval.[95] This fidelity came through in Meyerhold's production, for which Shpet served as both translator and dramaturg. Consulting with the director, Shpet advised him on tone and rhythm and encouraged him to explore the aesthetic potentials of a realistic staging. In the words of one Shpet scholar, "the inveterate theater experimenter yielded to the authority

Figure 2.1. Marguerite Gautier, played by Zinaida Raikh, and Armand Duval, played by Mikhail Tsarev, in *The Lady of the Camellias*, directed by Vsevolod Meyerhold at the Meyerhold State Theater, 1934. Copyright © Bakhrushin Theatre Museum, Moscow.

and experience of the philosopher."[96] Other sources offer more detail on this scantly documented working relationship:

> In an effort to open up the inner world of the play as deeply as possible for the actors, Meyerhold pulled into the rehearsals Gustav Shpet, author of the new translation of Dumas's drama, and gave him Zinaida Raikh [who played Marguerite Gautier] and Mikhail Tsarev [who played Armand Duval] as assistants. He [Meyerhold] needed for the actors not only to be performers but to become coauthors of the play. Meyerhold keenly followed the rhythm of a word, sometimes even slightly changing the sound of a Russian phrase to approximate the phonetics of French.[97]

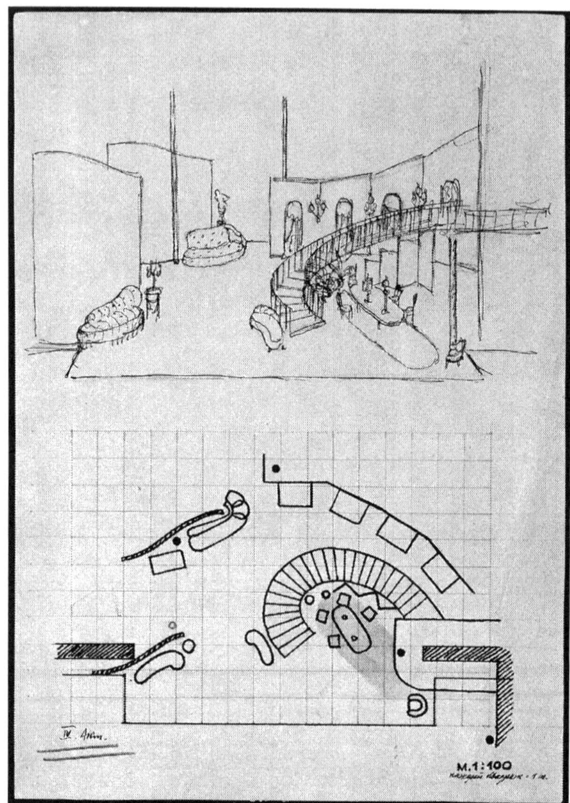

Figure 2.2. Sketch of the set by I. I. Leistikov for act 4 of *The Lady of the Camellias*, directed by Vsevolod Meyerhold at the Meyerhold State Theater, 1934. Copyright © Bakhrushin Theatre Museum, Moscow.

Just as a translator knows how images and phrases echo across a text, so an actor "coauthoring" a play must understand how one role is woven into the fabric of the others. Actors were directly involved in the development of the script, with the leads, Raikh and Tsarev (see fig. 2.1), making small edits and additions to Shpet's draft and being listed in the program as cotranslators with him. This participation of actors in creating the performance text reflects Shpet's own poetics, in which theater's creative artist is not the author but the actor.

Meyerhold was known for chopping up and reconfiguring literary texts onstage to reach an interpretation that he felt would speak to a modern audience, as in the case of his 1928 production *Gore umu* (*Woe to Wit*), based on Griboedov's classic play *Gore ot uma* (*Woe from Wit*, 1823). But *The Lady of the Camellias* was left largely alone.[98] The director oversaw Raikh

Figure 2.3. Photograph of act 4, part 2, of *The Lady of the Camellias*, directed by Vsevolod Meyerhold at the Meyerhold State Theater, 1934. Copyright © Bakhrushin Theatre Museum, Moscow.

and Tsarev's minor changes to Shpet's script, including the addition of fragments from Gustave Flaubert and Honoré de Balzac and Italian phrases for Marguerite.[99] Meyerhold also transposed the setting from the 1840s to the more colorful and spectacular 1870s. Impressionist artworks inspired the production design: "We are watching the play's characters through the eyes of Edouard Manet," Meyerhold wrote.[100] The mise-en-scène reflected elements of Pierre-Auguste Renoir and Edgar Degas, as well. Authentic French cartoons, fashion magazines, and illustrations from the era were mined when designing the production's verisimilitude. Period objects served as props against the simple backdrops. The most dramatic component of the set was a winding staircase that crisscrossed the stage (see figs. 2.2, 2.3). Musically, it was Meyerhold's most fully orchestrated production, with waltzes, scherzos, romances, and polkas from various French composers of the period.[101] In these aspects of the production, Meyerhold alluded to his own experiments at Borodinskaya a decade and a half earlier, when he asked actors to make stage properties (and music) the inspiration for their art.

Given Shpet's involvement in shaping the realism of the production, we can consider how this staging of his translation reflects his often abstract characterizations of realism in "Theater as Art." In December 1933 while at work on *The Lady of the Camellias*, Meyerhold delivered a public address in favor

Figure 2.4. Female costume design by I. I. Leistikov for *The Lady of the Camellias*, directed by Vsevolod Meyerhold at the Meyerhold State Theater, 1934. Copyright © Bakhrushin Theatre Museum, Moscow.

of realism. He asserted that his theater, though conventionalized (*uslovnyi*), was realistic: "Our approach to the construction of images, mise-en-scène, and performance as a whole is *profoundly realistic*. Every movement has its motivation, which is bound up with the idea of the performance and the psychology of the figure. We use conventionalized methods, but within the framework of the conventionalized theater, we build up profoundly realistic figures."[102] Like Shpet (and many others), Meyerhold notes possible symbiosis between the theatrical conventionality of the theater's imagery and the realism of the theater's meanings and characters. Conventionality can facilitate realism.

Meyerhold considered *The Lady of the Camellias* to be the beginning of French realist theater, linked closely to the style of Balzac's novels.[103] The realism of his *Lady of the Camellias* production consisted in its visual materialism and historical accuracy rather than abstraction, as well as its unexaggerated, realistic portrayal of characters—the aspect that would have especially appealed to Shpet's sensibilities. A sketch for a female costume shows both delicateness and an elevated, elegant realism (see fig. 2.4). Realism in the Russian theater at this time was often linked to a strong female lead, as in Tairov's much-lauded *Optimistic Tragedy* in 1933, with Alisa Koonen starring as the Bolshevik commissar, and in Dmitry Shostakovich's opera *Lady Macbeth of Mtsensk*, which premiered in 1934. These female protagonists, virtuous or sinful, sacrifice themselves in tragic situations, and in their deaths, their courage and purity triumph. Tragedy thus conceived—as a deeply individual struggle in which a strong woman, pitted against her surroundings, overcomes them—thus becomes a trademark path to socialist realism in the mid-1930s.

Along these lines, one critic wrote that in Meyerhold's *The Lady of the Camellias*, Raikh's Marguerite showed not the exaggerated seductiveness and smug pleasures of a stereotypical courtesan, but "all the features of Marguerite's human development. . . . The situation in which she finds herself is not shown as the result of her free choice but given as a fate that she did not deserve and from which she still hopes to save herself."[104] By this account, Raikh's delicate, subtle, and dynamic portrayal of Marguerite saved the character—and the production—from melodrama and crude social commentary. Such realism was a formidable task in Marguerite's death scene, which stage history had famously made operatic and melodramatic. Opera—inherently stylized—can draw out death, with a dying character illogically becoming a stronger singer as she dies. Realism, however, is challenged by the portrayal of death: can an actress, herself alive, represent the weakening and incoherence of the experience of a person dying? Shpet's text here notably scales back the dramatics of Dumas's original: Shpet's Marguerite does not exclaim in her last breath, "Ah! que je me sens bien!" (Ah! that I feel good!), as in Dumas. Instead, in Shpet's version she *wonders*, "And so, will I live? Oh, how good!" after which Shpet's Armand, realizing that Marguerite has died, cries out with a single "My god!" rather than the original "Mon Dieu! mon Dieu!" In the next moment in Shpet's text, Marguerite's suitor Gustave tells Armand merely "She loved you!"—a comment that is toned down from the lament in Dumas's original, "Elle t'aimait bien, la pauvre fille!" (She loved you well, the poor girl!).[105] In softening Dumas's conclusion, Shpet makes Marguerite's death more fitting to a nuanced portrayal of her character—as Meyerhold would ask of Raikh in rehearsal.

The capacity for precise and imaginative acting to carry the meaning of a production is the burden of Shpet's "Theater as Art," in which masterful acting "activates" the setting, props, and other stage effects, bringing them into the world created by the actor. In *The Lady of the Camellias* rehearsals, Meyerhold stressed the importance of the actors' creativity, beyond the director-driven approach for which he is known. To actress A. Kuliabko-Koretskaya, who played Marguerite's friend Adele, a dissatisfied Meyerhold said, as if echoing Shpet's treatise: "You don't have a motive. There's no song in your body, you carry your body separately, your voice separately, and have no coordination. . . . You must carry into practice the mastery of an actor, and not only carry out the commands of the director."[106] He instructed the members of the cast that they must create their own through lines between the directions he gave to them: "I can give only hints, the main signposts of actorly moments, and the actor should himself determine his behavior on the stage."[107] Acting has no breaks or holes; an actor on view is continually contributing to the stage creation. Meyerhold himself said as much at Borodinskaya: "The actor remains onstage the whole time, not only because there are no wings and therefore there is no backstage, but first and foremost so that, after having internalised the full significance of the pause, he does not halt the life of the onstage action."[108] Meyerhold's approach in *The Lady of the Camellias* insists on the actors developing individual nuance and detail that a director cannot plan out, a perspective that resonates with Shpet's assertion that improvisation must be embraced because it is "where [theater] was first nurtured."[109]

Upon hearing of the realism of Meyerhold's *The Lady of the Camellias*, Stanislavsky wrote to his assistant Ripsimé Tamantsova: "I find very interesting what you write about Meyerhold. He always was a naturalist, but without actors who could perform simply and well. He cannot teach them and therefore they need to be camouflaged by all sorts of trickery."[110] For Stanislavsky, as for Shpet, good acting is realist acting, acting without trickery. In *The Lady of the Camellias*, Meyerhold found a form of realism by giving actors greater agency and freedom.

Chapter 3

The Actor's Personhood

Konstantin Sergeevich Stanislavsky (1863–1938) worked for years on the manuscripts that would lay out the details of his acting system. A particular struggle that the already world-famous director faced was determining a set of terminology that this text would codify for actors both domestic and international. Stanislavsky's chief partner at taming and refining his rambling prose on the Russian side was his longtime friend Liubov' Gurevich, the literary editor and theater specialist at the Theater Section of the State Academy of the Artistic Sciences (GAKhN), who had worked with him from as early as 1908.[1] Gurevich, who was also responsible for the 1923 survey of theater actors discussed in the introduction, drew from her expert knowledge of the Soviet publishing industry, striving to turn Stanislavsky's writings into something both publishable and readable, as befitting such a prominent theatrical master. This task often required her to send the director suggestions for substantial revision.

Among the feedback Gurevich gave Stanislavsky over the several years he worked on the text (and before she resigned her post as editor in frustration), we find an especially interesting aside that speaks to both the attraction and the friction between Stanislavsky's acting system and Soviet psychology of the early twentieth century. In a letter from April 1929, Gurevich expressed her worry that the manuscript, with its discussion of "affective feelings" (*affektivnye chuvstva*) and other psychological concepts, employed scientific terminology its author did not properly understand: "I have long pointed out to you the imprecision of your terminology, but not wanting to rely on my own modest knowledge in this case, last winter and this winter I deliberately checked my hesitations with three prominent psychologists: [Georgy] Chelpanov, [Vladimir] Ekzemplyarsky, and the young [Lev] Vygotsky, who is very sensitive to art. All of them fully confirmed my opinion." Gurevich went on to reassure Stanislavsky that the question merely concerned word choice, not the concepts themselves: "However, this point should not worry you: this is just a matter of words. They can very easily be changed, and everything will fall into place."[2]

Gurevich would have known a handful of psychologists closely through her work at GAKhN, where psychological approaches to the stage were not merely welcome but explicitly written into the substructuring of the Theater Section. It is unsurprising that one of the psychologists she consulted was the soon-to-be world-famous Lev Semenovich Vygotsky (1896–1934), who had long nursed an interest in theater and had presented on the psychology of the actor's work at the Theater Section in 1928.[3] Vygotsky, who would become known for his contributions to psychology of education and children's psychological development, wrote on theater from the beginning of his adulthood, which would be foreshortened by tuberculosis. He completed a university thesis on *Hamlet* under the direction of esteemed critic Yuly Aikhenval'd in 1915–16, penned dozens of reviews of local theater productions in his hometown of Gomel in present-day Belarus (1922–23), and drafted an article on the psychology of the actor (written in 1932, published posthumously in 1936), which discusses Stanislavsky.[4] Given Vygotsky's massive influence on Soviet (and international) psychology and education, the fact that he considered Stanislavsky's terminology at a crucial point in Stanislavsky's efforts to publish his System is rich indeed.[5] Although, as far as is known, Vygotsky and Stanislavsky never directly connected (unlike the partnerships of Shpet/Meyerhold and Krzhizhanovsky/Tairov, discussed elsewhere in this book), this indirect exchange through Gurevich crystallizes the cross-pollination of ideas that underlay both of their bodies of work. For Stanislavsky drew from and contributed to ideas in psychology, just as Vygotsky did with ideas in theater.

Vygotsky made his national debut as a psychologist in 1924 with a paper defending the study of consciousness against reflexology, or the study of human behavior as the exclusive result of cortical activity. In the early twentieth century, the materialistic science of reflexology was just gathering steam, and it rejected psychological research on consciousness, deeming it too subjective and amorphous, inaccessible to scientific study. Even more so than Vygotsky (who would often strive to orient his work toward Marxism), the other two psychologists Gurevich contacted—Georgy Chelpanov (1862–1936) and Vladimir Ekzemplyarsky (1889–1957)—actively countered the materialism insisted on by the Marxist Soviet state.[6] The accomplished Chelpanov (who mentored Gustav Shpet, among others) was an open critic of materialism, declaring in 1913 that replacing references to consciousness with references to reflexes was not the domain of psychology but that of pure physiology. He met harsh criticism for his views at the First All-Russian Psychoneurology Congress, in January 1923, and lost his position as director of the Moscow Institute of Psychology. Ekzemplyarsky, meanwhile, was Chelpanov's student and left the institute with him. Both subsequently worked for the Psychology Section of GAKhN, which was a somewhat more free and liberal institution under the young Soviet regime, before the state closed it in 1930. While neither Chelpanov nor Ekzemplyarsky was connected to the theater (and neither's work shows the same theatrical-psychological exchange of ideas as we find in Vygotsky's), both presented at GAKhN on the psychology of art.[7] Gurevich's choice of these three psychologists as consultants on Stanislavsky's terminology speaks to her sense of the ideological bent of the director's thinking, as well as to the delicate lexical-political balancing act that awaited him as he strove to get his manuscript past Soviet censors.

In his experiences as a theatrical critic and spectator, Vygotsky used performance to think through the relation of the individual to society and to culture, and to develop an understanding of the mind's relationship to the body and its environment. Meanwhile, Stanislavsky, hard at work on his System, continually made the actor's mental training and mental state a central component of performance, alongside—even inseparably from—the actor's body. He explored the mind from his early experiments with naturalism and symbolism, through his ongoing development of the System, to his refinement of the System into the Method of Physical Action and Active Analysis in his final years. But so, too, did he pay attention to the actor's *spirit* and *soul*. The term "spirit" (*dukh*) is as integral to the human being for him as the mind or body is; we cannot understand his sense of "mind" (*um*) without understanding it, too. In fact, we might say that Stanislavsky's emphasis on the actor's mind and spirit in the theater constitutes the heart of his earth-shattering revolution in acting, which reverberates through all acting theories developed since.[8]

Both Stanislavsky and Vygotsky developed what we might consider a concept of the actor's (or individual's) personhood: the constitution of the actor as a person within the larger theatrical (or social) context. Stanislavsky declares the actor to be *human* and takes this as a premise of his System, wherein body, mind, and spirit are a unity; while Vygotsky, in borrowing Stanislavsky's terminology and concepts, instrumentalizes the actor as an example of human psychology. Both men sought resonances and insights for their work in the other's field; both found their interests in consciousness and other, more abstract, philosophical and psychological matters restricted by the state.

This chapter begins with a critical moment in the development of both thinkers: the landmark 1911 *Hamlet* at the Moscow Art Theater, which Stanislavsky cocreated with Edward Gordon Craig (1872–1966) and which the *Hamlet*-obsessed Vygotsky almost certainly saw. I use Craig's dialogues with Stanislavsky during rehearsals, captured by Moscow Art Theater stenographers, to examine the friction between Stanislavsky's understanding of the actor and other modernist discourses on the actor. Stanislavsky does not merely disagree with Craig: he wholly rejects Craig's terms, and, in doing so, he formulates an understanding of the actor that utilizes human contingency and individuality. Stanislavsky posits the human as a body-mind-spirit totality that thoroughly refutes other modernist efforts to reduce the actor to a sign, overturns a Platonic view of theater as imitation, embraces a human-centered aesthetics of being and presence, and—in its affirmation of the actor as person—entails ethical responsibility. From there, the chapter presents the debates over consciousness in Soviet psychology before turning to Vygotsky's lifelong fascination with theater's presentation of human psychology. I trace Stanislavsky's influence on the thought of Vygotsky, who reviewed Stanislavsky's drafts in 1929. Here my interest is not in identifying the extent of Vygotsky's direct borrowings from Stanislavsky, which scholarship has addressed (e.g., Vygotsky's use of Stanislavsky's concept of *perezhivanie*, or experiencing).[9] Instead, I interrogate the more intangible, more philosophical resonances between Stanislavsky's understanding of the actor and Vygotsky's understanding of the psychological subject in order to articulate the synergy between theatrical and psychological developments based in the actor's personhood that their work presents.

Hamlet (1911) and Modernist Debates on the Actor

Chapter 1 explained the Russian symbolist understanding of the actor that more or less opened the twentieth century, in which the individual quirks and imperfections of the actor are suppressed in the service of artistic unity, of art that foregrounds ethical, spiritual, and sexual ideals rather than a naturalistic reflection of reality. Nikolai Evreinov's response to symbolist discomfort with the corporeality and contingency of actors was ultimately not only to revel in the body's mortality and propensity to illness but to challenge the centrality of theatrical accoutrements like a stage, script, and paying audience to the concept of theater in itself. When Evreinov does embrace formalized theatrical performance, it is usually highly conventionalized—full of commedia characters and metatheatrical plots—to directly explore the ideas of his symbolist colleagues, who embraced conventionalization, though largely without Evreinov's spirit of parody. But within the formal performance tradition, we also find other paths to examining symbolist assumptions and refiguring the human in performance. Chapter 2, set in the context of the widespread notion of "actor as material" in early twentieth-century Russia and the USSR, showed that both Vsevolod Meyerhold at the Borodinskaya Street Studio and Gustav Shpet in his philosophical writings on theater also offer more individualized and phenomenological perspectives on the actor than symbolists and other early modernists practiced.

Key terms of early modernist polemics over the role of the actor were captured in the lengthy and contentious production process for *Gamlet* (*Hamlet*) at the Moscow Art Theater, steered by both Stanislavsky and England's maverick stage artist Edward Gordon Craig, with significant contributions by Leopold Sulerzhitsky (1872–1916). Premiering on December 23, 1911, the Moscow Art Theater's first *Hamlet* production was a much-anticipated dramatic feast that Valery Bryusov would call "indisputably an eminent

Figure 3.1. Engraving by Edward Gordon Craig of a scene from *Hamlet*, directed by Edward Gordon Craig and Konstantin Stanislavsky at the Moscow Art Theater, 1910. Copyright © Bakhrushin Theatre Museum, Moscow.

occurrence in the history of not only the Russian theater, but the entire European theater."[10] In *Hamlet* on the floorboards of the Moscow Art Theater, Craig realized ideas for a monodramatic theater that recalled proposals put forward by Evreinov and Fyodor Sologub in 1908 as a critique of the Moscow Art Theater's naturalism.[11] Many critics considered the most radical and exciting aspect of the production to be Craig's set design, which consisted of large, movable hinged screens that allowed for fluid reconfigurations of the stage space (see fig. 3.1).

The production's three years of rehearsals, 1908–11, were a source of ongoing stress for Stanislavsky and the Moscow Art Theater company, due to Craig's extravagant, ever-changing demands for the set and costumes. But the production also coincided with a critical moment in Stanislavsky's artistic development, as during its rehearsals he was in the thick of piecing together his initial plan for his acting system—at the time, fairly unpopular among his actors. His own first production to put it to use, a well-received staging of Ivan Turgenev's play *Mesiats v derevne* (*A Month in the Country*), premiered during the work on *Hamlet*, on December 9, 1909. Although Stanislavsky had hired Craig in part out of hope that the vibrant European would help bolster the Moscow Art Theater's fledgling experiments with symbolism and other efforts to counteract what many had perceived as the naturalism of the theater's first few years, stenograms of Stanislavsky and Craig's conversations during *Hamlet* rehearsals demonstrate the degree to which working with Craig in fact oriented Stanislavsky *away* from Craig's modish aesthetic beliefs and more firmly toward his own.[12] Against the background of Craig's symbolism and abstraction, Stanislavsky's own—more religious and humanistic—sense of theater and the actor comes into relief.

To be sure, Craig's perspective on the actor, articulated and recorded at the *Hamlet* rehearsals, clearly connects with familiar modernist discourses. Craig rejected many forms of acting, as he declared in his provocative essay "The Actor and the Über-Marionette" (1908), which he published in his own theoretical journal, *The Mask*. Craig's polemical essay entered into a vibrant European modernist fervor for the marionette that included voices such as Joseph Conrad, Walter Pater, Oscar Wilde, Maurice Bouchor, and Alfred Jarry.[13] In an extreme response to the paradox posed by Denis Diderot (that a great actor must convey emotion without actually feeling it), and following up on an essay by Heinrich von Kleist that was well known at the start of the twentieth century ("On the Marionette Theater," 1810), Craig had imagined that average, mediocre actors could be replaced by "über-marionettes," idealized puppets whose stage art would not be vulnerable to the unpredictability of the human body, with its uncontrollable emotions and physiology. Craig further considers the director and stage designer, not the actor, to be the exclusive artists in the theater, though he would later claim in *Hamlet* rehearsals that Vasily Kachalov, who played the lead, held a more important role than the director.[14] Craig wrote in the essay:

> Acting is not an art. It is therefore incorrect to speak of the actor as an artist. For accident is an enemy of the artistic. Art is the exact antithesis of Pandimonium [*sic*], and Pandimonium is created by the tumbling together of many accidents; Art arrives only by design. Therefore in order to make any work of art it is clear we may work in those materials with which we can calculate. Man is not one of those materials. . . . In the modern theatre, owing to the use of the bodies of men and women *as their material*, all which is presented there is of an accidental nature.[15]

Like many symbolists and other early modernists, Craig shifts the burden of theatrical authorship off the actor out of concern that the actor is incalculable. In direct contrast to Shpet and Meyerhold as discussed in chapter 2, Craig perceives the actor as material as an insurmountable problem for the stage, and he rejects the artistic potential in human unreliability or precarity.

Stanislavsky reports in his memoirs that Craig made a similar statement to him upon their first meeting in Moscow: "Further, Craig said that every work of art must be made out of dead material—stone, marble, bronze, canvas, paper, paint—and fixed once and for all into an artistic form. Thus the living material of the constantly changing actor's body is unstable, not suited to creative work, and Craig rejected actors, especially those who were void of bright and beautiful individuality, those who were not in themselves works of art, as Duse or Tommaso Salvini were."[16] Stanislavsky continues:

> Craig dreamed of a theater without women and without men, that is, completely without actors. He wanted to replace them with dolls, marionettes that don't have an actor's habits or an actor's gestures, nor painted faces, nor ringing voices, nor vulgar souls, nor the desire for cabotinage: dolls and marionettes would cleanse the atmosphere of the theater, they would endow the business with seriousness, while the dead materials out of which they were made would give the possibility to hint at that Actor with a capital letter who lives in the soul, the imagination and dreams of Gordon Craig himself.[17]

Stanislavsky's description of Craig's vision is thoroughly Platonic: the inanimate puppet as a substitute for an ideal Actor.[18] On Stanislavsky's remembering, Craig is a utopian whose work strives for an ideal it would never reach, a narrative that fits neatly with the many ways in which their *Hamlet* ultimately—due to disorganization and financial troubles—fell short of Craig's dreams for it.

Stanislavsky's own perspective on the actor, as articulated and recorded in dialogue with Craig at the *Hamlet* rehearsals, fits less comfortably within the familiar modernist tropes of man versus marionette and the failed utopia. In fact, Stanislavsky's responses to Craig in their discussions point not to ways in which Stanislavsky's views of the actor are conservative and out of touch with his era—a portrait of Stanislavsky that was at the time painted by symbolists and other colleagues—but rather to ways in which Stanislavsky questions and reshapes the terms of modernist performance.

We see in the rehearsal stenograms that as Craig begins to articulate something like his über-marionette concept, Stanislavsky pushes back. The following conversation was recorded in 1909:

> Craig: Not until the world flies away into a thousand pieces will we get from actors these simple forms rich in fantasy. Is it not better to use an actor like a half-instrument or a *half-child*?
>
> Stanislavsky: Through his soul or gesture?
>
> Craig: An actor has no soul.
>
> Stanislavsky: That is a big mistake.
>
> Craig: I've written about that. You evidently want an actor to be at the same time a person, while my entire theory lies in separating the person from the actor. When you manage to get from a person

> to the playing of external, learned movements and a face like a mask, then it is possible. You hold your hands forcibly, as you are an actor (*The Drama of Life*), but a person wants to spread these hands and make a gesture. A person and an actor are always enemies.
>
> . . .
>
> Stanislavsky: Here is your error—if you need movement, seek it through the actor's soul [*ishchite ego u aktera cherez dushu*].[19]

While Craig sees gesture as something to be imitated, something the actor "learns" from without, Stanislavsky prizes the specificity of the individual actor's expression and points to actors themselves as sources of knowledge or inspiration for movement, in particular through an incalculable and immaterial aspect of the actor: their *soul*. If Craig's vision of the actor takes the form of a Platonist narrative, Stanislavsky rejects the deference to an abstract ideal and instead latches onto a different, more individualized intangibility: the soul each actor possesses that can guide their art. Stanislavsky's choice to endow each actor with agency in performance, permitting actors to follow from their own soul rather than imitating something from without, is thus a rejection of the beliefs on which Craig's concept of the über-marionette is premised.

Craig's joking distinction between an *actor* and a *person* leads Stanislavsky to reinforce his conviction that not only is the actor a person (i.e., an individual with agency and identity) but the actor must lean into their personhood—embrace the creative resources of their own soul. Though the sentiment evokes some of the mysticism associated with other early modernists like Vyacheslav Ivanov and Maurice Maeterlinck, Stanislavsky sees the soul as a source of creativity that *counters* director-prescribed gestures, rather than as a direct conduit to universal truth. Meanwhile, Craig complained about Stanislavsky in his daybook: "[Stanislavsky] uses [actors] as one uses bookbinding tools or needles & threads—Can he *make* an actor this or that. If yes—then he considers him a good actor. It was this I feared. This point of view I have always tried to steer clear of. It is a practical one & valuable but quite inhuman—."[20] In other words, Craig and Stanislavsky's clash of visions for the production meant that both saw the other as inhuman—Craig for declaring humans unsuitable for acting, and Stanislavsky (in Craig's view) for using actors instrumentally.

For Craig the most compelling truth of the play was in Hamlet's spiritual nature. Early on, he informed Stanislavsky that he saw the play as a fight between spirit and matter, or material. Their Hamlet (see fig. 3.2) was to be not the mournful Russian Hamlet stuck in doubt and anxiety; nor would he be quite like the English Hamlet, intellectual and pensive, as played by Henry Irving in 1874. Craig saw Hamlet as spirit buried in matter: a true and transcendent individual surrounded by baseness and crudeness.[21]

Figure 3.2. Photograph of Hamlet, played by Vasily Kachalov, in *Hamlet*, directed by Edward Gordon Craig and Konstantin Stanislavsky at the Moscow Art Theater, 1912. Copyright © Bakhrushin Theatre Museum, Moscow.

Correspondingly, Craig wanted all of the characters except Hamlet portrayed as contemptible. All but Hamlet would merge into one uniform mass, rather than be distinguished by individual personalities. Further, even the symbolism of Hamlet's internal experience would be manifested visually. In a typescript prepared by Sulerzhitsky of Craig's conversations with him, Craig says: "I often imagine, I even dreamed a few times, that during Hamlet's monologues some sort of figure approaches him—light, golden, alluring—and it seemed that this figure accompanying Hamlet is death. Not the gloomy, grave one, as people normally imagine it, but light, joyful, as it appears to Hamlet, for whom it is the only escape from a tragic situation."[22] By giving a body to an abstract symbolic form, Craig further emphasizes that Gertrude, Claudius, and the others are themselves not *characters* with human personalities but representations of Hamlet's ideas.

Stanislavsky's work with Craig attests, by contrast, to the Russian director's commitment to character, a commitment that must not be confused with a commitment to any particular aesthetic style, such as naturalism or realism.[23] Unlike Craig, Stanislavsky approached *Hamlet* as a play whose narrative is driven by the interactions of its ensemble of individual personalities. In contrast to Craig's symbolism, Stanislavsky insisted that a spectator needs to see a compellingly real and fleshed out personality onstage in order to relate to the performance and make sense of it. Stanislavsky reportedly commented at a rehearsal in Craig's absence: "Because of his love for Hamlet, [Craig] shades everyone in dark colors, he makes all the rest of the characters into toads, buffoons, allows them nothing human."[24] This comment labels Craig's perspective as dehumanizing—and Stanislavsky's, by contrast, as affirming of the human. Craig's approach to actors themselves supports this interpretation of his perspective, as Craig stated in rehearsal: "There must not be different individualities, as there would be in a real [*real'n(aia)*] play. *No, here everything merges into one mass*."[25]

In her classic book on the death of character in mid-twentieth-century drama, Elinor Fuchs sums up the significance of each theatrical era's different understanding of character: "Each epoch of character representation—that is, each substantial change in the way character is represented on the stage and major shift in the relationship of character to other elements of dramatic construction or theatrical presentation—constitutes at the same time the manifestation of a change in the larger culture concerning the perception of self and the relations of self and world."[26] In line with Fuchs's statement, Craig and Stanislavsky's differences over character in the production suggest differing concepts of self and world. Stanislavsky appreciates the variability contained within a single self and the self's integration into a larger, variegated world, while Craig seems to see personality as more monolithic and the very concept of a self as at odds with a world that tries to subsume selves into generalities. Craig's approach to *Hamlet* shifted the burden of the narrative from the complex individual subjectivities often identified in Shakespeare's characters to an allegory about spirit and matter. The characters (as well as the actors) were seen as getting in the way of this allegory, and thus Craig intended to flatten out both characters and actors, by costuming actors in burdensomely heavy cloth that inhibited movement (see, for example, the drapery on the costume for the ghost of Hamlet's father in fig. 3.3), by emptying the delivery of Shakespeare's text of psychologically inflected tone, and

Figure 3.3. Photomechanical print of the ghost of Hamlet's father, played by N. A. Znamensky, in *Hamlet*, directed by Edward Gordon Craig and Konstantin Stanislavsky at the Moscow Art Theater, 1912. Copyright © Bakhrushin Theatre Museum, Moscow.

by transforming all characters but Hamlet into crude, even crass caricatures. Stanislavsky's resistance to these efforts conveys instead a belief that spectator interest is carried by emotional identification, by actors representing characters as human subjectivities—a representation that is not restricted to styles of naturalism or realism but that does reject the diminishment of the role of character within the performance. Character, as Stanislavsky would come to understand it, was always being actively created by the actor. Thus Stanislavsky questioned Craig's desire to use characters as symbols, such as Craig's suggestion of placing Hamlet at the corner of the stage in every scene to convey the monodramatic idea that the entire production was from Hamlet's perspective.

The *Hamlet* performance would be a legendary failure, its set memorialized in theater history for Craig's enormous movable screens, its design and acting remembered for their inconsistency and for the Moscow Art Theater's inability to implement the ideas of the British artist, ideas that they did not fully understand or appreciate. We do see in the final performance that Stanislavsky, along with Sulerzhitsky, who did much of the grunt work to make the production happen, succeeded at infusing the production with a stronger sense of individualized character, primarily by cutting back on some of Craig's efforts to eliminate it.[27] Hamlet was performed with subtlety and emotional range, in contrast to the Russian tradition of a declaiming Hamlet. Craig's hopes for elaborate theatrics, such as the Players flying in through the windows like trapeze artists, remained unrealized, leaving more responsibility to the actors themselves to convey character. In the face of Craig's suspicion of the human form, biology, and psychology, all of which were for him too uncontrollable, Stanislavsky strove to resurrect the person onstage in this *Hamlet* and to reclaim the person's place in art.

Thus we can see the Moscow Art Theater's *Hamlet* of 1911 as a production devoted to working out a philosophy of the actor. Not only were rehearsals filled with the two directors' debates over what actors are and how to direct them, but the unevenness of the final product also captured the unfinished, experimental, rough nature of these conversations and the ideas on acting that they developed. Where Stanislavsky sought to secure individual character and the agency of the actor, Craig sought an art that minimizes them, a point of conflict that indicates above all the instability of the concept of the actor in this era and its wide-ranging possibilities. Stanislavsky's defense of the actor who is an agent, which he would continue to endorse through his later work and writings, shines especially starkly in contrast to the extremity of Craig's perspective, but, importantly, both Stanislavsky's and Craig's positions take hold in modernist thought and practice.

Mind-Body-Spirit

Stanislavsky's System as it would develop both in practice and in his writings enriches the conviction he expressed during *Hamlet* rehearsals that the actor is a person. In the System actors bring their whole self—mind, body, spirit—to performance. Their personhood comes from their intentional investment of their full physical, cognitive, and spiritual capacities in the work of art, such that within the context of the performance they (as actors playing roles) are understood as people—or as what Stanislavsky calls a "human being–actor" (*chelovek-artist*)—a position that is radically opposed to the depersonalization of the actor by contemporaries of Stanislavsky such as Craig.[28] To acknowledge that an actor is a person is for Stanislavsky to acknowledge that the actor is a multifaceted being deserving of respect and individuality and capable of an ethics.

The maturation of Stanislavsky's acting theory roughly coincides with the development of the modern discipline of psychology, an instructive point because of the influence of psychology on the System (discussed most extensively by Rose Whyman), as well as Stanislavsky's influence, in turn, on Vygotsky.[29] Stanislavsky began to think carefully about acting while working at the Society of Art and Literature, which he founded in 1888, and he spent the rest of his adult life formulating his ever-evolving acting system. Meanwhile, the Moscow Psychological Society, Russia's first professional association for psychologists and philosophers, was founded in 1885 (it would close in 1922), and it included among its members theater critic Aikhenval'd. The first Russian psychological journal, *Voprosy filosofii i psikhologii* (*Questions of Philosophy and Psychology*), came out in 1889. While these early Russian psychologists were seeking out a scientific and philosophical understanding of the human mind and behavior in order to deliver more accurate, precise, experimentally verified conceptualizations of human psychology, Stanislavsky was working to eliminate declamation and exaggerated, conventionalized gestures onstage in favor of more sensitive, authentic displays of feeling. Indeed, Stanislavsky's thought evolved in tandem with its psychological context. An understanding of mind is not only crucial to the System (and its understanding of personhood); it also reflects psychological debates over the nature of mind and consciousness, particularly as Stanislavsky, like Soviet psychology itself, would face Soviet censorship.

Stanislavsky lays out the origins of his acting system thus. In the early years, he had practiced acting methods that move from the character's internal qualities to external ones: the actor experiences a certain *feeling* and, as a result, produces a certain *movement*. But, reportedly on a stay in Finland in the summer of 1906, he realized that his own performances as an actor in the role of Dr. Stockmann in Henrik Ibsen's *An Enemy of the People*, which had premiered at the Moscow Art Theater in 1900, had grown stale. In a moment that is echoed in the questions found two decades later in Gurevich's survey of actors for the GAKhN Theater Section, Stanislavsky asked himself: "Why is it that the more I repeat my roles, the more I go backward and grow wooden?"[30] He observed that a divide had sprung up between his internal and external experiences in performance: "That inner content that I had put into the roles when I first created them and that outer form which these roles grew into over time were as far from each other as heaven and earth. Previously everything had flowed out of beautiful, exciting inner truth. Now all that remained of it was a weathered shell, rot, rubbish that had stuck in the soul and the body for various random reasons that had nothing to do with genuine art."[31] The answer, Stanislavsky determined, required training the *spirit*: "Some kind of spiritual preparation [*dukhovnaia podgotovka*] was needed before beginning the creative act, every time, for every repetition. Not only a corporeal [*telesnyi*] toilette but principally a spiritual one [*dukhovnyi*] was necessary before a performance."[32] The insights with which he returned to rehearsals for the 1906–7 season would evolve into his System.

The System rejects the internal distancing from performance that Stanislavsky describes having experienced and overcomes his sense of a divide between inner content and outer form, which we might interpret as the mental, emotional, and spiritual investment in a role versus the physical performance of it. Whereas in the early years of the 1900s, Craig and the symbolists around him aspired to severely restrict, even eliminate, the place of the actor's personal psychology within performance, Stanislavsky saw the actor's psychology—in the form of introspection, self-awareness, empathizing, thinking, and feeling—as integral to the fabric of the artwork. He was revolutionary in making both the psychological and the physical a part of his System. In the words of Rhonda Blair: "Stanislavsky was the first to devise and disseminate broadly a systematic approach that connected the actor's behavior, body, emotion, and intelligence."[33] Bruce McConachie similarly suggests that Stanislavsky was the first acting theorist to "bridge the mind/body divide."[34] Although thinkers such as English philosopher George Henry Lewes, author of *Actors and Acting* (1875), had also arrived at the conviction that acting must be psychophysiological, Stanislavsky bears significant responsibility for Western acting's shift away from declamation and toward acting that involves the actor's internal work alongside the external.

What kind of "spiritual preparation" did the System require? Missing from assessments like McConachie's and Blair's are Stanislavsky's beliefs about the soul and spirit. In articulating his vision for their *Hamlet* production, Craig frequently used the term "spirit" (*dukh*), which would later prove central to Stanislavsky's System.[35] But Stanislavsky's understanding of spirit would derive from Russian Orthodoxy, as Maria Shevtsova argues, wherein God breathes the spirit into the person, rather than from the more secular lineage of symbolism, and it would be more invested in the actual human, with body and soul, than symbolism was.[36] Until recently, Stanislavsky's emphasis on the spirit has been underappreciated. Shevtsova asserts: "The spiritual dimension of a human being is of great consequence to Stanislavsky."[37] She writes: "In sum, the body, the soul and the spirit, together with their aspects and sides (like the feeling side of the soul), are a filigree of holistic interdependences that form the indivisible one of a human being."[38] Notably, the "spiritual preparation," or acting technique, Stanislavsky sought in Finland is what facilitates the integration of inner content and outer form. Making room for the spirit in the System permits the overcoming of mind-body dualism, which is not native to Russian Orthodoxy.

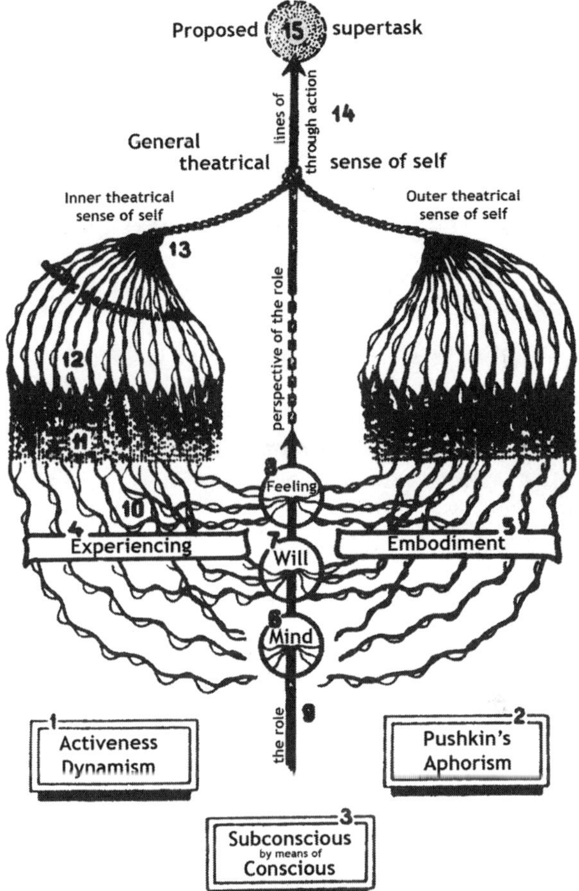

Figure 3.4. Diagram of Stanislavsky's System based on his "Plan of Experiencing," 1935. Wikimedia Commons.

Stanislavsky's merging of mind, body, and spirit manifests throughout the two books laying out his System, *Rabota aktera nad soboi v tvorcheskom protsesse perezhivaniia* (*The Actor's Work on Themself in the Creative Process of Experiencing*, 1938) and *Rabota aktera nad soboi v tvorcheskom protsesse voploshcheniia* (*The Actor's Work on Themself in the Creative Process of Embodiment*, 1953). Although the first book focuses more on training the mind/spirit and the second more on training the body, Stanislavsky makes clear that these two trainings work together harmoniously. The techniques he introduces for achieving a particular internal state, such as emotional memory, are as directed at purposeful physical action as they are at psychological conditioning. He writes of the physical and psychological:

"In every physical action there is something psychological, and in every psychological one, something physical."[39] Further, physical training has mental and spiritual purpose. Introducing the students in the book to acrobatics, his teacher character Tortsov says, "however strange it may seem, [acrobatics] is needed by the actor more for internal than for external use . . . *for the strongest moments of spiritual climaxes, for . . . creative inspiration*."[40] The inseparability of the physical and psychological, and of the internal and external, implies not a primacy of one over the other but a simultaneity and interdependence. For Stanislavsky both internal and external training aim at achieving "the creation of the life of the human spirit," the highest purpose of art.[41]

Late in his life, Stanislavsky drew up a rich diagram of his System, which he included in manuscripts in 1935 (see fig. 3.4). The diagram offers insights specific to Stanislavsky's integration of the total human being. Striking about it is that Stanislavsky arranges the terminology and concepts of the System along a sketch of a spine and pair of lungs, tying even his most abstract terminology to a concrete body in a way that subtly underscores the body's centrality to concepts like experiencing (*perezhivanie*) that might be misinterpreted as wholly mental/spiritual and thus body-less. In fact, Stanislavsky insists, the activity of the body, whether internal or external, is integral to acting. So too are mind (*um*), will, and feeling—terms that he arranges along the spine, which represents the role, with an arrow pointing upward and out of the lungs. Mind, will, and feeling are all connected directly to the two lungs by irregular wavy lines that suggest that they are essential starting points for the actor's breath and aspiration.[42]

This diagram also cites three bases to the System: activeness (or activity/action), the subconscious through the conscious, and "Pushkin's aphorism," which Whyman states as "the truth of passions, verisimilitude of feelings in proposed circumstances." Notably, Stanislavsky changed Pushkin's "supposed circumstances" to "proposed circumstances" for his rendering, emphasizing that the role, costuming, scenery, and so forth supply the actor with a set of "proposed" or "given" (as commonly translated) circumstances within which they must act.[43] As Whyman explains, Stanislavsky also cited a fourth base to the System elsewhere: "the aim of art is the creation of the life of the human spirit."[44] These bases suggest the purposefulness of System acting. It is rooted in action (*deistvie*) rather than play (*igra*), the term more commonly used in theater. It is also rooted in the response to "proposed circumstances," and the conscious filtering of the subconscious. "The creation of the life of the human spirit" implies concrete and material *making* out of an abstract and immaterial spirit. This is articulated by Patrick C. Carriere as: "The connection between inner and outer is a process of emanation in which the contents of the higher, ideal and more 'real' ('internal') plane are made incarnate in lower and material ('external') planes through the trained, sensitive and expressive body of the living actor."[45] Just as Craig insisted on the separation of "person" and "actor," Stanislavsky insisted on their unity (*chelovek-artist*) through deliberate, purposeful action.

That Stanislavsky maps his System onto a body's lungs and spine reinforces his belief that the capacity for creation is contained in the human, bodily actor—not the director, stage designer, or anyone else. Further, the role, which can be read as one of what Stanislavsky called the "given circumstances," is processed *through* the body's particular mind, will, and feeling through experiencing and incarnation (*voploshchenie*). The mind, will, and feeling are all placed anatomically closer to the location of the heart or gut than of the head, suggesting, again, a rejection of Cartesian dualism in favor of mind, will, and feeling *in* and *as* the torso, rather than as the more detached, distant, cerebral head.

The terminology for identifying Stanislavsky's beliefs is always a stumbling block, as scholars find themselves tripping over the fact that our language (and Stanislavsky's) for describing the actor makes discrete the components such as body, mind, behavior, and emotion that he in fact sees as integrated. In truth, Stanislavsky's System requires the participation of the totality of the actor however inadequately parsed—body, memory, mind, behavior, subconscious, unconscious, soul, spirit, intuition, and so on. That Stanislavsky himself uses multiple overlapping terminologies reinforces their incompleteness on their own. It is important to note, too, that much non-Russian scholarship that references the mind in Stanislavsky's thought may rely on mistranslations of his works that erroneously replace the spiritual with the mental. Stanislavsky translator and scholar Jean Benedetti consistently removes Stanislavsky's references to the spirit (*dukh*) or soul (*dusha*), replacing them with "mind" and "mental," as Shevtsova has pointed out.[46] With respect to Benedetti, this is not an uncommon substitution, as the Russian concept of *dusha* is far more grounded in the body than the Anglophone concept of *soul*, which suggests a wispy immateriality. Still, the translation seems to overly secularize and make scientific Stanislavsky's true meaning.

Experiencing, or emotional experiencing, a concept of Stanislavsky's that was especially interesting to Vygotsky, distills the director's vision of the human as a unity of mind, body, and spirit. In a state of experiencing, actors are fully, consciously present in the process of creating.[47] They are aware of their own acting while also being sufficiently invested in their role to identify with it in the first person—Stanislavsky's ambivalent (but earnest) response to Diderot's paradox of the actor. Because experiencing is grounded in the subjective perception of oneself and the surrounding (theater) world, it points to the phenomenological aspects of the System, which have been discussed by scholars including Daniel Johnston, Mark Fortier, and Robert Leach, and in which a unified vision of the human being is logical.[48] Seen in this way, the System prescribes to the actor a particular way of being in the world: a means of existing, and of interacting with the simultaneously imagined and real stage objects and people.

Process, Temporality, Ethics

Unlike Craig, what Stanislavsky, through terms such as "experiencing," offers is not so much an *ideal* but a process: that is, an atelic understanding of acting, whereby acting is based in process and presence, rather than in the striving for a particular result, a product. William B. Worthen articulates performance in the context of modernism not as "theater as an objectified thing-to-be-viewed" but as "a process, in which the position and power of the performers (actors, characters, spectators) are negotiable, changeable."[49] Indeed, Stanislavsky's sense of theater is continually vulnerable and in flux, with actors working to create their relationship to their roles and to the stage world. Acting takes place *now*, Stanislavsky would tell his performers. His System shifts the temporality of acting from past/future (preparing for performance / performing what one has prepared) to the present, cultivating something like "presence" as understood in theatrical scholarship today. Focusing on the *now* does not allow for a time delay between mind and body but rather insists on their simultaneity. This sense of presence is a consequence of the living and active nature of Stanislavsky's implicit concept of personhood. Johnston writes of the phenomenological tint to this sense of process: "*An Actor's Work* takes into account the intertwined nature of self and world, environment and body not with an origin, but as an entity continually in the process of becoming within temporality."[50] That is, the self is not the origin of truth; the self is continually negotiating truth in relation to the surroundings. Further, the self is experienced or lived in tandem with the world around it: process and presence are in themselves essential to the knowledge the actor achieves in this state.

The appendix to the second part of Stanislavsky's *The Actor's Work* includes "Études on Attention," in addition to "Études on Relations to Objects" and "Études on Freeing the Muscles," among others.[51] The études for attention are subdivided by the five senses, stimulating self-awareness. In a much-discussed episode, Stanislavsky describes the actor's ideal state of being:

> STUDENT: . . . Suddenly for some time I felt very good onstage; it didn't seem strange and unusual to me that I was acting, and all the others attentively watched my dilletante play. It seemed like it was normal, that this is needed and that I have the right to stand there and do what I was doing.
>
> TEACHER: This is a very important moment in the actor's state of being [*samochuvstvi[e]*] onstage. It even has its own special name. In actor's jargon we call this condition onstage "I am" ["*Ia esm'* "], that is I exist, I am located now, today, here, in the life of the play, onstage [*ia sushchestvuiu, nakhozhus' seichas, segodniia, zdes', v zhizni p'esy, na stsene*].[52]

The teacher goes on to explain that two things are needed for the students to progress as actors: one must conquer what gets in the way of creativity to form a state conducive to creating, and "one must learn how to awaken *one's organic nature and its subconscious*."[53] Good acting requires achieving a particular state of being that is in touch with one's own individual capacities—as given by God, we might presume, for Stanislavsky's religiosity is evident here. The possibility of doing this is particular to being human. As Shevtsova writes:

> Stanislavsky knew from church services, purification rituals and other such religious observances that "*ya yesm*" means nothing less than "I am in God and God is in me" in spirit and body; and the attitude underpinning "*ya yesm*" is "I am attentive to my state of oneness with God." . . . Stanislavsky is quite subtle in his affirmation that the spirit is *realized* in the actor, and this is of crucial importance, for the spirit does not float on high but is incarnate—in the flesh, in the body, of the human form.[54]

Again, we see Stanislavsky, through Orthodoxy, articulating a unified corporeal, spiritual self, achieved through a particular human relation to God. Further, the teacher's emphasis on "now, today, here," a phrase that has received attention in recent scholarship, shifts the time of acting to the rich thickness of the present moment, to *presence*, in all its purposefulness, incompleteness, and instability.[55]

For many thinkers in this book, acting is a means of actively understanding, even actively *being*, the human of everyday life. At times, Stanislavsky's work might suggest that he considered acting to be a special, even sacred activity—one that is unique from real life. In fact, his actor training aims explicitly to strip away an actor's inhibitions and theatricalized habits, to free the actor from staid forms. As Stanislavsky told Craig in a *Hamlet* rehearsal: "The main thing is to teach the actor to come onstage and not think anything. That is the most difficult thing. When that happens, then I can do with him what I want, but not before."[56] Although Craig was dismissive of this comment, claiming that Stanislavsky thought even worse of actors than he did, it captures part of Stanislavsky's drive for a natural, organic actor who is doing something real and purposeful that is akin to and part of life, though not strictly imitative of it.

By taking this atelic, process-oriented viewpoint, Stanislavsky rejects a modernist aesthetics of failure (because how can something fail if it is never finished) and rejects efforts to reduce the human to a sign. Instead, he sees the human actor as always in the process of becoming. This process entails responsibility: Stanislavsky's actor is an ethical being who must be disciplined in order to create art. Further, he stipulates that this actor is a public figure who must behave in a dignified manner in public spaces outside the theater.

They must be free of crime and scandal, and they must respect the art of acting and the collective creation of the theater to in turn receive respect from their colleagues and the public. The ethics of acting are thus tied intrinsically to the personhood of the actor and to Stanislavsky's sense of art's higher purpose.

Consciousness

By the late 1920s, while Stanislavsky was writing *The Actor's Work*, Gurevich's concerns about the scientific accuracy of his terminology were coupled with ever-increasing concerns about whether his manuscript would pass the censors. This meant a need to shift to more materialist language in order to shape his System to state-endorsed reflexology; as Sharon Marie Carnicke writes, "Body and flesh were acceptable, mind questionable (if it meant the subconscious), and spirit unacceptable."[57] And yet, Stanislavsky continued to emphasize spiritual and mental experience in performance, speaking in religious and metaphysical terms that capture the incalculable value of the human. Such terms complicate Stanislavsky's parallels with late imperial and Soviet psychology, suggesting that he has at least as much in common with antimaterialist thinking as with the leading physiological psychologists, whose work he references. As Whyman has demonstrated, Stanislavsky drew on Théodule-Armand Ribot, Alfred Binet, Ivan Sechenov, and Ivan Pavlov in understanding a physiological relationship between mind and body, though he stopped short of fully embracing their worldviews. These thinkers supported Stanislavsky's linking of bodily movement and emotion, as Whyman writes: "The thesis that all thought is accompanied by muscular activity seemed incontrovertible in Stanislavsky's time and the materialist reduction of mental states to activity meant that Stanislavsky saw emotion and action as inextricably linked."[58]

The dynamics of Soviet psychology help illuminate the context for how both Stanislavsky and Vygotsky understood the human. A materialist bent surfaced in Russian psychology of the prerevolutionary era, in the work of Sechenov (1829–1905) and Pavlov (1849–1936), as well as in the work of the developer of Russian reflexology, Vladimir Bekhterev (1857–1927). All three sought to eliminate abstract concepts of the soul, mind, and consciousness from scientific study by explaining mental processes through physiology. But the strong objectivist trend they introduced to Russian psychology did not go unchecked. Conceptions of the mind in Russian modernist culture at large were also shaped by Freudian psychoanalysis (which was far more introspective and subjective than the approaches of the physiological psychologists) and by the less materialist empirical psychology of Europeans Ribot, Wilhelm Wundt, and Emil Kraepelin (which was firmly bound to philosophy). Meanwhile, within Russian psychology, an ideological battle surged between reflexologists and their opponents. The versions of reflexology and physiological psychology that were uplifted by the Soviets bore no whiff of the abstraction, spiritualism, subjectivity, and introspection rendered suspect by the Marxist doctrine of the new Soviet state. Prizing instead a science and philosophy grounded in the objective, measurable, and material, the Soviet government began as early as 1922 to repress intellectuals who rejected Marxism, transporting these censored philosophers and scientists to foreign exile via steamship.

Sechenov's popular treatise *Refleksy golovnogo mozga* (*Reflexes of the Brain*, 1862) explosively argued that the central nervous system was the basis of all thought and motor activity, in a rejection of common concepts such as free will and the immortality of the soul. The soul was instead a function of the central nervous system. "The infinite diversity of external manifestations of cerebral activity can be reduced ultimately to a single phenomenon—muscular movement," he wrote.[59] At the time, Sechenov received significant resistance to his ideas from state censors and the Orthodox Church, which viewed his conclusions as at odds with morality. Meanwhile, his work was seen as revolutionary not only scientifically but also socially. Radical author Nikolai Chernyshevsky would base two protagonists in his novel *Chto delat'?* (*What Is to Be Done?*, 1863) on Sechenov, his acquaintance, solidifying the popular link between physiology and socialist utopia that would carry through to the Soviet era, although scientists themselves did not tend to espouse ideological views (and in fact Pavlov was strongly against the Soviets).[60]

Interest in Sechenov's ideas increased through the end of the Russian Empire. Pavlov followed in his footsteps as he developed his concept of the conditioned reflex, which determined that the body can learn new responses to otherwise neutral stimuli. This discovery put higher mental processes into wholly physiological terms, freeing them from discussions of consciousness and permitting their subjugation to laboratory experiments. Pavlov had found experimental means (with dogs, no less) to prove Sechenov's thesis that cerebral activity, including thought, could be identified as a reflex response. Meanwhile, Bekhterev's work in neurological science rivaled Pavlov's in revealing reflexes as the basis for brain activity, though Bekhterev devised successful experiments for measuring "association reflexes" in humans, rather than in dogs.[61] Bekhterev used the term "reflexology" for his theory of the integration of human physiology with human behavior and established a comprehensive center for this study in Saint Petersburg. Reflexology was subsequently officially adopted with the beginnings of the Soviet state because its emphasis on the physical, knowable, optimizable aspects of the human aligned well with Soviet Marxism, though Stalin would later have Bekhterev's name removed from textbooks.

A key figure in the opposition to materialist psychology was psychologist and philosopher Georgy Chelpanov (1862–1936), who countered materialism as early as his book *Mozg i dusha* (*Brain and Soul*, 1900). Chelpanov's conception of psychology was shaped by figures like Wundt (with whom he would study), who advocated for a psychological science that combined theoretical or philosophical investigation with empirical research. In particular, Chelpanov fiercely defended the place of consciousness (*soznanie*) in psychology, criticizing Pavlov and Bekhterev for replacing consciousness with reflexes. Chelpanov founded the Moscow Institute of Psychology in 1912 to educate students in his approach. Many of his students at the institute, including Konstantin Kornilov and Vladimir Ekzemplyarsky, joined him in critiquing Marxism's inroads in science, a critique no longer permitted by the 1920s—and Kornilov would in fact lead the movement against Chelpanov when Chelpanov was forced to resign from the institute in 1923. In the early 1920s, Chelpanov did accept a form of Marxist psychology as inevitable given his nation's politics, but he did not himself identify as Marxist, and he expressed that Marxism was no more suited to psychology than any other philosophical system was. I. V. Gladkova writes that the main topic of Chelpanov's work was "the topic of the soul and spirituality."[62] In fact, despite Stanislavsky's references to such physiological psychologists as Sechenov and Pavlov—scientists more favored by the censors—his System seems to resonate much more with the work of Chelpanov, who advocated for a more introspective and philosophical psychology.

Vygotsky would develop in more muted terms Chelpanov's defense of consciousness over reflexology in a presentation in 1924, declaring: "By ignoring the problem of consciousness psychology has deprived itself of access to the study of some rather important and complex problems of human behavior. It is forced to restrict itself to explaining no more than the most elementary connections between a living being and the world. That this is actually the case can easily be seen by a cursory glance at Academician V. M. Bekhterev's book *General foundations of human reflexology*."[63] In Chelpanov and Vygotsky, as in many of their contemporaries, we see both subtle and less subtle critiques of the militant alignment of psychology with Marxism, as well as critiques of reflexology and physiological psychology—theories not inherently Marxist in nature or origin. But although Stanislavsky drew on developments in reflexology and physiological psychology to understand the relationship between mind and body, this understanding can never be collapsed into the findings of these scientists; he refused to abandon valuing the impenetrable unconscious in tandem with the measurable body.

Psychology Meets the Stage (*Enter Vygotsky*)

Like most artistically conscious people in Moscow at the time, Lev Vygotsky appears to have seen the 1911 Craig-Stanislavsky *Hamlet*. He references it in his university thesis on *Hamlet* (1915–16) and in several of his theatrical articles and reviews. As it was for Stanislavsky, we can imagine that this production served as something of a launching point for Vygotsky, both sparking and shoring up his beliefs about actor, mind, soul, spirit, and social or cultural context—beliefs he would interrogate and refine in the roughly two decades to come. Shakespeare's play itself further underlies all of Vygotsky's thought: "To the end of L. S. Vygotsky's days, Shakespeare's tragedy was for him a reference book [*nastol'na(ia) knig(a)*]. He took it to the hospital from which he never returned," writes Mikhail Yaroshevsky.[64] Throughout his life, Vygotsky reaped from *Hamlet* examples of human psychology as filtered through aesthetic, cultural, and social lenses. He took interest not only in Shakespeare's play but also in the nuances of its reception within a particular society and culture.

The Moscow Art Theater *Hamlet*, which ran for three seasons, would have been one of the earliest Moscow performances Vygotsky attended. In a footnote reference to the production in his *Hamlet* thesis, which primarily focuses on interpreting Shakespeare's text, Vygotsky praises aspects of the production and admits that it came close to the views developed in his thesis, primarily in Kachalov's portrayal of Hamlet as a mystic.[65] Indeed, like Stanislavsky and Craig, Vygotsky articulates a view of Hamlet that owes as much to the predominance of symbolist discourse about matter and spirit as it does to religion, though Vygotsky sees the play not as an allegory of symbols, as Craig did, but rather as a myth. Vygotsky writes of *Hamlet* as a "tragedy of tragedies," taking place on the border between our visible world and the otherworldly.[66]

Even more interestingly, given Stanislavsky's own developing understanding of theatrical creation, Vygotsky calls his scholarly approach in the thesis "openly subjective criticism" (*kritika otkrovenno sub"ektivnaia*). Following the claim of his advisor, Aikhenval'd, that a literary work is created by its reader, he thus positions the reader-critic as the work's true author and suggests the act of reading as a kind of performance—a temporally unfolding aesthetic object.[67] As he writes in 1919, also with reference to the Craig-Stanislavsky *Hamlet* as a particular manifestation of the play: "A work itself is only an opportunity [*vozmozhnost'*] that is realized by the spectator or reader through his creativity [*svoim tvorchestvom*]."[68] This emphasis on impression and subjectivity in the readerly experience, setting aside the author and existing criticism, suggests something akin to a phenomenological interpretation that values subjective reception. Vygotsky's early-found obsession with *Hamlet* further reveals his inclination toward understanding the motivations and construction of the individual within a particular narrative and cultural structure, a drive to understand how the individual is shaped, even created, by various contexts. *Hamlet* for him represents a canonical text that has been continually of relevance and continually shaped and reinterpreted—and also a text that presents psychological puzzles.

Although Vygotsky's short adulthood is remembered for his contributions to developmental psychology, a closer examination of his biography reveals that theater played a consistent, ongoing role in his life. He followed his *Hamlet* thesis with an article on the Moscow theater, "Teatral'nye pametki (pis'mo iz Moskvy)" ("Theatrical Notes [A Letter from Moscow]"), published in the journal *Letopis'* (*The Chronicle*) in 1917. In it he reviewed three major, and stylistically diverse, 1916 productions. His article "Teatr i revolutsiia" ("Theater and Revolution") was published in 1919 in a volume devoted to art and literature of the October Revolution, alongside contributions from such authors as Alexander Blok, Andrei Bely, Zinaida Gippius, Maksim Gorky, and Vladimir Mayakovsky.[69] After the revolution Vygotsky returned to his hometown of Gomel and immersed himself in various teaching jobs. He also headed the theater subdepartment of the Gomel department of public education. He became a member of the town's art council, in which capacity he had free access to all theater performances in the region and was responsible for the publications about these performances in the Soviet press, and he traveled widely, to cities like Moscow, Kyiv, and Petrograd, to contract troupes to play in Gomel. He even made plans to jointly open a drama studio. It was also at this time, in 1922, that Vygotsky began specializing in psychological research. What began as a job teaching topics in psychology at the Gomel Pedagogical Tekhnikum turned into an administrative job managing the psychological laboratory of the tekhnikum, both its research and pedagogical activity. Vygotsky initially lacked the advanced training necessary for the psychological research that would go on at the tekhnikum, but he learned on the job, soon not only managing the lab but also running his own experiments and studies. Thus in Vygotsky's biography, his initiation into psychological research coincided with a period in which he frequently attended and thought about the theater.

Vygotsky's thesis on *Hamlet*, his book *Psikhologiia iskusstva* (*The Psychology of Art*, 1925) and even his 1932 article on the psychology of the actor are well known in the immense, interdisciplinary Vygotsky scholarship, which tends to see these texts as extensions of Vygotsky's work in psychology.[70] Far less familiar to scholars, however, is a set of sixty-eight theater reviews that Vygotsky wrote in his hometown of Gomel from September 1922 to December 1923. These sixty-eight reviews, originally published in a couple of local newspapers (*Nash ponedel'nik* [*Our Monday*] and *Polesskaia Pravda* [*Polesia Truth*]), chronicle Vygotsky's attendance at the two Gomel theaters. V. S. Sobkin and V. S. Mazanova call the theater reviews "sixty-eight special psychological experiments, sixty-eight observations of the manifestations of various personalities when life is defined in peculiar, 'extreme' situations."[71] Indeed, as Sobkin (who has done extensive work on the reviews, editing them for publication in 2015) has argued, Vygotsky saw in theater many of the key ideas he would develop in his psychological research, where he too asked what drives the "human." His reviews wrestle with the many layers of interpersonal, social, and societal relationships at play in each production. The reviews also attest to Vygotsky's immense theatergoing experience of these sixteen months, as many of them cover not one but two or three productions, which comes out to attending (and writing about) more than one production a week. They document not only local productions but also tours of major Soviet theaters, including the Second Studio of the Moscow Art Theater and the Crooked Mirror Theater.

Vygotsky's Gomel theater reviews both anticipate his work in psychology and reveal his affinity with Stanislavsky's ideas. In line with the work of the other theater thinkers in this book, his reviews stress the actor as primary artist in the theater, the actor's temporality and human qualities, and the value of the way in which a performance is perceived by a spectator. Vygotsky writes that his aim as a critic is not to hand out awards but "to critically help the spectator put on the production in their perception."[72] He references his own psychological reactions and experiences of the onstage events, which leads Sobkin to argue that Vygotsky's regular theatergoing in this period served as a psychological, even psychotherapeutic session for him—with the reviews serving as a kind of diary.[73] Vygotsky analyzes his own experience of a character, a gesture, a technical effect, alongside the production's sociocultural context and the way a generalized audience experiences the production. Stressing his own subjectivity in this way results in a phenomenological conception of the theater, in which the theatrical event is not the performance in itself, but the performance as it is experienced by a particular self or subjectivity. The spectator—in this case, Vygotsky—is thus a participant in the analyzed event. As an example, he writes of a melodrama performance: "The appearance of the worker was met by applause and even exclamations: 'That's it' [*Pravil'no*]—they applauded not the actor playing the role, they commended not the character, but they rejoiced in the melodrama that faithfully guessed the desires of the audience."[74] In this comment Vygotsky grasps the audience's psychology as witnessed by him at the performance: the audience's expectations of the genre of melodrama, and the fulfillment the audience achieves through the performance. He was especially attuned to genre conventions, always analyzing a production through the lens of expectations imposed by its genre.

In his reviews, Vygotsky saw in the Soviet theater a psychological model, one that brings together cultural context and the dynamics of a particular relationship, and one that emphasizes making meaning through subjective experience. Individuals and their emotional experiences in the theater space are defined within a relational context, in addition to the cultural context that both actors and spectators bring to a particular dramatic text or theatrical style. When Vygotsky mentions Stanislavsky in his reviews, it is in admiration, and he borrows Stanislavsky's terminology: *perezhivanie*, *samochuvstvie*. In what is less a review than a meditation on the joy of theater and dramatic characters, Vygotsky writes, in harmony with Stanislavsky's "now, today, here": "The happiest day in my life is today. To live without and outside of today is not to live at all."[75] Vygotsky makes this comment in a discussion of theater, such that the comment is another early twentieth-century articulation of theater's capacity for presence through the faculty of attention to the now.

Like Stanislavsky, Vygotsky also emphasizes the place of the corporeal human body in theater, in particular in contemporary theater, which he often describes as a strong break with the past:

> The general striving of the contemporary theater is directed now at the replacement of pictorial and cloth sets with three-dimensional, bulging architecture, which alone can be a real environment for the three-dimensional acting human body. . . . In connection with this even the very principle of the stage is changing. Previously it was understood naturalistically, as the place of the action—a forest, the sea, a room—and it strove to resemble it as much as possible.
>
> In today's theater the stage is only a conventional platform for the actor's play [*igra*], an environment for his action. It represents neither a room nor a forest. It is only a stage for the given play and is constructed as directed by the style and spirit of the play.[76]

Here Vygotsky commends contemporary theater for subordinating the set to the three-dimensionality of the human body. But he does not appear to be valuing the body over other aspects of the human being. Although he discusses gesture and speech in his reviews, he also writes of an actor's "emotional upheaval" (*volnenie*) and intellectual relationship to the role: "[Vershinin as Chechkov] was the best performance in the play—luscious, humorous. It was evident that the actor has something to say *about* the role and he said it well and convincingly: he destroyed Chechkov."[77] He delineates the actor's individual, unique contribution to the creation of a character, indicating that an actor navigates both conventions of how a particular role is played and their own individual capabilities: "A likeable and clean impression is left by Erina's performance of Queen Anna (and other roles). True, she plays little of the stage image of the role, but with sonorous and good speech and with some internal grace and restraint she evaded the vulgar and risky places."[78] In short, Vygotsky is attuned to multiple factors in the playing of a role, both societal and individual, and he is a shrewd critic, often quick to offer his own directorial vision for how a weak production should have been done.

Meanwhile, Vygotsky was gaining his footing in the discipline of psychology. A year after his final Gomel theater review, in 1924, Vygotsky presented his first major work in psychology at the Second All-Russian Psychoneurology Congress in Petrograd (within days to be renamed Leningrad). The speech deftly rejects behaviorism while endorsing its reliance on objective data, and it resurrects the study of consciousness. Vygotsky does not simply refute behaviorism, he offers a modification of it to overcome what he sees as its inherent dualism: "The main premise of reflexology, namely, the purported possibility in principle of explaining all human behavior without any recourse to subjective phenomena and of constructing a psychology without mind [*psikhiki*], is the hand-me-down dualism of subjective psychology, its attempt to study pure, abstract mind. This is the other half of the old dualism: then there was mind without behavior, now we have behavior without mind; in both cases mind and behavior are not one, but two."[79]

Vygotsky's rejection of dualism as an intervention into Soviet psychology is especially interesting in the context of Stanislavsky's integrated understanding of human behavior, or action (*deistvie*). Vygotsky's speech turns on a special delineation of what is *human*: he insists that human behavior not be studied as the "behavior of a mammal."[80] Michael Cole writes that Vygotsky "agreed that consciousness could not be viewed as the special property of the soul, but he insisted that it was an essential property of human beings, which mediated their experience with the external world and rendered them specifically human."[81] Further, Vygotsky articulates the special value of subjective perception of oneself, in a belief that resonates with Stanislavsky's attention to the actor as creating through their specific mind-body-spirit: "It is also now easy to explain the fundamental, fragmentary nature of experience: my mind is not like any other mind because it is affected by stimuli *sui generis* that occur nowhere else but in my own body. The movement of my arm, which is perceived by the eye, may also be a stimulus for both my eye and the eye of another; but the awareness of this movement, those proprioceptive excitations that occur in the process and elicit secondary reactions, exist for me alone."[82] Vygotsky sees objective, empirical significance in a subject's subjective account because he sees consciousness as a reflex of reflexes, stimulated by the actions of the body-mind-spirit.

Key in this speech as well is the similarity Vygotsky draws between one's relation to oneself (consciousness) and one's relation to others: "consciousness must be regarded as a particular case of social experience."[83] This concept has special resonance in the theater. It invites speculation as to whether theatergoing contributed to Vygotsky's idea, for theater is almost always a collective action of multiple actors who must be simultaneously self-aware and aware of one another, a belief Stanislavsky would endorse.

Like Stanislavsky, Vygotsky both acceded to materialism and stood against it, from this speech through the rest of his work in the coming decade. Vygotsky's emphasis on the sociocultural context in mental development is clearly in line with Marxism, and he strategically cites Marx, much as Stanislavsky references the concepts of Pavlov and Sechenov. But Vygotsky, like Stanislavsky, maintains a sense of the distinctiveness of the individual consciousness, although it can be objectively measured. Peter Smagorinsky characterizes Vygotsky's middle ground between Marxism and anti-Marxism as follows: "Vygotsky simultaneously aligns himself with Marx's materialist philosophy and makes space for the individual's role within a socially mediated world. This accommodation of individual constructs of reality . . . would later provide Stalin with the grounds to have Vygotsky's work suppressed posthumously for its ultimate attention to the individual, even one so heavily immersed in sociocultural context."[84]

Vygotsky's Actor-Subject

Vygotsky's emphasis on sociocultural context congeals in a belief that we develop through our experience of our environment. To describe the particularly emotional character of this experience, he uses Stanislavsky's term *perezhivanie*. Substantial attention in recent years has been given to Vygotsky's use of the term.[85] Vygotsky used it in his work as early as 1925, in his book *The Psychology of Art*, and also uses the term in a 1933 or 1934 lecture on the problem of the environment in pedology, stating: "*perezhivanie* is the essential factor for determining the influence of the environment on the psychological development of the child, on the development of his conscious personality. The *perezhivanie* of a situation, the *perezhivanie* of a part of his environment, determines what kind of influence this situation or this environment will have on the child."[86] Pedology, he claims, must study a child's environment not in itself but in its relationship to the particular child—in how the particular child has experienced or lived through it—emotionally, cognitively, and so on, a thoroughly phenomenological conception of human development. It is also clear that by *perezhivanie*, Vygotsky is referencing a totalizing way of experiencing that merges the cognitive, emotional, and physical; the concept, which he undoubtedly recognized in Stanislavsky given his numerous references to the director, underlies much of his thought. Michael Glassman, for example, argues that Vygotsky's zone of proximal development, in which a child learns from doing things just outside their capability, is closely connected to his use of the term *perezhivanie*.[87]

Vygotsky's understanding of the individual within the theater as constituted through both a cultural context and a relational context (between actor and spectator) is one of many themes in the Gomel reviews that heralds his work in psychology to ground individual development in a social, cultural, and historical context. This work shows the fundamental role of social interaction in the development of cognition, or of what Vygotsky sometimes terms "making meaning," a phrase that is particularly apt in the communicative and aesthetic context that is the theater: theater for him makes meaning through the contextualized experiencing of itself by the individuals involved.

Vygotsky's essay on the psychology of the actor, written at the end of his life, eloquently brings together his views of psychology and the stage to argue that the actor's psychology is determined culturally and historically, as well as individually: "We must not forget that the emotions of the actor, since they are a fact of art, go beyond the limits of his personality and make up a part of the emotional dialogue between the actor and the public."[88] He also acknowledges that Stanislavsky's System is not limited to a single style of performance, saying about the work of Evgeny Vakhtangov, who followed Stanislavsky, though his theater was far more spectacular: "We see how certain content dictates a new theatrical form, how a system proves to be much broader than the concrete application it is given."[89] That is, what Vygotsky argues here is that stage psychology is conditional on conventions specific to his cultural-historical moment, *as well as* on the capacities of the individual performers.

One potent resonance between Stanislavsky's and Vygotsky's thought is this belief that the actor creates by and through the contexts of the performance. Both thinkers see the actor as extremely aware of themself and their environment, creating something that is socially and culturally meaningful, or purposeful, but also specific to themself. Stanislavsky's terms *soul* and *spirit* both capture our place in the divine order; they serve the actor as a means of connecting the individual self to this order and to the environment as a whole.

Chapter 4

The Actor's Identity

The Theater Section of the State Academy of the Artistic Sciences (GAKhN)—that same academic body that commissioned the survey of actors discussed in this book's introduction—maintained a bustling calendar of meetings and events. These included several regular lecture series, totaling as many as forty lectures per year, which typically drew an intimate audience of five to fifteen people.[1] One such lecture, presented on December 20, 1923, for the subsection devoted to the study of the actor (led by Liubov' Gurevich), bore the curious title "Akter kak raznovidnost' cheloveka" ("The Actor as *Varietas* of Human"). That is, the actor, not as a theater professional or amateur enthusiast but as a zoological subspecies of *Homo sapiens*—a special kind of human being.[2] This lecture was authored and delivered by an individual whose contributions to the performing arts were wholly verbal rather than plastic or physical, an individual whose work has largely slipped through the cracks of theater history: the theater theorist, literary critic, and author Sigizmund Dominikovich Krzhizhanovsky (1887–1950).

But it was no run-of-the-mill academic argument. A thin, bespectacled man, Krzhizhanovsky is known to have captivated audiences with his oratory. The actor, he informed the acting scholars and theater professionals gathered for the lecture, has the peculiar status of lacking a stable identity. Each new role brings a change to the actor's sense of "I." While the text of the lecture has unfortunately not survived, we can assume that Krzhizhanovsky would have described for his listeners an existential gulf between the ordinary people of the theater audience and the ever-metamorphosing actor. We find such an image in his essay on which the lecture was based: "A creature able to burn through three hundred and sixty-five lives in the course of a year is surprising. The technique of changing 'I's surprises people with a name squeezed in between two passport stamps, who look out in amazement from within their identities, with their binoculars trained on what happens beyond the footlights, in the world in which identities come undone."[3] Theater spectators, who are firm in their own knowledge of themselves, encounter onstage a fundamentally different reality, one in which such firm self-knowledge is impossible. In Krzhizhanovsky's vision of the theater as "the world in which identities come undone"—or "the world of nonexistences," as he terms it in the same essay—actors are imagined as those who exist and even thrive in that identity-eluding world.[4] "They live as though *organized by plays* [*p'esoobrazno*]," he writes, the actor's life strangely constituted through dramatic art and structured by the changing personalities the actor takes on.[5]

Krzhizhanovsky's lecture, along with a second one that he gave to the Theater Section on March 10, 1924, titled "Otnoshenie aktera k kritike" ("The Actor's Relationship to Criticism"), marks his only documented involvement with the theater crowd at GAKhN, though it is possible that he attended other Theater Section gatherings.[6] Known today, and even in his own day, for being unknown (he declared as much himself: "I am known for being unknown" (*Ia izvesten svoei neizvestnost'iu*),[7] Krzhizhanovsky occupied a place in the Russian theatrical milieu that was almost exclusively behind the scenes, primarily working as a part-time employee at one of the premier Moscow theaters of the era: Alexander Tairov's Kamerny. There, Krzhizhanovsky wrote playscripts, delivered lectures to students, and worked out a vivid and distinctive philosophy of theater. But the most substantial elaboration of this philosophy—his 1923 essay "Filosofema o teatre" ("A Philosopheme for the Theater"), from which the above quotes come—was not published until 1989. Heavily informed by German Idealism and filtered through his own idiosyncratic writing style, his theatrical theory may be the most difficult as well as the most insightful of the Russian and Soviet modernist period. Like Gustav Shpet, Krzhizhanovsky aims not to prescribe a theatrical style but to understand the theater in its essence, an understanding interwoven with both the theatrical and intellectual innovations of his age. He developed his understanding of the actor in close connection with Tairov's efforts to distinguish the Moscow Kamerny Theater's repertoire, artistic style, and actor training methods from those of competing theatrical institutions. Fascinated by the actor as one who both lives through and lives separately from the roles he performs, Krzhizhanovsky uses his theatrical writings to examine the theater as a self-contained world in which the actor is the subject. This world has its own peculiar metaphysics, one that is different from the reality of ordinary life: if ordinary life is stabilized by sameness, then in the theater, "identities come undone." An examination of this metaphysics—the stage's temporality, its language, the permanence of objects in it, and the mental perception of it by both actor and spectator—drives Krzhizhanovsky's approach to a philosophy of theater.

Crucial to this chapter is Krzhizhanovsky's continual centering of his philosophy in the human mind: his emphasis on the fact that thoughts are thought *by a person*, that objects are experienced and even exist *only in our relation to them*, that the theater's imagery operates with the speed and illogic of imagery in the mind. Krzhizhanovsky's form of humanism serves the Kamerny well when he uses it to critique the rival Vsevolod Meyerhold's early 1920s interests in stage machinery. That the actor is a special kind of being means for Krzhizhanovsky that the actor has a special kind of self-conception, a special mental state. In previous chapters, we've seen how different thinkers and artists explored the philosophical underpinnings of the practical components of acting as reflections of the actor's mental processes: the experience of engaging in theatricality, the interaction with stage material (including one's own body), and the playing of a role. Here the chapter's central questions are more fundamentally philosophical, less obviously tied to acting practice: How do actors experience their own selves? How do actors conceive of the self within the planes of existence, both real and created, in which they operate? And what are the practical, philosophical, and aesthetic implications for what Krzhizhanovsky considers theater's recurring rupturing of identity?

While the actor's personhood was taken in chapter 3 as the constitution of the actor as a person within the stage context, and all that such personhood implies, identity is here a more fundamental question of who the actor is and where the actor belongs. Larry D. Bouchard, writing about theater, explains that identity is at heart an *identifying-with*: it "refers to how the self is organized in relation to extrinsic yet internalized matters: traditions and families, tribes and nations, affiliations, vocations, missions, and so forth. Identity is part of how the self persists by being situated with meanings and relations that allow it to transcend itself."[8] An actor's identity, then, might be determined by their sense of community with other actors, as well as by their gender, sexuality, race, ethnicity, and cultural background. Identity, as Bouchard explains, has hidden aspects, for the ways in which we conceive of ourselves in relation to outside structures are not always discernable by another person. Theater further complicates the elusiveness of identity through role-playing's concealing of identities, and in so doing, as Michael Goldman describes, theater makes identity present: "All the unique qualities of awareness that theater makes available to us are finally best understood as contributing to a very special awareness of identity, a unique mode of experiencing both our own identity and that of others."[9] In Goldman's words, theater draws attention to our ways of understanding ourselves and others because theater enables a special kind of awareness.

Krzhizhanovsky places these concerns about identity at the heart of his understanding of theater, but more than Bouchard or Goldman, he interrogates an existential form of identity: the actor's identity as human. This inquiry propels Krzhizhanovsky's work, from his defense of Tairov's theatrical aesthetic against Meyerhold's, to his 1923 adaptation of G. K. Chesterton's novel *The Man Who Was Thursday* for the Kamerny stage, to his phantasmagorical prose tales, in which his view of the actor's way of being serves as a continual metaphor and point of reference. This chapter pulls from both Krzhizhanovsky's theory and his creative works to explore his ideas on the actor's unstable identity, before turning to his work with

Tairov at the Kamerny. It concludes with a case study of *The Man Who Was Thursday*, which interrogates the very concept of identity, or self-conception, within the unstable ontology of performance.

The Famously Crossed-Out, Unknown, Nonexisting Krzhizhanovsky

Of the main figures in this book, Krzhizhanovsky is historically the most unknown, even in his homeland: only since 1989 has the majority of his writings been published, a delay caused by a combination of factors: his writings' mismatch with Soviet censorship and priorities, bad luck, and his own unwillingness to comply with editors' requests for revisions. Born into a Polish Catholic family outside of Kyiv, he studied law at Kyiv University. A polyglot and polymath, he gave lectures at theaters and conservatories in Kyiv before moving to the Soviet capital in 1922 with his life partner, actress and theater pedagogue Anna Bovshek. In Moscow, though immersed in Bovshek's theatrical circles, which included Konstantin Stanislavsky and others (Bovshek had worked at the Moscow Art Theater's First Studio), Krzhizhanovsky devoted himself to writing fiction, but for a living he was compelled to freelance for whatever opportunities arose, cobbling together part-time work as an editor, translator, lecturer, and occasional writer of commentary and encyclopedia articles. In 1923 a friend of Bovshek's passed a manuscript of one of Krzhizhanovsky's short story collections to Alexander Tairov. The director requested an introduction to its author immediately, and they quickly developed a rapport.[10] From 1923 to 1948, Krzhizhanovsky was listed on the Kamerny Theater's payroll. He lectured on the psychology of the actor at the theater's Experimental Theater Workshops (EKTEMAS) and in 1923–24 contributed to the theater's publicity newspaper, *7 dnei M.K.T.* (*7 Days of the Moscow Kamerny Theater*), which Tairov and Krzhizhanovsky dreamed up together.[11] Of the publication's twenty issues, his work appears in sixteen, giving articulate and poetic voice to the methodology of the Kamerny and defending it against competing aesthetics. His essay "A Philosopheme for the Theater," written in 1923, was likely intended for the Kamerny's more substantial journal, *Masterstvo teatra* (*The Craft of Theater*), in which Shpet published his "Theater as Art" (1922). That journal folded after two issues, however, and Krzhizhanovsky's piece remained unpublished in his lifetime.

Krzhizhanovsky's creative biography is filled with such missed opportunities, along with many graver misfortunes. For most of his adult life, he was poor, hungry, and solitary by choice, preferring to live alone in a tiny room, rather than with his partner. He was very particular about what he wanted to write and too proud and stubborn to let his words be manipulated by editors. He made several attempts to write for the stage, but these contributions rarely came to fruition. Of at least ten dramatic scripts he composed in a range of genres, including operetta and farce, only two reached opening night: his *The Man Who Was Thursday* and a patriotic libretto for the 1942–43 opera *Suvorov* (music by Sergei Vasilenko) at the Stanislavsky Opera Theater.[12] For the Kamerny's contribution to the nationwide celebration of Alexander Pushkin's death centennial in 1937, Krzhizhanovsky adapted *Eugene Onegin* for the stage, taking liberties with Pushkin's near-sacred novel in verse to make it more playable. The text was neither approved nor banned, and the Kamerny canceled the production before the start of rehearsals.[13] Krzhizhanovsky also contributed to two film scripts and served as head proofreader for the *Bol'shaia sovetskaia entsiklopediia* (*Great Soviet Encyclopedia*). As a literary critic, he wrote on Pushkin, William Shakespeare, George Bernard Shaw, Anton Chekhov, Edgar Allan Poe, and Alexander Ostrovsky, and he almost certainly advised on the Kamerny's 1934 production *Egipetskie nochi* (*Egyptian Nights*), a hybrid of the Cleopatra tales of Shakespeare, Pushkin, and Shaw. But he especially dedicated himself to fiction: phantasmagorical short stories that echo or anticipate the modernist sensibilities of Evgeny Zamyatin, Andrei Platonov, Mikhail Bulgakov, Vladimir Nabokov, and Daniil Kharms, as well as Jorge Luis Borges, Franz Kafka, and Tom Stoppard. These stories meditate on the materiality and theatricality of language, the life of a thought, the cracks and seams that prevent true intimacy, dreams within dreams, nightmares, time-space travel, poverty, hunger, the Moscow housing crisis, and the death of words, dreams, and a consciousness. All but nine of these darkly fantastical stories remained unpublished until they were rescued from the archives by scholar and poet Vadim Perelmuter beginning in 1989.

All of Krzhizhanovsky's work is infused with his wide-ranging knowledge of literature, philosophy, history, and science, and he claims to have read such authors as Shakespeare and Immanuel Kant from a young age.[14] Though he studied law in college, the curriculum included a heavy dose of philosophy, and he also audited various history and literature courses.[15] Russia's philosophical milieu in the early 1910s was occupied with debating German-derived Kantianism and neo-Kantianism, and thus it is unsurprising that Krzhizhanovsky as a person drawn to philosophy, though not a professional at it, would be familiar with Kant's work through its resurgence in relevance. Kant and neo-Kantianism represented for early twentieth-century Russia a *scientific* approach to philosophy, a newly exciting counterweight to the religious and spiritually inflected branches of Russian philosophy popular around the turn of the century. In Krzhizhanovsky's thought we find an often self-contradictory effort to embrace philosophical methodology and modes of inquiry—and to embrace famous philosophers of the past as characters contributing to a historical drama of human thought—while rejecting philosophy's insistence on abstraction. More specifically, what Krzhizhanovsky rejects in Idealist philosophy is what he appears to see as the bleakness and loneliness of its worldview. Theater, he believes, is the antidote.

The World of the Theater: The World of As-If

Before we can turn to mind and identity in Krzhizhanovsky's theatrical thought, however, we must start by understanding the theater as Krzhizhanovsky envisions it, as the world of "As-if," a world in itself with its own physical and metaphysical laws, which are different from the laws of the everyday world. Krzhizhanovsky's theater phenomenology is structured around three key terms that have the richness and physicality of living thoughts. He presents the following playful schemata in his 1923 "A Philosopheme for the Theater," moving from the realm of Idealist metaphysics to the theatrical through the skimming off of letters:

Бытие (Bytie)	*Being, metaphysical existence*
Быт (Byt)	*Everyday life*
Бы (By)	*If, the subjunctive*
0	*Zero*

The schemata elegantly *moves* from one term to the next as the words become increasingly briefer and more agile: "I do the same with meaning as I do with letters: just as from one word to the next there are fewer phonemes and symbols, so too from one meaning to the next: ever fewer essences, Being recedes and diminishes."[16] For Krzhizhanovsky these three categories are not in themselves abstract concepts. They map onto an interrelated set of belief systems, and for each one, Krzhizhanovsky latches onto a character to illustrate it: the metaphysician, the everyday person, the actor. Each of these beings has a particular understanding of the world and a particular relationship to it, and each relies on the world's understanding of them to confirm their way of being. As for the zero at the bottom, Krzhizhanovsky himself sets it aside: "Further I will not go: however black my ink may be, the night of nonexistence is blacker."[17]

The first term, Being, or metaphysical existence, according to Krzhizhanovsky, articulates a belief in unity, essence, and, thus, the virtue of permanence by perceiving the physical world as a mere shadow of what it considers to be the real world beyond. It is the place of Plato's Forms and Kant's noumena (Kant's term for posited things that are unknowable because they exist independently of human perception). The world of Being is necessarily unseen. "Even [Johann Gottlieb] Fichte complained: 'everything hinders seeing—even the eyes,'" writes Krzhizhanovsky, referencing one of Kant's early followers.[18] Being's existence is purely known; it is not perceived or sensed by a subject. Krzhizhanovsky imagines that the metaphysicians at home in Being have hyperopic vision: they can see only from a distance, and things up close appear blurry and out of focus, as though not real. Next, Everyday Life is the physical world experienced by ordinary people. In it objects clutter up space, have weight and consequence. In Everyday Life we cling to our beliefs in our ownership of things and our connections to real others: "A person from Everyday Life . . . strongly believes in the reality of his three rooms, the body of his wife, and in postmarks that can be clearly seen."[19] Such objects and companions appear to the everyday person to confirm their own reality. Finally, the world of the theater is the subjunctive world of the As-if, which is a joyous affirmation of irreality. It is in its essence ever changing and *only* seen. Further, it is a framed world, set off from the Everyday: *because* we deliberately suspend our disbelief while in the theater, we can experience its illusions as actually real. While the Everyday world is in many ways not "seen" by us since we move around in it through blind habit, we see the framed world of the theater more clearly because it is set off from our usual experience.

With the As-if's resistance to causality and consequence, its defining feature, philosophically, is that it cannot be flattened into expected, conventional patterns of thought: "The world of As-if cannot be cognized; pure freedom, happening upon our thinking, which moves by its own laws, is subjected to the regularities of thought, that is, it ceases to be free."[20] In the world of the stage, we are liberated from a certain kind of knowing, as the stage does not demand to be known beyond what actually appears. Everything that is beyond what is immediately presented to the senses is bracketed, including a consciousness or self that is not sensible from the visual representation. In this world, people and things continually appear, disappear, and change with the lightness and quickness of the imagination or a dream.

The entire system of theater is modeled on *change*: "art, especially in its highest theatrical expression, serves, with the help of a special changeable being (an actor), *the principle of change as such*. For science and religion it is important *what* changes; for the theater it is important that *something* changes, what matters is the very process of variation."[21] Krzhizhanovsky compares the theater to undeveloped film, which must remain in the laboratory, lest the sun's rays (or any light source) turn it black. But in *this* laboratory, the developer has at their disposal only a developing agent and no fixing agent: the photographs' images appear and then quickly disappear. Theater's time is the future, which is a call to freedom and revolution, but is also a burden—theater can only bring about transient images and fictions.

It is here that we see the centrality of the mind in Krzhizhanovsky's vision of theater. Krzhizhanovsky describes the task of the theater in terms of pacing, or velocity. In his 1934 essay "Komediografiia Shekspira" ("Shakespeare's Comediography"), he writes that in our everyday world, thoughts move faster than "facts." We daydream, anticipate, hope, dread—all of which cause us to move mentally ahead of real-world time, which cannot keep pace with our imaginations. Theater, however, not being weighed down by the heft of real-world action, moves its facts along like thoughts: "Theater—from the viewpoint of durations—*is the art* of imparting facts with the speed of thoughts."[22] Such a world is modeled on the world in the mind: "Theater presents itself like a huge skull constructed for hundreds and thousands of spectators, in which a series of events takes place, as if adopting from the tiny human skull its technique of instantaneous change."[23] The world onstage appears and disappears with the lightness of images in the mind, its only residue being "the scenery that is quickly taken out to storage and the actors who have taken off their makeup."[24]

Theater from this perspective is analogous to dreaming, which holds a special place in Krzhizhanovsky's philosophy. He presents our understanding of fictionality as comparable to a dream within a dream. While dreaming, a person assumes the dream to be reality, Krzhizhanovsky claims, but the dream dreamt within the dream you take to be what it actually is, a fantasy. The As-if is not possible without the line of footlights that separates the stage from the audience, just as the entire theater space must be walled off from any encroachment by real-life understandings of the world. Both dreams and theater externalize the thought, as Krzhizhanovsky notes in his discussion of the speed of thoughts and facts in Shakespeare: "A dream is the only instance *when we perceive our thoughts as outer facts*: in a dream the contradiction between outer and inner is removed, moreover the advantage of speed held by the inner, ideal series is not taken away. Thoughts, more or less artfully playing the role of facts, create a resemblance, albeit often incoherent, to 'theater for oneself.' "[25]

Krzhizhanovsky's perception of theater as operating on the movement of thoughts attributes to theater the modality of human cognition. If metaphysics views Being as a physical manifestation of ideas originating from beyond the human, then theater is the physical manifestation of human ideas and, more specifically, the forms of human thinking that have not yet been normalized into ordinary logic. Things and thoughts in the theater can become actors alongside humans when everything takes on the lightness and quickness of embodied fictionality.

A Self-Conscious Fiction

For Krzhizhanovsky, the theater world is a self-conscious fiction: essential to the demarcation of this world is the fact that we, as participants in it, know that it is a constructed fantasy. The passage from Being to Everyday Life to As-if is set in motion by phenomenalization: the act of something manifesting as a phenomenon. Krzhizhanovsky harnesses the language of philosophy to articulate the relationships among the three categories: Being, Everyday Life, and As-if. The result is a perhaps over-complicated but nonetheless philosophically grounded attempt to define the boundaries of theater and philosophy via perception. Although Krzhizhanovsky first presents theater and philosophy (here largely German Idealism) as opposed, their places in his own philosophical system are remarkably similar. We sense his desire to overturn the classic notion that theater only presents falsehoods and deception, while philosophy offers insight into truths. He insists on the opposite: there is a greater authenticity in theater's self-awareness of its own fictionality and in the complicity of all theater's participants than in the truths aspired to by metaphysical systems.

Krzhizhanovsky identifies appearances, or phenomena, in the theater as undergoing a second degree of appearing, or phenomenalization (a move that resonates with Shpet's concept of "detachedness," as I discussed in chapter 2). This second appearance heightens fictionality. From the perspective of Being in this imaginative metaphysics, Everyday Life makes fictionally physical the world of Being: the tables and chairs of Everyday Life, for example, are not real to the eternal truths of Being. In the move from Everyday Life to the As-if, As-if ascribes an extra fictionality to the everyday objects and people that appear in it. This allows for what would be a fictional physicality from the perspective of Everyday Life—the embodiment of what a spectator from the Everyday would acknowledge as fictions. Just as Being and Everyday Life share a close relationship (brought about by the transformation from noumena to phenomena), Everyday Life shares a close relationship with As-if: theater must bring the Everyday (the audience) into its space, where the audience recognizes what is onstage as being *like* objects and people in the everyday world. And yet these objects and people are destabilized, functioning within a fictional creation on the other side of the dividing line that is the footlights. In this respect, Alexander Spektor has offered an astute analysis of the relationship between the material and immaterial in Krzhizhanovsky's work. Spektor terms this relationship a "tessellation effect": "a setting in which each of the binary set's elements enters into a relationship of interpermeability with its opposite. While concepts, abstract categories, and ideas struggle to find their way into material existence, the inner world accretes attributes and characteristics of physical reality. Each member of the binary set becomes heavily hybridized with elements intrinsic to its opposite."[26] It would seem that both Everyday Life and As-if contain a tessellation of material and immaterial, for both the Everyday and the As-if wrestle with the relationships of objects and ideas.

The path from Being to As-if is a path from abstraction (Being) to the embodiment of fictions (As-if) by way of the tactility of the Everyday, as well as a path from the eternal (Being) to the ever changing (As-if) by way of Everyday mortality. Hence the importance of *time* to the construction: the subjunctive offers a transcendence of both the eternal and the mortal. While objects in Everyday Life are weighed down by the causality and consequence of the everyday world, theater—with its multiplicity and potentiality—suffers no such fate. As-if takes on instead the lightness, flexibility, and liberating discontinuity of thought.

And thus the theater presents possibilities or potentialities: wholly free, creative images that require the self-consciousness of the As-if/theater world to exist. Krzhizhanovsky illuminates this notion of possibilities in his 1927 novella *Klub ubiitsv bukv* (*The Letter Killers Club*). The novella describes a group of seven "conceivers" who meet every Saturday in a room lined with empty bookshelves to tell one another stories, with the proviso that none of the stories will ever be written down. The club's founder and chairman is Zez, a formerly successful writer who became disillusioned with the demands and constraints of publishing. On the first night described in the novella, Rar, the skeptic of the club, presents his tale "Actus Morbi" ("History of an Illness"), a drama about *Hamlet*, which problematizes the actor-role relationship.[27] The choice of genre in itself angers Zez, who objects that the stage dampens ideas and stops their growth by bundling them up into a real body: "To dramatize is to vulgarize. A conception intended for the stage is pale and insufficiently . . . fertilized. . . . Beware the footlights!"[28] Plays, needing bodies to perform them, are incomplete in themselves.

The subsequent argument between Rar and the other Letter Killers over his drama exposes tensions in the theatrical way of being. Rar is attracted to *Hamlet* for all its theatrically interesting mysteries: a ghost seen by the audience but alternately seen and not seen by the characters, the fantasy of a fictional being deliberating over "to be or not to be," and the fact that we never know the title of the book in which Hamlet is reading his "words, words, words." Most importantly, and contrary to Zez's objection, pure conceptions (which the Letter Killers so desperately love) thrive in Rar's drama. Creativity is not crushed by bodies; it multiplies them. Characters and roles are divided in two: Guildenstern becomes two actors, Guilden and Stern (both vying to play Hamlet); Shakespeare's Ophelia becomes an actress whose name alternates between "Phelia" (*Feliia*) and "Phelya" (*Felia*), depending on whether she is being tragic or comic. Roles exist independently of actors, in an echo of Luigi Pirandello's revolutionary 1921 metaplay *Six Characters in Search of an Author*. And in the Land of Roles, we see a succession of phantom Hamlets sitting and reading "words, words, words." These are the acted roles of the past, including Richard Burbage's original Hamlet for the Globe, Sarah Bernhardt's, Edmund Kean's, and an invented drunken actor Zamtutyrsky's.

What we learn from *The Letter Killers Club*, then, is that the stage has no problem with multiple Hamlets or with a role and an actor both taking on a body before us. As the stage does not attempt to lock down or freeze an idea, so the actor is firmest in his chosen identity knowing that his embodiment does not preclude other equally live and real embodiments. Every character-role exists as but a possibility, a promise made by the infinity of empty chairs reserved for future Hamlet incarnations in the Land of Roles. Rar understands that in fact the club's private Saturday story performances are already a kind of embodiment. He accuses the Letter Killers of "matterphobia," which is a fear not of *things*, but of *raw material*—those potentials and possibilities with which theater deals. The actor, he shows, is a fascinatingly irreal character type, who himself exists only as this multitude of appearances. The ontology of the theater world is founded on this multitude, as Krzhizhanovsky writes in "A Philosopheme for the Theater": "But colorfulness and multiplicity—it is not them and only them that the theater seeks: dramatic characterhood [*personazhnost'*], dialogue, and conflict are its fundamental devices."[29]

The Actor's Inherent Instability

In this theater world, the actor is the exemplary subject, the being "at home" in the world of the As-if. Krzhizhanovsky's understanding of the actor is thoroughly divorced from the realities of training, labor, professionalization, work-life distinctions, and so on. Rather, he focuses on the actor as a person for whom the theater's laws are the most native ones: the actor as someone who barely seems to exist when not playing a role. The actor embodies a tension between existence and nonexistence, individual and collective, and they continually reinvent themselves as they take on other characters and other roles.[30]

For Krzhizhanovsky, the actor is thus a variegated body in a "world of nonexistences":

> When an actor enters a room, it becomes peopled. An actor is always made out of many; he is a creature torn apart into roles: he does not exist because he many times exists. Anyone, even an angel by means of falling, can come to know solitude: only an actor is refused solitude. He is not allowed to remain with himself as an individuum. . . . Torn away from individual and social life, a stranger both to monks' cells and to town squares, [the actor] is compelled to cross the boundary: beyond the boundary is the world of nonexistences: only in it can the no longer existing individuality and the not yet existing collective find protection: the half-crossed-out "I" and the half-meaningful "we."[31]

The actor is neither a private individual nor a social collective but a set of individuals vying for existence. The line of footlights is a boundary that "protects" the actor, separating them from the collective that is the audience, while also ensuring that these two kinds of beings, actors and audience, are brought together into the same space. Here the actor is *not* alone: they are *watched*. The actor's ability to "people" a room extends their actorly mode of being beyond the stage; they do not have a self that is separate from the theater. This is not grounds for distrust of or dissatisfaction with actors; for Krzhizhanovsky, the continual playing of roles implied in the actor's "half-meaningful 'we'" and the deficiency of self that comes with it (in the "half-crossed-out 'I'") have phenomenological significance. This is because the actor, for Krzhizhanovsky, finds their place only in relation to a spectator, while the boundaries between actor and role are constantly renegotiated. Such a reading of theater seeks not only to define what tasks the actors perform but also to articulate a philosophical system that takes the theater as a model.

The act of being seen bestows existence on the actor, as Krzhizhanovsky remarks in "A Philosopheme for the Theater": "An actor lives—while he is *seen*: the rising curtain he senses as the huge eyelid of an eye gazing at him. All the spectators need only close their eyes at the same time, and the actor won't exist."[32] The actor, whose mode of being is defined through their continual changing of roles, finds confirmation in the gaze of a spectator. In fact, *seeing*, the sense privileged by phenomenology, is theater's primary act for Krzhizhanovsky, the act into which a whole philosophy of theater can be concentrated. Indeed, the eye (*glaz* and *oko*) is everywhere for Krzhizhanovsky the perceptual organ of choice, with its ability to orient toward sources of light, as in the Platonic cave allegory.[33] In his 1937 essay on the changing function of stage directions through history, Krzhizhanovsky claims that the shortest article about theater for the shortest encyclopedia would read: "THEATER—cf." In other words, "THEATER: See."[34] He continues: "know how to be a spectator: the rest will follow."[35]

The Land of Roles from *The Letter Killers Club*, with its empty chairs awaiting new inhabitants, is a fitting tribute to fictions and to actors as roles once their brief time "before the eyes" has run its course. But many of Krzhizhanovsky's stories end with their dreamers and thinkers turned into corpses; there is always a dark side to fantasy for Krzhizhanovsky. In order to exist in the theater/As-if world, the actor gives up the kind of stable identity that we are familiar with in the everyday world. The actor can only "be" as their roles prescribe them to be. The question of how much of one's experience exists only within one's own "I" appears throughout Krzhizhanovsky's fiction. Important for him is the "crack" between the "I" and the "not-I." This crack, like the footlights that divide actors from audience despite their proximity, can feel insurmountable and confining. In "Avtobiografiia trupa" ("Autobiography of a Corpse," 1925), the corpse-protagonist, whose suicide letter our narrator transcribes for us, takes an intellectual approach in his attempt to find the boundaries of his "I." Researching the "philology of 'I,'" he discovers that "I" has no satisfying positive meaning. Only life in the dative case—a passive "to me" and "for me" in which the "I" is excused from being a subject—feels fitting to his own experience.

Acting is a means of changing oneself, of liberating oneself through attuning oneself to and taking on other identities. The narrator of "Chut'-Chuti" ("The Slightly-Slightlies," 1922) allows the miniscule "Slightly-Slightlies," a kingdom of beings the size of dust particles, to enter into his body and to spread themselves out on the surfaces of the world around him so as to alter it "slightly." With tiny adjustments, the second-rate painting on his wall and the aging woman next door appear more beautiful and appealing. The proper placement of a few tiny Slightly-Slightlies transforms the signatures he analyzes as a forensic examiner from counterfeit to authentic, making our narrator's work more hopeful and affirming. Change is under his control, until, in a tragic moment, he kisses his new love and a tear wells in his eye that washes away and drowns the king of the Slightly-Slightlies, who had perched there to personally oversee his subjects' arranging of our narrator's happiness. Yet, we see in this meta-aesthetic story how living in a world altered by acting and by the As-if brings hope, liberation, and possibility.

The positive potential of the tension between thought and body, a consciousness taking on a body or a body taking on an additional consciousness, is perfectly reflected in the professional responsibility of the actor, who is their own raw material as well as their own work of art. In the most creative moments, the weight of the human body onstage or in a story is not essentially different from that of the shadow-body, letter-body, or thought-body: all exist as appearances and by "not existing." This is how they receive themselves and one another. All serve an imaginative potentiality that is free from politicization and ideological obligations. Theater and creativity do not derive from the laws and agendas of the outside world, they anticipate them—but only because they anticipate all possibilities.

In sum, the actor is both the paradigm for Krzhizhanovsky's view of theater's potentialities and coexisting multiplicities and the subject who lives his theatrical worldview. Theater functions for Krzhizhanovsky as a philosophical experience or argument about selfhood: the structure of the theater—with spectators who are there to watch and actors who need to *be watched*—implies the interactivity of the world and the presence of others outside the subject. In other words, the theater's fictions are made real through the encounter between actor and spectator, an event that can be abstracted to a more general observation: seeing ourselves being seen confirms that we exist. For Krzhizhanovsky theater is not only a model of the "real" world (a classic *theatrum mundi*) but also a more potent and self-confirming metonymy for the world we live in. He seeks to redefine via the stage the relationships among humans, thoughts, and things.

It is in the creative space of the theater that we can multiply our consciousness, escape from our "I," and free ourselves from fixed or doomed identities. The narrator of *The Letter Killers Club*, horrified by the club's tragic end, reveals one of the meta-moral Kantian subtexts of Krzhizhanovsky's orbiting identities, the relationship of solipsism to compassion: "And yet I did, if only briefly, for a few scant instants, break out of my orbit and step out of my 'I.' "[36] In acts of creativity, one is less heavily invested in who one is because the alternative—being or experiencing someone else—feels more true. We see in *The Letter Killers Club* a modernist version of Fyodor Dostoevsky's *Zapiski iz podpol'ia* (*Notes from Underground*, 1864), but without the bitterness or spite, with only the verbal resources, mental agility, and loneliness.

Krzhizhanovsky and Tairov: Defining the Kamerny Actor

Krzhizhanovsky wrote his philosopheme—as well as the majority of his theoretical writings on the theater—while employed at the Moscow Kamerny Theater. Like Stanislavsky and Meyerhold, Alexander Yakovlevich Tairov (1885–1950), director of the Kamerny, began his stage career as an actor. Born to a Jewish family in Ukraine, Tairov caught the eye of the Saint Petersburg theater manager Vera Komissarzhevskaya, who saw him perform in small roles in Kyiv. At her behest, he moved to Petersburg and played such minor roles as the Blue Mask in Meyerhold's *Balaganchik* (*The Little Show Booth*) at Komissarzhevskaya's Dramatic Theater. Even to the young and novice Tairov, Meyerhold seemed to diminish the role of the actor and overemphasize the importance of scenic design. As he finished up his law degree at Petersburg University, Tairov took up directing, first in the company of actor and theatrical manager Pavel Gaideburov, and subsequently at Georgian director Konstantin Mardzhanov's Free Theater. Tairov was excited by Mardzhanov's vision for a "synthesized theater" that united divergent styles of music and movement. Performers would be trained thoroughly in singing, dancing, and acting, with acrobatic training as well. At the Free Theater, Tairov also met his future wife, the Stanislavsky-trained actress Alisa Koonen, who would become one of Russia's greatest tragediennes. But the Free Theater was poorly managed and forced to close in 1914, so Tairov, together with Koonen and many of Mardzhanov's actors, founded his own theater on similar principles later that year.[37]

The Moscow Kamerny (Chamber) Theater, located in the city center, at 23 Tverskoi Boulevard, was designed as an intimate, chamber-like space evocative of the experimental "studio"-type theaters that Stanislavsky had established as satellites of the Moscow Art Theater. The Kamerny would last until it was closed by the state in 1949; the Pushkin Drama Theater took over the space in 1950 and remains in operation today. When Tairov founded the Kamerny, he saw it as a rebellion against many of the trends of the day, in particular against his crude characterizations of Stanislavskian "naturalistic" theater and Meyerholdian "conventionalized," or "stylized," theater. Neither pole, Tairov felt, utilized an actor's full capabilities: the naturalistic theater prized the imitation of life over deeper artistic truth, and the conventionalized theater was concerned only with overt theatricality, circus tricks, and the composition of an image, with the actors merely following instructions to stand where needed. Accordingly, he argued that the artistry of the theater should be based neither in the director nor in the dramatic text, but in the skilled actor, whom he envisioned as a "master actor" or "über-actor" (both an homage to and a critique of Edward Gordon Craig's "über-marionette").[38] As Dassia N. Posner writes, "Tairov's definition of theater made the actors the central generators of a production."[39] Unlike Craig, who chased an elusive ideal of what actors could achieve and was perennially disillusioned, Tairov felt that the actor could develop the requisite mastery with extensive training. He sought an actor with refined sensibilities in rhythm and movement, capable of performing in a range of genres, including dance, pantomime, singing, acrobatics, and all manner of dramatics. Musical rhythm would unify the actors' movements and speech, as all productions at the Kamerny would be accompanied by music. Even in the most grotesque distortions, Tairov sought an overall impression of beauty and harmony achieved through an aesthetically pleasing synthesis of forms. Because he felt that the theater should be an independent art not tied to the authorial intentions of a dramatic text, in the early years of the Kamerny, Tairov often based his productions on nondramatic literature adapted in-house by Kamerny staff. He frequently drew from E. T. A. Hoffmann's stories, rich in theatricality and the grotesque, and even believed that one day the Kamerny actors would be skilled enough to act without depending on any text at all.[40]

Krzhizhanovsky began lecturing at the Kamerny's school, EKTEMAS, when it was founded in 1923 as a new iteration of the Kamerny's Studio-Workshop (Masterskaia-studiia), which Tairov started in 1918.[41] In these early Soviet years, Tairov felt pressured by the polemical atmosphere of the Moscow theater community to show that the Kamerny had its own theoretical approach that was just as distinctive as those of Stanislavsky and Meyerhold. Krzhizhanovsky—as a well-educated and multilingual writer—was at the center of the Kamerny's efforts to position itself intellectually on the Russian and international theater scenes. Tairov was developing the Kamerny into a community for theater studies: theoretical and historical, as well as practical. As of October 1924, EKTEMAS offered evening lectures in the history and theory of theater that were open to all.[42] Additionally, the theater published the journal *The Craft of Theater* (two issues, 1922–23, print run of two thousand), in which Shpet's essay "Theater as Art" appeared, as well as the weekly newspaper *7 Days of the Moscow Kamerny Theater* (twenty issues, 1923–24, print run of one thousand), to which Krzhizhanovsky contributed many short articles. In addition to updates on the productions in development at the Kamerny, the work of EKTEMAS, and theater happenings in Europe and America, *7 Days* featured short theoretical pieces by Krzhizhanovsky and others defending the Kamerny's actor-centered approach to theater against what these authors perceived as the actor-restricting puppetry and machinery popularized by Meyerhold. The expressive covers of the newspaper depicted elements of the Kamerny's latest work, such as the score for the movement of the mechanical set for *The Man Who Was Thursday*, on the cover of issue 13 (see fig. 4.1). As expressed by longtime Kamerny actor Yuly Khmel'nitsky, "Not a single theatrical debate in Moscow went by without the participation of Tairov. Often his opponent was Vsevolod Meyerhold."[43] Krzhizhanovsky, for his part, championed the Kamerny's theoretical foundation from a philosophical rather than strictly practical perspective.

The competition between Tairov and Meyerhold was at its peak in 1921–23, and Krzhizhanovsky was an active participant in the debates. Biomechanics

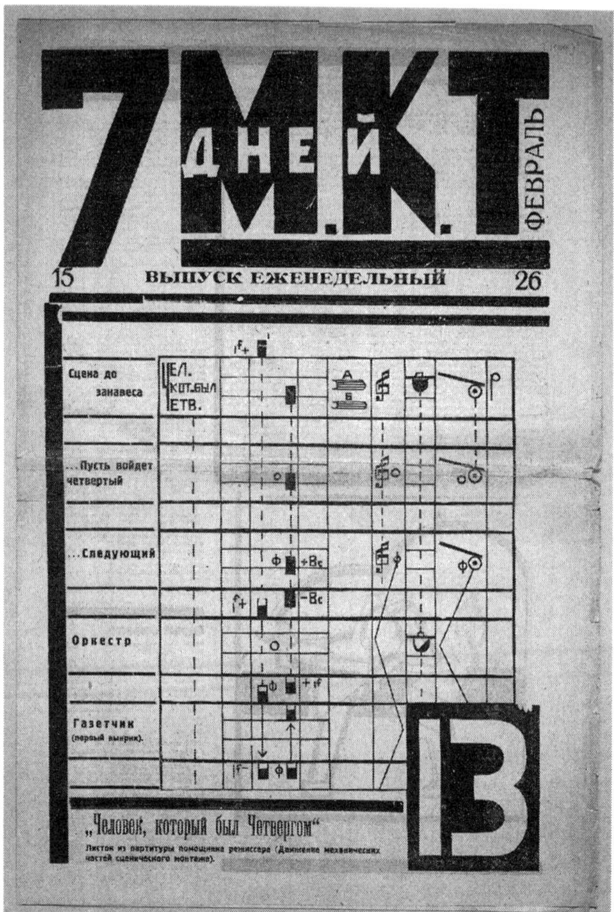

Figure 4.1. Front cover of *7 Days of the Moscow Kamerny Theater*, no. 13, 1924. Reproduced from the original held by the Department of Special Collections of the Hesburgh Libraries of the University of Notre Dame.

was fundamentally at odds with Tairov's and Krzhizhanovsky's understanding of the actor. Meyerhold made use of a constructivist set for *Velikolepnyi rogonosets* (*The Magnanimous Cuckold*, 1922) that celebrated mechanization by integrating the style of the actors' Biomechanical movements with those of the set itself. Krzhizhanovsky decried this sort of staging, viewing the stage machine as a lethal weapon to the vulnerable human actor. In 1924 he published an article in the Kamerny newspaper that was implicitly targeted at Meyerhold, as readers would have rightly understood:

> Just as the monstrous engineering of the war had one goal: to kill a person, so stage engineering, having captured the theater, has one goal: to kill the actor. His body is built into its construction, his voice is muffled by the sounds of the moving montage; the actor has gotten lost in a complex wickerwork among flat planes and ropes, like a soldier thunderstruck by a cannonade in a tangled wire and the "communication trenches." . . . But a person, naturally, wants to play a person, not a diagram; to have a body, not a flat, colored sketch. And the right asserted by the actor is elementary: the right to *be alive*. . . . What the person-spectator needs from the person-actor is a person.[44]

Krzhizhanovsky's piece has the whiff of PR, creating stark dichotomies between the unnatural and the natural, the flat and the embodied, the destructive and the creative. He suggests that an actor subordinated to constricting designs and structures is deprived of the possibilities—or even rights—that are natural and proper to human beings. The military imagery of cannonades and trenches would have been especially vivid to contemporaries, as the Russian Civil War had ended just over a year previously. Further, Krzhizhanovsky pushes back on what he sees as Meyerhold's misguided focus on the practical limits of the human body. The limits that interest Krzhizhanovsky and Tairov are not *practical* limits (such as limits on how far a body can bend or how fast it can move). They are metaphysical limits: the conceptual boundary between the stage world and the real one, the world of the audience, and the way that actors experience this boundary as they look over the footlights at an audience that (in this kind of theater) can only look back at them.

Writing for the Kamerny's weekly, Krzhizhanovsky engaged in two major discussions about the status of the actor: (1) whether the actor should or even could be replaced by a puppet or a machine, or trained to mimic them—an ostensible polemic with Meyerhold; and (2) how an actor relates to their role. Both questions turn on the theme of the *double*. One insufficiency of machinery or puppetry onstage is that people need to connect to *people* over the border of the footlights, Krzhizhanovsky claimed: "the most interesting and the only interesting thing for a person is a person."[45] When theater recognizes its two fundamental dualities of actor-role and actor-audience and incorporates them self-consciously into the repertoire, theater itself is theatricalized—a transformation that Krzhizhanovsky calls "theater raised to the power of theater," or "T^T." "The Kamerny Theater has almost always given *playing about playing*," he writes, "*thus becoming* a theater of high theatricality."[46] And he goes on to explain that dualistic themes are the Kamerny's specialty: Phaedra's dual loves, the double identities of undercover agents, twins, the inverted double that is carnival, and the binaries of reality and dream, life and death. Metatheatricality for Krzhizhanovsky, then, stems not only from the explicit showing of theater or artifice onstage, but also from doubles, dialogue, disguise, and inversions—anything that complicates or erases the singularity of the person. Machinery and puppets perceived in this way are confined to singularity; as replacements for human actors they are not robust doubles for the human audience, nor do they evolve as they accumulate experience by playing more and more roles. Theatricality must be cultivated as a living value.

While Krzhizhanovsky became a close friend and interlocutor for Tairov, enriching Tairov's practical sense of the actor with abstract philosophizing about theater as world, the seeds of attending to the actor's phenomenological condition can be found in Tairov's only lengthy theoretical treatise, *Zapiski rezhissera* (*Notes of a Director*, 1921). Here Tairov presents the history of the Kamerny's early years along with his thoughts on the actor, set, costumes, and other elements of a production. The book positions the Kamerny's work as neither naturalistic nor stylized but as following a new path that rejected both of these mainstays of the Russian theater of the time: "Leaning on only the *negative provisions* that our path was not the path of the Naturalistic theater or path of the Stylized theater, and having agreed only that we were going to strive for a new, self-sufficient stage form and that in our search we would consistently proceed from the particular nature of the actor's material, we took up our work."[47] In rejecting the trends around him to seek new stage figures that were "self-sufficient," Tairov implies a distinctly phenomenological system of meaning. Gesture, emotion, and movement in the Kamerny would not signify outside systems of meaning but would be independent and new, making meaning on their own terms. There are limits to this, to be sure: Tairov did not create a theater that thoroughly rejected language, for example (unlike the Futurists' *zaum* experiments around the same time). But Tairov sought to replace both naturalistic imitation of lifelike gesture and stylized *systems* of gesture (like Biomechanics) in order to find new, original scenic forms. Further, in saying that his work proceeded from "the particular nature of the actor's material," Tairov stresses that he bases his work in the actor's particular body and its abilities.

Gestures and movements in Tairov's theater were not systematized but were individualized. The actor's "internal technique," as he terms it in a chapter subheading in the book, cannot be predicted. Tairov writes: "The first moment—the moment of seeking a stage figure does not succumb to any particular rules or systems. It is a *deeply individual* moment, different for each actor, and the secret of the origin of the figure is just as wonderous and inscrutable as the mystery of life and death."[48] The actor for Tairov is an individual being—not a machine—whose art depends on the internal mysteries specific to them. By endowing the individual with such mystery, Tairov presents a sense of the actor's selfhood within a production.

Tairov envisions a highly versatile, responsive actor. This actor is aware of and sensitive to both the theatrical world onstage and the metatheatrical world of the auditorium. Tairov's statement, quoted in chapter 2, that the actor must be simultaneously conscious of both the persons and objects onstage and the spectators in the hall, suggests that the actor for him is an aware and perceptive being whose real-time experience affects their art: "When communicating with his partner, the actor must at the same time sense that before him is the audience hall and not the fourth wall of naturalism."[49] Tairov's über-actor must be conscious of both the real and the fictional; in a production with various real and fictious realities, the actor must be aware of and responsive to all of them. In stressing the actor's attention, Tairov points to the role of the actor's mind and mental experience in artistic creation.

Tairov further describes the role of the actor's mind in imagining and creating the artistic product: "The stage figure is a synthesis of emotion and form born by the actor's creative fantasy."[50] That is, inner emotion and outer form spring from the actor's fantasy. Even though Tairov's theater was highly physical, he did not view physical movement as the starting point for a production. Instead, as Posner argues, Tairov viewed inner emotion and external form as inseparable and simultaneous.[51]

Describing the rigorous physical training his actors underwent along with his vision of how the actor would move and emote onstage, Tairov often uses the language of "freedom." Indeed, this concept comes up in his work multiple times: he worked at the Free Theater in Moscow prior to founding the Kamerny, and his *Notes of a Director* was called *The Unchained Theater* in translation. "Freedom" captures something essential about how Tairov understood the actor. His actor was extremely well trained in such techniques as ballet, Swedish gymnastics, acrobatics, fencing, and eurhythmics, but his actor was also free *from* using any single physical language in performance. Tairov's actor has such masterful control over their body that they can express and gesticulate in new ways trained by but not dictated by classical movement techniques. In a direct rejection of symbolist criticism of the actor, Tairov enthusiastically calls the actor's body "his capricious and eternally changing material," and we sense that it is the capriciousness of the actor's body that allows it freedom for Tairov, for Tairov's actor is constantly aware of their body in the moment and always ready to improvise with it.[52] Tairov's language of freedom also connects to his references to the essentially human nature of the actor. Svetlana Sboeva writes that Tairov dedicated his entire life to the confirmation and development of the creative potential of the human.[53] She also notes that Tairov "wanted to reveal the unknown possibilities and abilities of the human to his contemporaries."[54] Thus Tairov's view of the actor is distinctly humanist, invested in celebrating, rather than restricting, the magnificence of the human mind and body onstage. In Posner's words, Tairov's actor creates "joyfully," a term that captures the ethics of the actor's freedom.[55] As Sboeva writes: "Tairov's theater wanted to speak not about everyday affairs, but about the problems of existence; it rejected the momentary and personal and sought the eternal, the essential in the human, humanity, and the world."[56] Tairov sought an understanding of the human through his actor, who was both incredibly capable—internally, externally—and thoroughly free from theatrical tradition. The means and consequences of this understanding were not limited to stage movement and stage emotion. Instead, *Notes of a Director* and the work of the Kamerny suggest that Tairov, though not inclined to philosophical rumination in writing, sought to understand the actor ethically and phenomenologically—as did Krzhizhanovsky.

Theatrical Allegory, Phenomenological Truth

On December 6, 1923, the Kamerny premiered an unusual adaptation of G. K. Chesterton's anarchist spy tale *The Man Who Was Thursday: A Nightmare* (1908). In a requisite revision for the newly Soviet era, the adaptation—written by Krzhizhanovsky and directed by Tairov—dispensed with the Christian allegory that underpins Chesterton's story. The novel depicts a club of London anarchists whose code names are the days of the week (with Sunday as their leader), who *all* turn out to be undercover policemen. Instead of Chesterton's religious symbolism, the Moscow production's visuals foregrounded the crime, corruption, avarice, and excitement of a capitalist city, featuring over-the-top, fashionable costumes and a spectacular constructivist set, designed by architect Alexander Vesnin, that was in constant motion.

Tairov's choice of *Thursday* was a deliberate effort to shape the identity of the Kamerny. Drawing Tairov to Chesterton's novel were most likely its London setting and its resemblance to the Pinkerton detective genre, which was popular in early 1920s Russia, especially in the form of "Red Pinkertons," a phrase coined in 1923 for detective-adventure tales in which proletarians triumphed over Western capitalists. Urbanism was also celebrated in the Russian theater of the time, and the Kamerny, which specialized in European (and the occasional Asian) classics, had yet to do an urbanist production, though Tairov had been planning one since at least 1917.[57] The show's constructivist set and costuming, as well as the hyperbolic contemporariness of its imagery and quick tempo, contrasted with the more historical or atemporal designs of the Kamerny's previous productions. Though unusual, the show marked not an anomaly but a turning point in the Kamerny's repertoire, as Tairov sought in *Thursday* a new theoretical direction for his theater. Intended as the opening of the 1923–24 season (but delayed by three months), the *Thursday* production appears to have been dedicated in part to reexamining the Kamerny's aesthetic principles in the face of competition with other Russian theaters, and especially with Meyerhold's work, and it resonated with the theoretical work being done in the Kamerny's publications.

Crucially, Tairov assigned Krzhizhanovsky in 1923 to completely rewrite the script for *The Man Who Was Thursday*, throwing out a draft that had already been prepared by the regular Kamerny writing team. Just as Krzhizhanovsky gave intellectual depth to Tairov's arguments with other theaters in his newspaper articles, so did he thicken and complicate the playscript for *Thursday*. The result was a production that combined Chesterton's darkly fantastical and funny storyline with an attempt to embody Tairov's and Krzhizhanovsky's actor-centered, humanist vision of theater. Although Krzhizhanovsky did not come up with the idea to adapt Chesterton's novel, the script reflects many clear marks of Krzhizhanovsky's hand: in the characters' discussion of Kant and Fichte, in the themes of doubling and the theatricality of chess, in direct echoes of phrases from Krzhizhanovsky's essay "A Philosopheme for the Theater" (written in the same year), and in an extended meditation on the experience of playing a role. But even the text of the adaptation is properly seen as a collaboration with the director, as evidenced by Tairov's many corrections and additions in the promptbook, which I reference here.[58]

The Kamerny production of *Chelovek, kotoryi byl Chetvergom* (*The Man Who Was Thursday*) represents a creative meeting point between Tairov and Krzhizhanovsky in which special attention is given to the nuances of the actor's identity and modes of experiencing it. Their *Thursday* advances a philosophy of the actor through visual juxtapositions of the human and the mechanical, along with metatheatricality in the characters' lines and in the performance's shifting dimensions of fiction and reality. Further, even though the *Thursday* production is stripped of Chesterton's Christian allegory, this theistic framework—with its dynamic conflict between God and man, good and evil—is reworked by Krzhizhanovsky and Tairov into a theatrical allegory of the actor's place in the universe that is the theater. The actor's ostensible freedom to play anything onstage is kept in check by the inability of the performed world to exist on the same level of reality as the audience's experience.

When the Kamerny performed *Thursday* on a tour of Germany and Austria in 1925, it bore the subtitle "A grotesque kino-revue-sketch in 3 acts (27 episodes)," referring to its filmlike intertitles, quick pace, and pastiche of exaggerated acting styles.[59] The show ran for forty performances in Russia and nineteen on tour in Europe. Chesterton, who had converted to Roman Catholicism in 1922, was appalled to hear that his novel had been adapted to the godless Soviet stage without his permission and with no fidelity to his text: "The Bolshevists have done a good many silly things; but the most strangely silly thing that I ever heard of was that they tried to turn this Anti-Anarchist romance into an Anarchist play. Heaven only knows what they really made of it; beyond apparently making it mean the opposite of everything it meant. . . . In other words, they are barbarians and have not learnt how to laugh."[60]

In the Russian press, the performance received somewhat negative reviews, particularly for its Bolshevist rewriting of Chesterton's ending. Chesterton's novel ends with the revelation that the plot has all been a dream; the Kamerny production, in contrast, ends with the triumph of revolution: the assassination of the king of France. Audiences found the new ending discordant and ideologically ambivalent: "an unconvincing production," wrote a typical

Figure 4.2. Photograph of the set and actors of *The Man Who Was Thursday*, directed by Alexander Tairov at the Moscow Kamerny Theater, 1923. Reproduced from the original held by the Department of Special Collections of the Hesburgh Libraries of the University of Notre Dame.

Russian critic, although foreign audiences were overall more favorable.[61] The production is most often remembered in theater history for Vesnin's elaborate set (the first instance of constructivism at the Kamerny, see fig. 4.2), with the dynamic horizontal and vertical movement of its moving sidewalks and elevating platforms. Many reviews were primarily devoted to weighing the *Thursday* set against the set for Meyerhold's staging of Aleksei Faiko's play *Ozero Liul'* (*Lake Lyul*) at the Theater of the Revolution earlier in 1923. *Lake Lyul* had also featured moving walkways, and Meyerhold took Tairov to court for plagiarism. Tairov produced good evidence that the *Thursday* design was created first, and the case was thrown out of court, but the scandal delighted the press. In light of the production's mediocre reviews, scholars have continued to assume that the *Thursday* production was underdeveloped, inconsistent, and torn between conflicting ideals. Maria Malikova, for example, concludes: "Its authors' attempts to unite their own interests with an effort to be timely result in a cliché, a parody, an ambiguity, and a loss of authorship."[62] But if we view the production in the light of Krzhizhanovsky's theory and Tairov's objectives at the time, it takes on new meaning.

Tairov used this production to extend his polemics from the pages of his newspaper. The most directly polemical aspect of the production was its set, which Tairov used to express an opposition between the mechanical and the human onstage. Vesnin's design evokes the atmosphere of a bustling city born of the mechanical and technological. The structure filled the entire stage, both vertically and horizontally, leaving no large open surfaces on which actors could perform. In addition to the moving walkways and elevating platforms, it featured light-up advertising signs, streetlamps, an ironwork bridge, and structures representing skyscrapers and oil derricks. The prompter's notes show that occasional phrases were projected onto a screen like film intertitles to announce key scenes, such as "The Secret of Gabriel Syme" and "The Man in Dark Glasses."[63] Spotlights directed the spectator's attention to the action. But unlike the celebration of mechanization that we find in Meyerhold's constructivist sets, like those for *The Magnanimous Cuckold* and *Lake Lyul*, the set for *The Man Who Was Thursday* was cumbersome and the atmosphere bleak. It appeared to critique the machine—and capitalism. Alisa Koonen wrote in her memoir that Tairov "wanted to show a city that, with its monstrous standardization and mechanization of everyday life, bears down on man like a storm cloud."[64]

While the set for *The Man Who Was Thursday* may have resembled the Meyerhold sets that Krzhizhanovsky had so enthusiastically criticized, Tairov's actors engaged in a range of performance styles that purposefully contrasted with the crowded and angular set. There are no detailed scene-by-scene records of the acting, but reviews indicate that it ranged from the rigid and mechanical movements consistent with the aesthetics of Vesnin's design (and Chesterton's nightmare) to the grace and smoothness of the fox-trot. Pantomime might have also been included. Koonen recalls: "In the production there appeared an entire gallery of people-mannequins who spoke with standardized, identical intonations. The unbroken change of rhythms underlined by the mechanicity of movements and intonations announced for the production an expressionistic character."[65] Most likely, given what is known about Tairov's other productions in this period, the *most* stylized gestures would have taken place during scene changes, with the range of styles unified by the music. The overall impression of the production stylistically has indeed been called expressionist and grotesque. While Tairov's actors moved their bodies in forms ranging from the most rigid to the most graceful, the Vesnin set could only be rigid; its moving parts could only grind out the same motion again and again. The most skillful theatrical transformations rested not with the modish technology but with theater's oldest agent—the actor.[66]

Through the visual opposition between actor and set, Tairov for the first time brought into sharp relief the human features of the actor that he felt were most important for theater to build on—and most under threat by his contemporaries. These include the actor's physical flexibility and capacity for spontaneity. This interpretation is supported by a curious undated review of

Thursday by Kamerny actor and writer Boris Glubokovsky under the pseudonym "Tsvibel'fish": "In this production the gentleman is not an automaton, not a machine, but a living person." Glubokovsky wrote many such pieces in favor of the Kamerny.[67] Tairov advocated strongly for theater that fully uses and displays the actor's ability to creatively make *with* their own body a work of art that *is made of* their own body. Tairov writes: "only in the art of the actor are the creative personality, the material, the instrument, and the very work of art organically combined into a single entity, which cannot be separated."[68] In Tairov's view, theater that is imitative or representational (crudely, Stanislavsky's and Meyerhold's) does not allow the actor to truly create. Such an actor could *only* be material, instrument, and tableau vivant, not also a performance virtuoso.

Thursday's Metaphysical Actor

The staging of *The Man Who Was Thursday* highlights the physical and emotional capabilities of the Kamerny actors through the contrast of their movements with the constructivist set. But the promptbook also engages in a more metaphysical investigation of acting (as opposed to a *practice*-oriented one). Throughout the production's playscript, the characters known as the Days (Monday through Saturday, excluding their chairman, Sunday) are portrayed as *actors* within the frame of the story. In line with Krzhizhanovsky's distinction between actor and machine, the promptbook also emphasizes the characters' multilayered *humanness*. This theme of the actor that surrounds the Days raises philosophical questions—about the experience of human mortality, self-identity, and the awareness of the limits of one's own agency. In the promptbook we witness Tairov and Krzhizhanovsky exploring not the practical questions of how an actor draws on the copresence of fiction and reality to execute their creative task, but the philosophical questions of how an actor mentally and physically experiences that copresence. In the very plot of *Thursday*, the borders between the actors' fictional and real planes of existence are continually renegotiated.

While Chesterton's novel features disguises, false names, and a character who is an actor by profession (Wednesday), the adaptation makes even more prominent the further layers of acting in the novel, and those added by the fact of performing the work onstage. When the audience is first introduced to the six Days at the initial Council of Anarchists meeting, all the Days except Thursday are heavily stylized and disguised, with flashy clothing, wigs, large hats, and glasses. The Days are, as we know, policemen pretending to be anarchists; their anarchist disguises are dramatic and exotic, as depicted in Vesnin's costume designs (see fig. 4.3).[69] Following theatrical convention for the stylized world of this production (like the deceptions at the masquerade ball in *Much Ado about Nothing*), none of the characters see through the

Figure 4.3. Sketch of male costumes by Alexander Vesnin for *The Man Who Was Thursday*, directed by Alexander Tairov at the Moscow Kamerny Theater, 1923. Copyright © Bakhrushin Theatre Museum, Moscow.

others' disguises. The promptbook indicates that each of these characters has two voices, two manners, two names: one stylized persona for their anarchist self, and the other, relatively unstylized, for their policeman self. Tairov had the actors alternate between the two voices and manners, even from one sentence to the next in some scenes.[70] These shifts in style convey the fluidity of but also distinctions between the different realities that the characters inhabit: some realities more real, others more fictional.

The sense is created that the Days have been recruited to the police force to *act a part*—the part of an anarchist on the Council of Anarchists. The opening scene resembles the casting for a role in the theater as Syme-Thursday (see fig. 4.4) is interviewed and then hired by a "Voice from the Darkness" (which is actually Sunday). A voice is heard coming from the very back of the stage: "Let the fourth come in." The silhouette of Syme appears at the front of the stage. Voice: "Name?" Syme: "Syme." Voice: "Profession?" Syme: "Person. Or is that not sufficient?" Voice: "Sufficient. Struggle and death await you. Go."[71] Being a person (*chelovek*) is both necessary and sufficient for the role: their humanness makes them suitable candidates for Sunday's plan.

This initial scene "casting" Syme for the role of Thursday is echoed by the Day that is most interesting from the perspective of metatheatricality:

Figure 4.4. Sketch of the costume for Thursday by Alexander Vesnin for *The Man Who Was Thursday*, directed by Alexander Tairov at the Moscow Kamerny Theater, 1923. Copyright © Bakhrushin Theatre Museum, Moscow.

Wednesday (see fig. 4.5). He is known to the Council of Anarchists as the decrepit old Professor de Worms.[72] By profession Wednesday is a young actor named Wilks, but for some time now he has been living the role of the withered old nihilist Professor de Worms (a parody of Nietzsche). The backstory of Wilks's disguise, elaborated in the novel, reflects on the authenticity of theatrical transformation: once at a party Wilks was imitating the famous old professor when the professor himself showed up. The two sparred until the professor was laughed out of the room because Wilks played the old man better than he "played" himself. In the Kamerny production, Wilks tells

Figure 4.5. Sketch of the costume for Wednesday by Alexander Vesnin for *The Man Who Was Thursday*, directed by Alexander Tairov at the Moscow Kamerny Theater, 1923. Copyright © Bakhrushin Theatre Museum, Moscow.

Syme-Thursday that when he was summoned to be a policeman (by the same unseen Sunday in a dark room), he was told he was wanted on the police force not because he *is* the old de Worms, a feeble figure with no control over his own body, but because Wilks is so good at *playing* de Worms. In a line original to the Kamerny promptbook, Wilks reports being told: "We don't need stage makeup. We need a makeup artist."[73] Being a person and being someone who can play roles qualify him for the job.

Just as the Kamerny production builds up the analogy between the Days and the actors, so does it stress their bodily experience. Dialogue alludes to the Days' sensory experience as they play the role of anarchists on the Council of Anarchists. For example, Tuesday, who is exposed as a policeman early in the production, is glad to take off his bushy black beard and wig because they are stifling him. Wednesday describes thinking as both Wilks and de Worms simultaneously: it is a mentally confusing experience, but one that he accepts as integral to his personality. These references to the Days' bodily experience are underscored by their association with temporality. In the Kamerny production the names are connected to the emphasis on these characters as humans and as actors. The dialogue in the promptbook repeatedly suggests that the convention of naming the characters after the days of the week is not meaningless and absurd; in fact the Days' sense of life is connected to their naming convention. Analogies are drawn between "killing time" out of boredom and killing the Days. Sunday tells them that neither God nor Satan can die, only a person can. The *human* role the Days play on the Council of Anarchists thus marks them for death.[74]

The association between the Days and time in the promptbook also consigns the characters to the temporality of *theater*. The audience is made aware of the passage of time: the promptbook indicates that in most scenes there was a large tear-off calendar hung up to the side marking the day, an object that often occurs in Krzhizhanovsky's stories to underline the materiality of time. The events take place from Monday through Sunday, and the stage lights come up and then dim day by day, taking the audience through the quick cycles of daylight and darkness. Close to the end of the production, on Saturday night, the character Sunday tells the Days (who by now have discovered that they are all policemen) that *their* time has "passed" or "run out": "I have waited for you, Days. You came because you *passed*."[75] And fittingly, for all of them except Thursday, this is their last scene in the production.

In underscoring the Days' experience of time and role-playing, alongside this emphasis on the Days as *actors* within the temporal and existential reality of the story, Tairov and Krzhizhanovsky are reconsidering the Kamerny Theater's principle of actor-centered theater through a metaphysical exploration of what an actor is, an exploration that is based not in an examination of biomechanical abilities but in the actor's mental self-conception. What kind of agency does an actor have within the temporally finite and *prescribed* universe of a production? Sunday as a godlike—or director-like—figure appears by contrast to be limited neither by his body nor by time. The status of the Days as vulnerable human actors troubles their self-identity: not only are the six Days not really anarchists, they are not really policemen either—a point that is implied but never developed in Chesterton's novel. Tairov's promptbook would suggest that the play used very few hand props, save for the blue identification card (*golubaia kartochka*) that each of the Days has been given after being hired by the voice in the dark room. Curiously, seven blue cards are listed as appearing in the first scene, which from the script would appear to only require one, Syme's. This shade of blue in Russian, *goluboi* (as opposed to the similarly common but darker shade *sinii*), has spiritual connotations, as it is the translucent color of the sky. One looks through it to the heavenly spheres. In the course of the production, the Days frequently bring the cards out as proof that they are policemen. The cards are identical, and all have a blank line where a name should go. When Syme-Thursday gets his blue card in the first scene, he comments: "No name. I'm in the position of a person who doesn't know what his name is."[76] He has secured an identity (he is now a policeman) but also is lacking an identity (the line is blank).

The state of both having an identity and not having one is framed as a problem peculiar to the actor when the character of the actor Wilks (Wednesday) reflects back on the roles he has played, in both theater and life: "I've in essence never had a name, and at the same time you couldn't count them all."[77] But how do the Days understand the blank line on their blue police cards? After they have discovered that they are all policemen and finally catch up with Sunday, they are hopeful that he can offer some explanation. Chesterton, in the novel, has the Days ask Sunday: "who are *you*?" But in Krzhizhanovsky and Tairov's version, the more pressing question for the Days is "who are *we*?" For the Days, the art of acting (as anarchists or policemen or, really, neither) is a way of coming to knowledge about their world. Being an actor is framed as a special gain *and* loss of agency. This perspective takes actors as a philosophical problem, as a special kind of person.

As the production progresses, the six Days become increasingly cognizant of the real theater audience. Their first look out toward the audience is speculative. Wilks reflects on having played roles onstage as a professional actor and on having pretended for so long to be the elderly Professor de Worms: "We actors have a confounded, bothersome habit of changing 'I' for 'I.' Cut off from the theater, I tried to do the same for myself. If we reason soundly—here and everywhere is the theater. Even right now, right here, are you certain, Mr. Thursday, that you and I aren't on a stage, that out there (*gesture in the direction of the audience*), there aren't a hundred pairs of eyes, following our search [or, following our following]."[78] Wilks's line sets up a metatheatrical parallel: while the characters are chasing one another trying to catch anarchists, the audience is doing the same shadowing of the characters.

The second time the characters look out to the audience, they are no longer speculating about whether an audience is there. Chased by Sunday and herds of other men, they ask the audience for help. Saturday shouts out into the hall of the auditorium: "You people sitting quietly. . . . Why are you keeping quiet behind the footlights? Now we need not eyes but muscles."[79] Wednesday cuts in: "I'm an actor. And I know: one can't call on them. Worlds have been destroyed and resurrected before them. Wars staining the Earth with blood have passed before their eyes, but they always stayed there, behind the footlights. They have only that, eyes. And what do we need eyes without people for?"[80] Again, a narrative is created of the Days *coming to the knowledge* that they are in a theater. It is a horrifying knowledge, because it would then seem that they have no means of escape and no future. At the same time, the experiencing of the theater event by both actor and spectator is unique to theater as an art, as Tairov emphasizes in his *Notes of a Director*: "And only in the theater is the spectator present for the unmediated creative process of the actor, being as it were a witness to the creative process of a production."[81]

The two moments in which the Days look out to the real theater audience are echoed in the final scene of the Kamerny production. Gregory, who at the beginning seemed to be a harmless street-corner soapbox anarchist, reveals to Syme-Thursday that he is a *real* anarchist and has killed the king of France. The promptbook emphasizes the theatrical relationship between Gregory and the Days. When Gregory and Thursday meet in the final scene, Gregory mocks Thursday and claims that the Council of Anarchists was all a deliberate ruse to allow the real anarchists to do their work. Gregory says: "We used you six like hired play actors [*komedianty*]. Now you can repeat your comedy wherever you'd like, maybe in the theater. We no longer need it."[82] The one true anarchist, Gregory, just sweeps in and kills the king: the people Gregory refers to as *actors* (the "policemen" playing anarchists) are all unable to do *their* task: catching the anarchists. In these final lines of the play, we now see an incompatibility between Gregory's world and Thursday's, an incompatibility that exposes the insurmountable gap between a real world and a theatrical one. The theater world here—the world of Thursday and the Council of Anarchists—can do nothing in the real one, that of Gregory and the king of France. Gregory lives in *a different reality*, and it is his reality that triumphs. Even as the Days shed the pretense of being anarchists, they do not cross the boundary from the "theater" of the Council of Anarchists into the "reality" of Gregory the real anarchist.

At the end of the adaptation, the "policemen" don't catch anyone, Sunday remains a bizarre mystery, and the real anarchist escapes. This plot twist at the end repeats the genre of the Red Pinkerton: workers (the anarchists) versus capitalists (the propertied classes, the policemen).[83] Krzhizhanovsky did not himself come up with this ending (he inherited it from the previous adaptor), but the pacing of the final moments resembles the heavy tone of the endings to his bleaker stories like "Autobiography of a Corpse," "Chuzhaia tema" ("Someone Else's Theme," 1930), and "Most cherez Stiks" ("Bridge over the Styx," 1931). These narratives share sobering conclusions: the realization that even seemingly unbounded fantasy and possibility run up against a hard barrier, a dead stop.

The Man Who Was Thursday as produced by the Kamerny Theater *performed* a philosophy of the actor by showcasing the creative possibilities of the human actor in opposition to the finite predictability of machines. The human actor was shown to be irreducible to signs and continuously in the process of making meaning out of the acting experience. In its transcendence of materiality, the production's suggestion of an inhuman Sunday who governs the mortality of the Days does not entirely eliminate the hierarchies of Chesterton's allegory of metaphysical freedom before God. The atheism of the Kamerny rendition, however, finds meaning not in Christianity but in the metaphysics of the theater, where actors are subject to role-playing. The actor-Days relinquish their identities to their blue ID cards, much like how, in the Christian tradition, God owns the person's "I." But in the theater, this "I" is multiplied. An actor can engage in innumerable kinds of movements and performance traditions (according to Tairov, the practitioner), and an actor can take on multiple, shifting identities when playing one role after another (according to Krzhizhanovsky, the imaginative philosopher).

Yet the production of *Thursday* seems ultimately ambivalent about theater. Tairov and Krzhizhanovsky show self-reflexively the limitations of their own humanizing project. The actor as human involves both a freeing experience and a constraining one; self-identity is both gained and lost. The ambivalence is confirmed in the concluding moments of the show, which amplify the tension between a material-political and a metaphysical-theatrical reading of the person. In the material-political view, we are all mortal creatures, death is final, and the end of the production is the end of Syme. In the metaphysical-theatrical view, all is not over: future roles and possibilities always await. This is theater's inherent potentiality. Although the Days' awareness and understanding of the theater in which they find themselves has not yet transcended the sense of finality they feel at the conclusion of the production, Sunday has advised them that their roles will be called on again, "for the playing of Days there will always be a demand on the Earth."[84]

Actors are uniquely positioned to create another self no less real than any other, a belief that is shared by the thinkers and artists investigated in this book. For all of them, the actor mediates between a real world and a possible one and therefore performs a uniquely human task. Thus in the modernist era, in which literature, art, and film critiqued, broke up, and erased the human figure, a current in the Russian theater investigated, upheld, and strove to manifest not only the mind but the human in performance. This is true both of these thinkers' emphasis on the individual, creative human agent onstage, and of their emphasis on understanding the many layers of human perception and consciousness that are made present through the theater's synthesis of the physical and metaphysical. In an actor-centered theater, the actor is the one who changes the most and *is changed* the most by their roles. As Krzhizhanovsky proposes in his concept of the changeability and "velocity" of theater, that which changes the most is the *most* real. A changing theater is, like life, organic and temporal.

Coda

✦

Thinking the Actor under Stalinism

By the peak of high Stalinism, the thinkers and artists in this book had mostly emigrated or died. Nikolai Evreinov emigrated to France in 1925, Lev Vygotsky died of tuberculosis in 1934, Gustav Shpet was executed in 1937, Konstantin Stanislavsky died of heart disease in 1938, Vsevolod Meyerhold was executed in 1940, Liubov' Gurevich died in 1940, and Sigizmund Krzhizhanovsky (succumbing to alcoholism) and Alexander Tairov (stripped of his Kamerny Theater) both died in 1950. Meanwhile, the State Academy of the Artistic Sciences (GAKhN) was dissolved in 1930, and the scholars and practitioners of its Theater Section dispersed to find work elsewhere, often in politically safer venues like translation, the path taken by both Shpet and Krzhizhanovsky.

The gutting of philosophy and psychology of all but the crudest materialism by the 1930s happened in the theater, as well, thereby fundamentally changing the intellectual contexts for new acting theory and technique. Theaters staged both new Soviet plays and approved Russian classics, but the general atmosphere under high Stalinism was cautious. So-called "formalist" theater (a term that could mean almost anything, depending on the transient needs of party propaganda) and any other theater charged with indifference toward the socialist education of the audience came under threat. Nonetheless, theater of the era is rich at offering new ways of making meaning from language, narrative, and human actors. The search for these ways was in equal parts dispiriting and creatively stimulating. As Nicholas Rzhevsky writes, in the era of socialist realism, "long before postmodernism and its discontents, Russian men and women of the arts had to face their loss of control over words and the open-ended meaning of aesthetic signs they created once they entered the social sphere."[1] Stalinist censorship imposed new forms of signification on the Soviet theater, new meanings to the bodies and consciousnesses that appeared onstage before the audience, and new ways for the audience to interact with actors.

The 1930s–40s in Russia saw a reduced production of theoretical texts about theater, due to censorship that rendered suspect abstract theorizing and any pure philosophizing. Furthermore, there was less space for new theory. A watered-down version of Stanislavsky's System in the form of psychological realism was adopted across the USSR as the model for theatrical performance. Only in the Thaw era, after Stalin's death, would the Soviet theater find means of first supplementing, and then resisting, this psychological realism.

One thinker who wrote on acting in the Stalinist era is of special interest here: Pavel Maksimovich Yakobson (1902–79). A follower of Shpet and Edmund Husserl and a relatively obscure psychologist specializing in the psychology of art and feelings, Yakobson did significant work in the Theater Section of GAKhN as a recent college graduate before its dissolution. His ongoing debates about theater with a more senior GAKhN colleague, director Vasily Sakhnovsky (1886–1945), became a central locus of attention in the Theater Section's discussions in the late 1920s. Sakhnovsky defended a more practical but less intellectually rigorous perspective that prized the actor's subconscious, while Yakobson championed a more philosophically precise perspective derived from Shpet.[2]

After the closure of GAKhN, Yakobson would write up his ideas on the actor in the 1936 book *Psikhologiia stsenicheskikh chuvstv aktera: Etiud po psikhologii tvorchestva* (*The Psychology of the Actor's Stage Feelings: Étude on the Psychology of Creativity*), in a print run of five thousand. The volume included as an appendix the first (and posthumous) publication of Vygotsky's essay on the psychology of the actor. The foreword to the book was written by Viktor Kolbanovsky, a graduate of the Institute of Red Professors (which from 1921 through 1938 prepared a generation of Marxist social science professors) and director of the Moscow Institute of Psychology (which had been founded by the anti-Marxist Georgy Chelpanov). The book is adorned with epigraphs from Georg Hegel and Vladimir Lenin—near prerequisites for publication in the Soviet 1930s. It also draws heavily on the GAKhN actor surveys from the 1920s, a curious choice for a book published over a decade after the first surveys were collected. Yakobson would even reintroduce and reprint some of these survey responses for the Soviet public in 1948 in his essay "Aktery o svoem tvorchestve" ("Actors on Their Work").[3]

Yakobson's 1936 book carefully analyzes the actor's "stage feelings" (*stsenicheskie chuvstva*), relying on evidence from the surveys of actors to account for such things as how actors' stage feelings differ from feelings in life, how long stage feelings last, and how actors feel about their stage feelings. Although Yakobson was trained in philosophy and had delivered lectures on the theory of theater at GAKhN, this book engages in little philosophical speculation. Its points are defended by detailed evidence in the words of famous Russian actors. Yakobson writes scientifically and concretely, rarely generalizing without substantiation. Much of his attention goes to the social forces shaping the actor (a topic amenable to Marxism) and to the conscious efforts the actor makes to present appropriate stage feelings. Given the censor's eye, Yakobson has little to say about many of the topics important to other thinkers in this book, such as the unconscious or subconscious mind, the actor's soul or spirit, the actor as a mind-body totality, or the actor's personal identity. His book is a sanitized extension of the work of GAKhN into the Stalinist era.

Like the acting theorizers of the 1900s–1920s, Yakobson stresses the livingness of the role and the actor's internal work. At times, his writing ventures into the more philosophical territory of the worldviews detailed in this book. Describing the specificity of the actor's art, for example, Yakobson hints at the problem of the actor's selfhood:

> Any artist who creates is aware of his power over himself, is aware that he can and must direct all of his energy toward the work he has thought up. The actor masters himself not only in this sense. He disposes of his soul's world, his attention, feelings, thoughts, as of some kind of material, alongside his movements, gestures, intonations: this is a particular type of power over oneself.[4]

Yakobson does not assume that the actor is able to master wholly his own creative self, nor does he resort to the model in which the actor turns agency over to the director. Rather, he claims an interesting middle ground, the ground of an engaged, collaborative actorly personalism, whereby the actor maintains both full potency *and* agency over the performance. He continues:

> The actor becomes conscious of his own specific skills, conscious of his own craft that permits him to sculpt the stage image in just the way that his intuition [*chut'e*] prompts him. And the consciousness of his skills, the sensing of the freedom of handling his own material, which is valuable for the actor not only in itself but also as it leads to the creation of a convincing and socially influential image, is one of the essential ingredients of the actor's creative consciousness.[5]

Yakobson's term "creative consciousness" (*tvorcheskoe soznanie*) may seem to resonate with a more intangible view of the acting process, like that embraced by the thinkers in this book. In fact, however, he has in mind a cerebral picture of the actor as consciously aware of the variety of external influences on his art and aware of his own act of creation. Yakobson's actor seems almost bodiless: there is little sense of the fluid relation between body, mind, and self that we find so startingly present in Stanislavsky and Evreinov. Yakobson is also uninterested in how we on the outside—the audience and observer—perceive the actor or what significance we derive from the multiple simultaneous meanings of the actor's body, important to Shpet and Krzhizhanovsky. "Consciousness" (*soznanie*) for him is closer to Marx's use of the term, meaning social awareness, or awareness of how one compares to others in society, and thus a tool for equalizing oneself to others. It is a far cry from early twentieth-century philosophy and psychology, in which consciousness is rendered a somewhat imprecise repository for introspective self-awareness, cognition, and perception.

Where many of the thinkers in this book seem to turn the actor into a vehicle for commenting on human experience of the world as a whole, Yakobson is fully concentrated on the actual actors who filled out the GAKhN surveys and on the specificity of their reported stage experiences. We might surmise that Stalinist thought on the actor, even from figures like Yakobson who had previously worked at the liberal and philosophically oriented GAKhN, had to be grounded in the words of actual actors, captured and coded as in a scientific (read: materialist) experiment, rather than in the free thinking and speculation of directors, philosophers, psychologists, and other ancillary figures. The Stalinist stage body was rendered meaningless as a phenomenological object; its existence had significance solely for the enactment of socialist narratives.

The Russian Modernist Theater and the Concerns of Today

Today human beings are increasingly compressed into data points by governments, businesses, the medical field, instructors of massive impersonal courses, and, increasingly, the progress and pretenses of AI. The internal functions of our bodies are scanned and analyzed by machines to produce new research in neuroscience and other fields of biological study. The thinkers in this book fought against such schematization of the human organism and outsourcing of human abilities, citing instead the value of individuality, concepts of selfhood and self-narrative, the spirit, the soul, the religious meaning of a body, and the body's personhood. Their explorations of mind in theater strove to make the actor's body whole and self-reliant, rather than augmented by machinery, visually dissected and disjointed, or used primarily for spectacular effect. They did not oppose mind to body but generally saw the two as unified and interdependent, and they valued the actor's, and spectator's, unique subjectivity.

Although the conceptualizations of the actor held by the people covered in this book are not identical to one another, they suggest potent trends in modernist thought that can reorient our understanding of the place of the human in art of the era. They also suggest the function of theater as a laboratory, whether in actual praxis or as a mere thought experiment, for articulating and advancing beliefs about the human. Vygotsky, Shpet, and Krzhizhanovsky used theater as a source of intellectual inspiration and instruction, drawing truths about the human being from theatrical performance. Meyerhold and Tairov, though opponents, both understood movement in tandem with the actor's mental state and individual sense of self. Meyerhold's work at Borodinskaya and Tairov's work at the Kamerny sought to cultivate the most human qualities of the actor. Meanwhile, recent research on Stanislavsky has shown his ideas to anticipate our contemporary discoveries in neuroscience, and Evreinov's beliefs about theater's capacity to heal are echoed in drama-therapy today. Similarly, the theater of Evreinov, Stanislavsky, Meyerhold, and Tairov often experimented with concepts that only in hindsight could be intellectually formulated as coherent theories. Indeed, the work by scholars and practitioners to accurately conceptualize their theory and practice continues. The prescience of the figures in this book, who speak so compellingly to issues in our world today, reinvigorates us to look not only to science, but also to art for deeper, lived, and experiential understandings of the human being, buffeted about by society and culture but still determined to create value in embodied forms.

NOTES

Introduction

1. Technically, the institution was named the Russian Academy of the Artistic Sciences (RAKhN) from its formation in 1921 until 1925, when it became the State Academy of the Artistic Sciences (GAKhN). Scholars tend to apply the latter name retroactively to the initial years. The Theater Section was founded on January 1, 1922, by incorporating the State Institute of Theater Studies (Gosudarstvennyi institut teatrovedeniia), established a few weeks earlier. For the survey, see, for example, the questions asked of Kamerny Theater actor Alisa Koonen, in Alisa Koonen, "Anketa po psikhologii akterskogo tvorchestva," ed. Nina Panfilova and Oleg Fel'dman, *Voprosy teatra*, 2014, 232–40. Cf. the questions asked of Moscow Art Theater actor Vasily Kachalov, in V. I. Kachalov, "Anketa Gosudarstvennoi akademii khudozhestvennykh nauk po psikhologii akterskogo tvorchestva," in *Sbornik statei, vospominanii, pisem*, ed. V. Vilenkin (Moscow: Iskusstvo, 1954), 637–48. Cf. also the list of questions reprinted in Pavel M. Iakobson, "Aktery o svoem tvorchestve," in *Teatral'nyi al'manakh: Sbornik statei i materialov*, ed. M. S. Grigor'ev (Moscow: Vserossiiskoe teatral'noe obshchestvo, 1948), 7:117–40. Yakobson's essay contains survey responses by Maria Ermolova (121–23), Elena Leshkovskaya (123–27), Andrei Petrovsky (127–36), and Vasily Luzhsky (136–40).

2. Tairov's term *sinteticheskii* has traditionally been translated as "synthetic," which wrongly implies artificiality. In this book I follow the lead of Dassia N. Posner's forthcoming work on Tairov, in which she more accurately translates the term as "synthesized."

3. Some of the responses would be reprinted in various publications and would form the basis of Russian writings on the nature of the actor's art for years to come, including Gurevich's own *Tvorchestvo aktera: O prirode khudozhestvennykh perezhivanii aktera na stsene*, first published in 1927 by GAKhN. Pavel Yakobson's book *Psikhologiia stsenicheskikh chuvstv aktera: Etiud po psikhologii tvorchestva* (1936) is another volume that extensively references the surveys.

4. Iakobson, "Aktery o svoem tvorchestve," 7:132–33.

5. Kachalov, "Anketa Gosudarstvennoi akademii khudozhestvennykh nauk," 646.

6. V. V. Gudkova, *Teatral'naia sektsiia GAKhN: Istoriia idei i liudei, 1921–1930* (Moscow: Novoe literaturnoe obozrenie, 2019), 40.

7. Ana Hedberg Olenina, *Psychomotor Aesthetics: Movement and Affect in Modern Literature and Film* (New York: Oxford University Press, 2020); Anna Toropova, *Feeling Revolution: Cinema, Genre, and the Politics of Affect under Stalin* (New York: Oxford University Press, 2020). Note, too, David Joravsky's line: "The anti-mentalist crusaders of the early twentieth century were

concentrated in the United States and Russia, two peculiar provinces of European culture, each with its own form of the provincial tendency to seize a metropolitan fashion—in this case the mechanization of man—and to exaggerate it, sometimes to a grotesque extreme." David Joravsky, *Russian Psychology: A Critical History* (Oxford: Basil Blackwell, 1989), 150.

8. Jonathan Pitches, *Science and the Stanislavsky Tradition of Acting* (London: Routledge, 2006), 48–76.

9. Vsevolod Meyerhold, "Biomechanics," in *Meyerhold on Theatre*, trans. and ed. Edward Braun, rev. ed. (London: Methuen Drama, 1998), 199.

10. Qtd. in Robert Leach, *Revolutionary Theatre* (London: Routledge, 1994), 133.

11. Rose Whyman, *The Stanislavsky System of Acting: Legacy and Influence in Modern Performance* (Cambridge: Cambridge University Press, 2008), 67–76.

12. Maaike Bleeker, Jon Foley Sherman, and Eirini Nedelkopoulou, eds., *Performance and Phenomenology: Traditions and Transformations* (New York: Routledge, 2015); Stanton B. Garner Jr., *Bodied Spaces: Phenomenology and Performance in Contemporary Drama* (Ithaca, NY: Cornell University Press, 1994); Daniel Johnston, *Theatre and Phenomenology: Manual Philosophy* (London: Palgrave, 2017); Alice Rayner, *To Act, to Do, to Perform: Drama and the Phenomenology of Action* (Ann Arbor: University of Michigan Press, 1994); Bert O. States, *Great Reckonings in Little Rooms: On the Phenomenology of Theater* (Berkeley: University of California Press, 1985); Bruce Wilshire, *Role Playing and Identity: The Limits of Theatre as Metaphor* (Bloomington: Indiana University Press, 1982); Phillip B. Zarrilli, *(Toward) a Phenomenology of Acting* (London: Routledge, 2020).

13. Dick McCaw, *Rethinking the Actor's Body: Dialogues with Neuroscience* (London: Methuen Drama, 2020); Zarrilli, *(Toward) a Phenomenology of Acting*.

14. Bruce McConachie, *Theatre & Mind* (Houndmills, UK: Palgrave Macmillan, 2013), 1.

15. McConachie, *Theatre & Mind*, 1; McCaw, *Rethinking the Actor's Body*, 4–5.

16. Rhonda Blair, *The Actor, Image, and Action: Acting and Cognitive Neuroscience* (London: Routledge, 2008); Rick Kemp, *Embodied Acting: What Neuroscience Tells Us about Performance* (London: Routledge, 2012); McCaw, *Rethinking the Actor's Body*; Bruce McConachie, *Evolution, Cognition, and Performance* (Cambridge: Cambridge University Press, 2015); Matthew Wilson Smith, *The Nervous Stage: Nineteenth-Century Neuroscience and the Birth of Modern Theater* (New York: Oxford University Press, 2018).

17. Joseph R. Roach, *The Player's Passion: Studies in the Science of Acting* (Ann Arbor: University of Michigan Press, 1993), 15.

18. Olenina, *Psychomotor Aesthetics*, see esp. chapters 3 and 4.

19. Edward Gordon Craig, "The Actor and the Über-Marionette," *Mask* 1, no. 2 (April 1908): 3, Blue Mountain Project, https://bluemountain.princeton.edu.

20. Martin Puchner, *Stage Fright: Modernism, Anti-Theatricality, and Drama* (Baltimore, MD: Johns Hopkins University Press, 2002), 5.

21. Olga Taxidou, *Modernism and Performance: Jarry to Brecht* (Houndmills, UK: Palgrave Macmillan, 2007), 12, 32.

22. Marvin Carlson, *Shattering Hamlet's Mirror: Theatre and Reality* (Ann Arbor: University of Michigan Press, 2016), 18.

23. Olenina, *Psychomotor Aesthetics*; Julia Vaingurt, *Wonderlands of the Avant-Garde: Technology and the Arts in Russia of the 1920s* (Evanston, IL: Northwestern University Press, 2013).

24. Tim Armstrong, *Modernism, Technology, and the Body: A Cultural Study* (Cambridge: Cambridge University Press, 1998), 3.

25. See, for example, Robert Gordon, who writes, after a chapter on Stanislavsky and psychology: "Directly opposed to the naturalistic conception of the actor as imitator of human behavior was the notion of the actor as an instrument. . . . In the first two decades of the twentieth century, Adolphe Appia, Edward Gordon Craig, and Vsevolod Meyerhold each resolved that the realism of dominant nineteenth-century traditions—privileging the repertoire of gesture and facial expression representing the performer's histrionic personality—should be replaced by a mode of acting in which a more aesthetically controlled vocal and bodily expression might be fully integrated within a unified artwork." Robert Gordon, *The Purpose of Playing: Modern Acting Theories in Perspective* (Ann Arbor: University of Michigan Press, 2006), 89.

26. Whyman, *Stanislavsky System of Acting*, xii.

27. Closest to this book in perspective is Irina Sirotkina and Roger Smith's analysis of sensation and feeling in the bodily movement of dance in Russian modernism. See Irina Sirotkina and Roger Smith, *The Sixth Sense of the Avant-Garde: Dance, Kinaesthesia, and the Arts in Revolutionary Russia* (London: Methuen Drama, 2017). Their approach emphasizes the bodily aspects of phenomenological perception, while mine focuses more on the mental aspects.

28. Irina Shevelenko, "A Centennial Perspective on Modernist Studies," introduction to *Reframing Russian Modernism*, ed. Irina Shevelenko (Madison: University of Wisconsin Press, 2018), 5. She writes: "This scholarship largely relied on conceptual frameworks immanent to modernist culture itself, be it the taxonomy of 'schools,' programmatic declarations, or partisan judgments of taste." Cf. Leonid Livak, *In Search of Russian Modernism* (Baltimore, MD: Johns Hopkins University Press, 2018), 72–73.

29. Dassia N. Posner, *The Director's Prism: E. T. A. Hoffmann and the Russian Theatrical Avant-Garde* (Evanston, IL: Northwestern University Press, 2016), 31.

30. Konstantin Rudnitsky, *Russian and Soviet Theatre: Tradition and the Avant-Garde*, trans. Roxane Permar, ed. Lesley Milne (London: Thames and Hudson, 1988), 8.

31. Amy Skinner, ed., *Russian Theatre in Practice: The Director's Guide* (London: Methuen Drama, 2019); Stefan Aquilina, *Modern Theatre in Russia: Tradition Building and Transmission Processes* (London: Methuen Drama, 2020); Maria Ignatieva, *Stanislavsky and Female Actors: Women in Stanislavsky's Life and Art* (Lanham, MD: University Press of America, 2008); Catherine Schuler, *Women in Russian Theatre: The Actress in the Silver Age* (London: Routledge, 1996).

32. Livak, *In Search of Russian Modernism*, 7.

Chapter 1

1. Nikolai Evreinov, *Chto takoe teatr: Knizhka dlia detei* (Saint Petersburg: Svetozar, 1921), 5.

2. Evreinov, *Chto takoe teatr*, 68.

3. Platon Ivanovich's name signifies the "Platonic Everyman," perhaps implying that he is a representative not merely of the acting profession but of the truth-seeking person. Ivan, the Russian form of John, is often used like John Doe to refer to either an anonymous person or an everyman, as in the combination of first name and patronymic Ivan Ivanovich (the formal equivalent of "Mr. Doe") or the full name Ivan Ivanovich Ivanov.

4. Evreinov, *Chto takoe teatr*, 69.

5. Nikolai Evreinov, *Teatr kak takovoi*, in *Demon teatral'nosti*, ed. A. Zubkov and V. Maksimov (Moscow: Letnii sad, 2002), 96.

6. This production, titled *Tsarevna* (*The Tsar's Daughter*), was staged at Vera Komissarzhevskaya's theater in Saint Petersburg, with a set design by Nikolai Kalmakov. After a single dress rehearsal on October 27, the Holy Synod charged it with obscenity and barred it from performance. See Tat'iana Dzhurova's discussion of the production in "'Salomeia' v Teatre na Ofitserskoi: Triumf formy," in *Nikolai Evreinov: K 130-letiiu so dnia rozhdeniia (materialy nauchnoi konferentsii, sostoiavsheisia 16 fevralia 2009 goda)*, ed. T. S. Dzhurova (Saint Petersburg: Rossiiskii institut istorii iskusstv, 2012), 23–32. Contrary to some scholars' reports, the set design was not modeled after a vulva or vagina but rather depicted an outdoor landscape featuring a gateway framed by monstrous caryatids. See Elena Strutinskaia, "Legenda o 'Salomee,'" *Russkoe iskusstvo*, no. 1 (2004): 140–49.

7. An actress, Kashina saw Evreinov's *V kulisakh dushi* (*Backstage at the Soul*) in 1916 and then attended a lecture by him in 1920, the latter of which caused her to declare him the most talented speaker she had ever heard. They married in 1921. Anna Kashina-Evreinova, *N. N. Evreinov v mirovom teatre XX veka* (Paris: Les Editeurs Réunis, 1964), 11–12.

8. V. N. Evreinov, *"Moia zhizn'—teatr": Vospominaniia o Nikolae Evreinove* (Saint Petersburg: Zhurnal "Zvezda," 2018), 64.

9. Iulii Aikhenval'd, "Otritsanie teatra," in *V sporakh o teatre: Sbornik statei*, by Iu. Aikhenval'd et al. (1914; repr., Moscow: RATI-GITIS, 2008), 6, 19.

10. B. V. Kazanskii, *Metod teatra: Analiz sistemy N. N. Evreinova* (Leningrad: Academia, 1925), 89–90.

11. Oliver M. Sayler, *The Russian Theatre*, rev. ed. (New York: Brentano's, 1922), 247.

12. Kazanskii, *Metod teatra*, 4.

13. Spencer Golub comments that Evreinov's theories consistently leave little room for the work of the professional actor: "His body of dramatic theory is not so much actor-affirming as actor-proof, whether by conscious design or unconscious disposition." Spencer Golub, *Evreinov: The Theatre of Paradox and Transformation* (Ann Arbor, MI: UMI Research Press, 1984), 211.

14. Nikolai Evreinov, *Istoriia russkogo teatra: S drevneishikh vremen do 1917 goda* (New York: Chekhov, 1955), 390, 391.

15. For details on Evreinov's work at the Crooked Mirror, see Golub, *Evreinov*, 145–90.

16. Jonathan Stone, *The Institutions of Russian Modernism: Conceptualizing, Publishing, and Reading Symbolism* (Evanston, IL: Northwestern University Press, 2017), 11–19.

17. V. Ia. Briusov, "Nenuzhnaia pravda (po povodu Moskovskogo khudozhestvennogo teatra)," in *Sochineniia v dvukh tomakh*, ed. A. A. Kozlovskii (Moscow: Khudozhestvennaia literatura, 1987), 2:63.

18. Dassia N. Posner, *The Director's Prism: E. T. A. Hoffmann and the Russian Theatrical Avant-Garde* (Evanston, IL: Northwestern University Press, 2016), 2. I use Posner's translation of *uslovnost'* as "conventionalization." It is also sometimes translated as "convention."

19. Viacheslav Ivanov, "The Need for a Dionysian Theatre," in *The Russian Symbolist Theatre: An Anthology of Plays and Critical Texts*, trans. and ed. Michael Green (New York: Ardis, 2013), 115.

20. Daniel Gerould, "Introduction: The Politics of Theatre Theory," in *Theatre/Theory/Theatre: The Major Critical Texts from Aristotle and Zeami to Soyinka and Havel*, ed. Daniel Gerould (New York: Applause, 2000), 33.

21. Fyodor Sologub, "The Theatre of the Single Will," in Green, *The Russian Symbolist Theatre*, 150.

22. Aikhenval'd, "Otritsanie teatra," 8.

23. Sharon Marie Carnicke, *The Theatrical Instinct: Nikolai Evreinov and the Russian Theatre of the Early Twentieth Century* (New York: Peter Lang, 1989), 39.

24. Michael Wachtel, *Russian Symbolism and Literary Tradition: Goethe, Novalis, and the Poetics of Vyacheslav Ivanov* (Madison: University of Wisconsin Press, 1994), 144.

25. Wachtel, *Russian Symbolism and Literary Tradition*, 144.

26. Aleksandr Blok, "The Puppet Show," in Green, *The Russian Symbolist Theatre*, 47. Harold B. Segel writes: "In the best theatricalist style of the early twentieth century, Blok uses the appearances of the Author as a way of distancing the audience from the surface eeriness and Romanticism of the play and of reminding them that the whole thing is no more or less than a spoof." Harold B. Segel, *Pinocchio's Progeny: Puppets, Marionettes, Automatons, and Robots in Modernist and Avant-Garde Drama* (Baltimore, MD: Johns Hopkins University Press, 1995), 229–30.

27. Blok, "The Puppet Show," 44.

28. Vsevolod Meierkhol'd, foreword to *O teatre*, in *Stat'i, pis'ma, rechi, besedy*, ed. A. V. Fevral'skii and B. I. Rostotskii (Moscow: Iskusstvo, 1968), 1:103.

29. Martin Puchner, *Stage Fright: Modernism, Anti-Theatricality, and Drama* (Baltimore, MD: Johns Hopkins University Press, 2002), 5.

30. Carnicke, *The Theatrical Instinct*, 42.

31. V. Maksimov, "Filosofiia teatra Nikolaia Evreinova," introduction to Evreinov, *Demon teatral'nosti*, 17.

32. Maksimov, "Filosofiia teatra Nikolaia Evreinova," 16.

33. Nikolay Evreinov, "Introduction to Monodrama," in *Russian Dramatic Theory from Pushkin to the Symbolists: An Anthology*, ed. and trans. Laurence Senelick (Austin: University of Texas Press, 1981), 183.

34. Evreinov, "Introduction to Monodrama," 183.

35. Evreinov seems to view spectacles negatively here, which would appear to contradict the showiness of some of his performances. But the key distinction between theater that resonates with its actor or spectator and theater that seems indifferent, or that is pure show, holds across Evreinov's thought.

36. Evreinov, "Introduction to Monodrama," 183.

37. Nikolai Evreinov, preface to *Predstavlenie liubvi*, in Dzhurova, *Nikolai Evreinov*, 68.

38. Aleksandr Kugel', *Utverzhdenie teatra* (Moscow: Teatr i iskusstvo, 1922), 197.

39. Sologub, "The Theatre of the Single Will," 160.

40. Evreinov, "Introduction to Monodrama," 185.

41. Evreinov, "Introduction to Monodrama," 187. While monodrama bears much resemblance to the concurrent movement of expressionism in theater—namely, an emphasis on emotion that permeates and determines the scenic design—monodrama is focused on conveying one particular protagonist's perspective.

42. Iu. B. Lisakova, "Rol' traditsii Starinnogo teatra v sozdanii teatral'noi teorii N.N. Evreinova," *Vestnik Novogorodskogo gosudarstvennogo universiteta im. Iaroslava Mudrogo*, no. 27 (2004): 89.

43. Evreinov, "Introduction to Monodrama," 195.

44. Evreinov, *Predstavlenie liubvi*, 103.

45. Laurence Senelick, ed. and trans., *The Crooked Mirror: Plays from a Modernist Russian Cabaret* (Evanston, IL: Northwestern University Press, 2023), 270.

46. Spencer Golub says that the speech is meant to satirize Stanislavsky for his fascination with psychologists and philosophers. Golub also compares this to the fact that Evreinov's productions at his Ancient Theater "were preceded by lectures delivered by noted scholars which not only oriented the audience but lent credibility to the productions they were about to see." Golub, *Evreinov*, 45.

47. L. Tikhvinskaia, *Kabare i teatry miniatiur v Rossii, 1908–1917* (Moscow: RIK "Kul'tura," 1995), 280.

48. Evreinov, *Teatr kak takovoi*, 34.

49. Louise McReynolds, *Russia at Play: Leisure Activities at the End of the Tsarist Era* (Ithaca, NY: Cornell University Press, 2002), 5.

50. Nicholas Evreinoff, *The Theatre in Life*, ed. and trans. Alexander I. Nazaroff (New York: Brentano's, 1927).

51. See Richard Schechner, *Performance Studies: An Introduction*, 3rd ed. (New York: Routledge, 2013), 126.

52. Josette Féral, "Theatricality: The Specificity of Theatrical Language," trans. Ronald P. Bermingham, *SubStance* 31, no. 2/3 (2002): 106.

53. Nikolai Evreinov, *Teatr dlia sebia*, in *Demon teatral'nosti*, 180–81.

54. Evreinov, *Teatr dlia sebia*, 309–10.

55. Evreinov, *Teatr dlia sebia*, 310.

56. Evreinov seems to repeatedly establish a vague line between acting "as oneself" and acting "not as oneself" as a boundary between not-theater and theater. He complicates this naive approach in his play *The Main Thing*, in which we continually discover that what we thought was a character being themself is actually a case of acting, and after many layers of metatheatrical uncovering, we are left not with bare actors but with theatrical types—Harlequin, Columbine, and Pierrot.

57. Evreinov, *Teatr dlia sebia*, 310.

58. Evreinov, *Teatr dlia sebia*, 401–2.

59. Evreinov, *Teatr dlia sebia*, 402.

60. Carnicke, *The Theatrical Instinct*, 80.

61. Silvija Jesterovic, in a *SubStance* forum on theatricality, makes a compelling comparison between theater for oneself and the Russian Formalist concept of estrangement (*ostranenie*), but she does not consider the relationship between theatricality and theater. Silvija Jesterovic, "Theatricality as Estrangement of Art and Life in the Russian Avant-Garde," *SubStance* 31, no. 2/3 (2002): 50–51.

62. Puchner, *Stage Fright*, 18.

63. Féral, "Theatricality," 106n11.

64. Thomas Postlewait and Tracy C. Davis, "Theatricality: An Introduction," in *Theatricality*, ed. Tracy C. Davis and Thomas Postlewait (Cambridge: Cambridge University Press, 2003), 12.

65. Evreinov, *Teatr dlia sebia*, 385.

66. Evreinov, *Teatr dlia sebia*, 379.

67. Evreinoff, *The Theatre in Life*, 292.

68. Evreinoff, *The Theatre in Life*, 292.

69. Sil'viia Zasse, "'Mnimyi zdorovyi': Teatroterapiia Nikolaia Evreinova v kontekste teatral'noi estetiki vozdeistviia," trans. Elena Novak, in *Russkaia literatura i meditsina: Telo, predpisaniia, sotsial'naia praktika; Sbornik statei*, ed. K. A. Bogdanov, Iurii Murashov, and Rikkardo Nikolozi (Moscow: Novoe izdatel'stvo, 2006), 214.

70. Nikolai Evreinov, "Teatroterapiia: Quasi-paradox N. Evreinova," in *Original o portretistakh*, ed. T. S. Dzhurova, A. Iu. Zubkov, and V. I. Maksimov (Moscow: Sovpadenie, 2005), 259.

71. Evreinov, "Teatroterapiia," 259.

72. Eric Caplan, *Mind Games: American Culture and the Birth of Psychotherapy* (Berkeley: University of California Press, 1998), 62.

73. Angela Brintlinger, "Writing about Madness: Russian Attitudes toward Psyche and Psychiatry, 1887–1907," in *Madness and the Mad in Russian Culture*, ed. Angela Brintlinger and Ilya Vinitsky (Toronto: University of Toronto Press, 2007), 174.

74. Irina Sirotkina, *Diagnosing Literary Genius: A Cultural History of Psychiatry in Russia, 1880–1930* (Baltimore, MD: Johns Hopkins University Press, 2002), 96–97.

75. Sirotkina, *Diagnosing Literary Genius*, 97–98.

76. Alexander Etkind, *Eros of the Impossible: The History of Psychoanalysis in Russia*, trans. Noah Rubins and Maria Rubins (Boulder, CO: Westview Press, 1997), 112–18, 121.

77. Zasse, "Mnimyi zdorovyi," 212. Etkind briefly mentions Evreinov's theatrotherapy in his study of psychoanalysis in Russia, but he does not provide an explicit argument that theatrotherapy has psychoanalytic roots; see Etkind, *Eros of the Impossible*, 125. Sasse further critiques Etkind's assessment of theatrotherapy; see Zasse, "Mnimyi zdorovyi," 215–16.

78. William James, *The Varieties of Religious Experience: A Study in Human Nature* (Mineola, NY: Dover, 2002), 94.

79. Incidentally, Quimby's transformative carriage ride is echoed, probably unintentionally, in Evreinov's writings on theater for oneself, when the director notes that a friend of his occasionally hires a driver and rides around town in a carriage to take in the sights as a "living cinematograph" (*zhivym kinematografom*), in other words, perceiving what he sees outside the carriage window as a

theatrical (or cinematic) spectacle for the sake of pure personal enjoyment. Evreinov, *Teatr dlia sebia*, 310.

80. Wakoh Shannon Hickey, *Mind Cure: How Meditation Became Medicine* (New York: Oxford University Press, 2019), 33.

81. The 1915 publication was in a combined volume with psychiatrist Richard Maurice Bucke's mystical, transpersonal treatise *Cosmic Consciousness: A Study in the Evolution of the Human Mind* (1901). Despite these publications, there appears to be little research on the reception of New Thought in Russia.

82. Prentice Mulford, "The Doctor Within," in *The White Cross Library: Your Forces, and How to Use Them* (1888; New York: F. J. Needham, 1910), 2:3.

83. Evreinov, "Teatroterapiia," 260.

84. Evreinov, "Teatroterapiia," 260.

85. New Thought was not the only movement promoting a mind cure in this era: French psychologist Émile Coué (1857–1926) became well known for his practice of "autosuggestion," a form of self-healing through the mind. Evreinov does not mention Coué, however.

86. Evreinov, "Teatroterapiia," 261. While scholars debate the exact meaning of Aristotle's *catharsis*, we can be certain it refers to an improvement in one's state of being through witnessing a dramatic performance, whether this improvement is in the form of intellectual or emotional clarification, purification, or purgation. Examples of Freud's use of dramatic references include his Oedipus complex and Electra complex.

87. Hilarion G. Petzold, *Gestalttherapie und Psychodrama* (Kassel, West Germany: Nicol, 1973), 99–105; Phil Jones, *Drama as Therapy: Theory, Practice and Research*, 2nd ed. (London: Routledge, 2007), 34–38; Fintan Walsh, *Theatre & Therapy* (New York: Palgrave Macmillan, 2013), 39.

88. Other scholars appear to have struggled with this line of inquiry, as well. Sasse conflates philosopher Vladimir Il'in as cited by Hilarion G. Petzold with psychiatrist Ivan Il'in as cited by Alexander Etkind, though Etkind does not attribute to Ivan Il'in any involvement with dramatherapy; see Petzold, *Gestalttherapie und Psychodrama*, 99–105; Zasse, "Mnimyi zdorovyi," 218n3; Etkind, *Eros of the Impossible*, 63–65. More primary research into the work of Vladimir Il'in is needed to better substantiate Petzold's claims, which seem to be the root of all scholarly discussions of Il'in's work in therapeutic theater. I have been yet unable to find independent evidence of the books by Il'in on therapeutic theater that Petzold names.

89. Walsh, *Theatre & Therapy*, 40.

90. Evreinov, "Teatroterapiia," 261.

91. Caplan, *Mind Games*, 62–63.

92. Carnicke, *The Theatrical Instinct*, 9–13.

93. Walsh, *Theatre & Therapy*, 1.

94. Carnicke, *The Theatrical Instinct*, 15–16; Robert Leach, *Revolutionary Theatre* (London: Routledge, 1994), 132.

95. The other two plays in this trilogy are *Korabl' prapovednykh* (*The Ship of the Righteous*, 1925) and *Teatr vechnoi voiny* (*The Theater of Eternal War*, 1929).

96. The theological thread runs through Evreinov's original name for the play, *Christ-Harlequin*.

97. Nikolai Evreinov, *The Main Thing*, in *Theater as Life: Five Modern Plays*, trans. and ed. Christopher Collins (New York: Ardis, 2012), 74.

98. Evreinov, *Teatr kak takovoi*, 41.

Chapter 2

1. S. M. Volkonskii, "Chelovek kak material iskusstva," in *Chelovek na stsene*, 5th ed. (Saint Petersburg: Lan' / Planeta muziki, 2019), 100.

2. Aleksandr Ia. Tairov, *Zapiski rezhissera*, in *O teatre*, 2nd ed. (Moscow: Akademicheskii proekt, 2018), 85.

3. Gustav Shpet, "Theater as Art," *Soviet Studies in Philosophy* 28, no. 3 (Winter 1989–90): 73.

4. Vsevolod Meyerhold, "The Naturalistic Theatre and the Theatre of Mood," in *Meyerhold on Theatre*, trans. and ed. Edward Braun, rev. ed. (London: Methuen Drama, 1998), 24. Notably, and as Meyerhold surely knew, both *Antigone* and *Julius Caesar* were in the Moscow Art Theater's repertoire. Meyerhold had at one time acted for Stanislavsky and had also recently led the Moscow Art Theater–affiliated Theater-Studio on Povarskaya, but he moved to Vera Komissarzhevskaya's theater in 1906 after the Theater-Studio failed.

5. Vsevolod Meyerhold, "Biomechanics," in *Meyerhold on Theatre*, 199.

6. Vsevolod Meyerhold, "*The Lady of the Camellias*," in *Meyerhold on Theatre*, 275.

7. Meyerhold, "Biomechanics," 199.

8. Vsevolod Meyerhold, "Vsevolod Meyerhold's Class. Stage Movement," trans. Dassia N. Posner, in "The Commedia Dell'arte Origins of Biomechanics," in *The Routledge Companion to Vsevolod Meyerhold*, ed. Jonathan Pitches and Stefan Aquilina (London: Routledge, 2023), 220.

9. Robert Leach, *Stanislavsky and Meyerhold* (Bern: Peter Lang, 2003), 8. Leach elsewhere writes: "Stanislavsky and Artaud worked 'from the inside' outwards, whereas Meyerhold and Brecht worked in the contrary direction." Robert Leach, *Makers of Modern Theatre: An Introduction* (London: Routledge, 2004), 3.

10. For a discussion of Meyerhold and reflexology, see Alma Law and Mel Gordon, *Meyerhold, Eisenstein and Biomechanics: Actor Training in Revolutionary Russia* (Jefferson, NC: McFarland, 1996), 36–37.

11. Posner, "The Commedia Dell'arte Origins of Biomechanics," 212.

12. For an extensive discussion of commedia as understood by Meyerhold and his colleagues at Borodinskaya, see Posner, "The Commedia Dell'arte Origins of Biomechanics," 213–17.

13. Alexander Mgebrov, excerpt from *A Life in the Theatre*, trans. Posner, in "The Commedia Dell'arte Origins of Biomechanics," 232.

14. Vsevolod Meyerhold, "Vsevolod Meyerhold's Class. Stage Movement Technique," trans. Posner, in "The Commedia Dell'arte Origins of Biomechanics," 227.

15. Meyerhold, "Vsevolod Meyerhold's Class. Stage Movement Technique," 228.

16. Meyerhold, "Vsevolod Meyerhold's Class. Stage Movement Technique," 228.

17. Jonathan Pitches, "Tracing/Training Rebellion: Object Work in Meyerhold's Biomechanics," *Performance Research* 12, no. 4 (2007): 99.

18. Jonathan Pitches, *Vsevolod Meyerhold* (London: Routledge, 2018), 58.
19. Mgebrov, excerpt from *A Life in the Theatre*, 232.
20. Meyerhold, "Vsevolod Meyerhold's Class. Stage Movement Technique," 228.
21. Posner, "The Commedia Dell'arte Origins of Biomechanics," 244n37.
22. Meyerhold, "Vsevolod Meyerhold's Class. Stage Movement," 220.
23. Bert O. States, *Great Reckonings in Little Rooms: On the Phenomenology of Theater* (Berkeley: University of California Press, 1985), 8.
24. Dassia N. Posner, *The Director's Prism: E. T. A. Hoffmann and the Russian Theatrical Avant-Garde* (Evanston, IL: Northwestern University Press, 2016), 38.
25. Vsevolod Meyerhold, "The New Theatre Foreshadowed in Literature," in *Meyerhold on Theatre*, 38.
26. N. V. Pesochinskii, "Akter v teatre Meierkhol'da," in *Russkoe akterskoe iskusstvo XX veka*, ed. S. K. Bushueva (Saint Petersburg: Rossiiskii institut istorii iskusstv, 1992), 99.
27. I am grateful to Dassia N. Posner for pointing out this distinction to me.
28. Tairov, *Zapiski rezhissera*, 93.
29. Tairov, *Zapiski rezhissera*, 95.
30. Meyerhold, "Biomechanics," 198.
31. Vadim Shcherbakov, "Meyerhold and the Russian Commedia Dell'arte Myth," trans. Dassia N. Posner and Kevin Bartig, in *Three Loves for Three Oranges: Gozzi, Meyerhold, Prokofiev*, ed. Dassia N. Posner and Kevin Bartig with Maria De Simone (Bloomington: Indiana University Press, 2021), 225.
32. Julia Vaingurt, *Wonderlands of the Avant-Garde: Technology and the Arts in Russia of the 1920s* (Evanston, IL: Northwestern University Press, 2013), 65.
33. With this criticism Meyerhold weighs in on Denis Diderot's paradox of the actor. Tairov says something similar when he writes that Edward Gordon Craig is wrong to say that the actor is overcome by emotion: "Here [in naturalism], having aroused his nervous system, the actor often loses power over it and even himself falls under its influence. But one must look at this as a *symptom*, generated not by emotion but by the incorrect approach to it." Tairov, *Zapiski rezhissera*, 95.
34. Meyerhold, "Biomechanics," 199.
35. Qtd. in Law and Gordon, *Meyerhold, Eisenstein and Biomechanics*, 234.
36. Caryl Emerson, "The Actor's Task as Philosophical Quest in the Russian 1920s: Two Case Studies," in *Russian Performances: Word, Object, Action*, ed. Julie A. Buckler, Julie A. Cassiday, and Boris Wolfson (Madison: University of Wisconsin Press, 2018), 227–34; Frederick Matern, "Stanislavski, Shpet, and the Art of Lived Experience," *Stanislavski Studies* 2, no. 1 (2013): 44–63; Galin Tihanov, *The Birth and Death of Literary Theory: Regimes of Relevance in Russia and Beyond* (Stanford, CA: Stanford University Press, 2019), 81–85; Galin Tihanov, "Gustav Shpet's Literary and Theater Affiliations," in *Gustav Shpet's Contribution to Philosophy and Cultural Theory*, ed. Galin Tihanov (West Lafayette, IN: Purdue University Press, 2009), 73–74. For responses to Shpet's essay, see Liubov' Ia. Gurevich, *Tvorchestvo aktera: O prirode khudozhestvennykh perezhivanii aktera na stsene*, 2nd ed. (Moscow: Knizhnyi dom "Librokom," 2012), 22–23; and the following essay, which I read as a loose response to Shpet in its entirety: Sigizmund Krzhizhanovsky, "A Philosopheme for the Theater," in *That*

Third Guy: A Comedy from the Stalinist 1930s with Essays on Theater, trans. and ed. Alisa Ballard Lin (Madison: University of Wisconsin Press, 2018), 17–57.

37. Shpet's translation work included English Romantic and realist works (Dickens, Byron, Shakespeare) and philosophy by George Berkeley and Georg Wilhelm Friedrich Hegel. He helped prepare the prestigious eight-volume Academia edition of Shakespeare's works (1937).

38. "The Purge of Gustav Shpet (Extracts)," in John E. Bowlt, "RaKhN on Trial: The Purge of Gustav Shpet," *Experiment* 3 (1997): 302.

39. Tairov, *Zapiski rezhissera*, 57. Unfortunately, we do not know the pretext for these discussions or the extent of them, though Shpet's friendship with Tairov would continue for the rest of his life.

40. Elena Iakovich, *Doch' filosofa Shpeta v fil'me Eleny Iakovich: Polnaia versiia vospominanii Mariny Gustavovny Shtorkh* (Moscow: ACT, 2014), 45.

41. T. G. Shchedrina writes that Shpet attended all the premieres at the Moscow Art Theater, Moscow Art Theater II, Kamerny Theater, Vakhtangov Theater, Meyerhold Theater, and others. T. G. Shchedrina, *"Ia pishu kak ekho drugogo . . .": Ocherki intellektual'noi biografii Gustava Shpeta* (Moscow: Progress-Traditsiia, 2004), 258.

42. The Theater Department's head was Anatoly Lunacharsky, and its deputy was Meyerhold. The other two members of the theater theory section were Andrei Bely and Fyodor Stepun. Stepun was deported from the USSR in 1922 on one of the infamous "Philosophers' Steamships" and would publish his own theoretical book on theater, *Osnovnye problem teatra* (*Foundational Problems of the Theater*), in Berlin in 1923.

43. Indicating the importance of "Theater as Art" for his body of work, Shpet included it in a concise list of his principal works in the 1929 *Granat Encyclopedic Dictionary*. A. A. Mitiushin, commentary to "Theater as Art" by Gustav Shpet, *Soviet Studies in Philosophy* 28, no. 3 (Winter 1989–90): 89.

44. V. V. Gudkova, *Teatral'naia sektsiia GAKhN: Istoriia idei i liudei, 1921–1930* (Moscow: Novoe literaturnoe obozrenie, 2019), 44, 233. Gudkova details Shpet's extensive involvement with the GAKhN Theater Section, even though his only official role in it was to be made a member in November 1929. Incidentally, Sigizmund Krzhizhanovsky also gave a presentation to the Theater Section in December 1923, exactly one week later than Shpet's, as I discuss in chapter 4. Though the two men never collaborated, their biographies overlap extensively, from birth in the Kyiv region, to friendships from youth with Tairov, to work on the Academia Shakespeare editions in the 1930s.

45. Gudkova, *Teatral'naia sektsiia GAKhN*, 233.

46. V. V. Aristov, "G. G. Shpet i proekt sozdaniia im Akademii Moskovskogo khudozhestvennogo teatra," *Voprosy psikhologii* 3 (2009): 108–15. Although Shpet is cited as having prepared a translation of *Julius Caesar* for the Maly, it does not appear to have reached the stage. Cf. Gudkova, *Teatral'naia sektsiia GAKhN*, 232.

47. K. S. Stanislavskii to Mariia Lilina, October 1934, in K. S. Stanislavskii, *Sobranie sochinenii v deviati tomakh*, ed. O. N. Efremov (Moscow: Iskusstvo, 1988–89), 9:611.

48. For a full discussion of Shpet's work with the theater, see the careful scholarship of Tihanov, "Gustav Shpet's Literary and Theater Affiliations," 72–76.

Further research, in particular regarding Shpet's work with the GAKhN Theater Section, can be found in Gudkova, *Teatral'naia sektsiia GAKhN*.

49. Iakovich, *Doch' filosofa Shpeta v fil'me Eleny Iakovich*, 146–47.

50. Not until 1990 was it officially stated that Shpet was shot in 1937; previously he was said to have died from collapse of the lungs in 1940. See the timeline in N. V. Serebrennikov, ed., *Shpet v Sibiri: Ssylka i gibel'* (Tomsk: Vodolei, 1995), 324–27.

51. Vasilii Kachalov to Iosif Vissarionovich [Stalin], 1938, in Serebrennikov, *Shpet v Sibiri*, 284. Shpet's last home before his exile was at 17 Briusovskii pereulok in Moscow, where Kachalov and many other Moscow Art Theater artists also lived. Aristov, "G. G. Shpet i proekt sozdaniia," 109.

52. Randall A. Poole, "Gustav Shpet: Russian Philosopher of the Human Level of Being," *Kritika: Explorations in Russian and Eurasian History* 14, no. 2 (Spring 2013): 397.

53. See Vladimir Zinchenko and James V. Wertsch, "Gustav Shpet's Influence on Psychology," in Tihanov, *Gustav Shpet's Contribution*, 45–55; Vladimir Zinchenko, "Thought and Word: The Approaches of L. S. Vygotsky and G. G. Shpet," in *The Cambridge Companion to Vygotsky*, ed. Harry Daniels, Michael Cole, and James V. Wertsch (Cambridge: Cambridge University Press, 2007), 212–45.

54. Pannill Camp discusses Husserl's comments on theater's peculiar modes of representation in understudied notes from 1905 through 1918, in "The Stage Struck Out of the World: Theatricality and Husserl's Phenomenology of Theatre, 1905–1918," in *Performance and Phenomenology: Traditions and Transformations*, ed. Maaike Bleeker, Jon Foley Sherman, and Eirini Nedelkopoulou (New York: Routledge, 2015), 20–34.

55. Bert O. States, "The Phenomenological Attitude," in *Critical Theory and Performance*, ed. Janelle G. Reinelt and Joseph R. Roach, rev. and enlarged ed. (Ann Arbor: University of Michigan Press, 2010), 28.

56. Maaike Bleeker, Jon Foley Sherman, and Eirini Nedelkopoulou, introduction to Bleeker, Sherman, and Nedelkopoulou, *Performance and Phenomenology*, 1.

57. Gustav Shpet, "Differentsiatsiia postanovki teatral'nogo predstavleniia," in *Iskusstvo kak vid znaniia: Izbrannye trudy po filosofii kul'tury*, ed. Tat'iana Shchedrina (Moscow: ROSSPEN, 2007), 18.

58. Shpet, "Differentsiatsiia postanovki teatral'nogo predstavleniia," 18.

59. Shpet, "Differentsiatsiia postanovki teatral'nogo predstavleniia," 18. See commentary in Tihanov, "Gustav Shpet's Literary and Theater Affiliations," 72–73.

60. Gudkova, *Teatral'naia sektsiia GAKhN*, 44. In particular, Gudkova notes that the debates between Vasily Sakhnovsky and Pavel Yakobson that dominated GAKhN Theater Section discussions in the mid-1920s stemmed from Shpet's assessment of the nature of theater in this essay.

61. See Tihanov, "Gustav Shpet's Literary and Theater Affiliations," 73.

62. Shpet, "Differentsiatsiia postanovki teatral'nogo predstavleniia," 16. In the same issue of *The Craft of Theater* as Shpet's essay appears an interpretation of the Kamerny's *The Man Who Was Thursday*, which I discuss in chapter 4.

63. A. Tairov, "Fokusnichestvo v nauke teatral'nogo iskusstva," *Masterstvo teatra: Vremennik Kamernogo teatra*, no. 1 (December 1922): 25–30, Sankt-Peterburgskaia gosudarstvennaia teatral'naia biblioteka, https://sptl.spb.ru.

64. Shpet, "Theater as Art," 62–65.

65. Gustav Shpet, "Teatr kak iskusstvo," in *Iskusstvo kak vid znaniia*, 24. Shpet's use of the term *akt* here is unusual, especially given Russian's several terms to denote an action (*delo*, *deistvie*, *postupok*, *deianie*), all of which Krzhizhanovsky differentiates in relation to the stage in his 1923 essay "A Philosopheme for the Theater," 49–50.

66. Shpet, "Theater as Art," 61–62.

67. Shpet, "Theater as Art," 67–68.

68. Shpet, "Theater as Art," 71 (translation modified). Cf. Shpet, "Teatr kak iskusstvo," 27. According to Robert Bird, Lev Vygotsky may have picked up Shpet's term *detachedness* in his essay on Ivan Bunin's story "Legkoe dykhanie" ("Light Breathing"). Robert Bird, "The Hermeneutic Triangle: Gustav Shpet's Aesthetics in Context," in Tihanov, *Gustav Shpet's Contribution*, 41.

69. Shpet, "Theater as Art," 71; Shpet, "Teatr kak iskusstvo," 27.

70. Bird, "The Hermeneutic Triangle," 33; see also Bird's explanation of the concept of detachedness as developed throughout Shpet's writings on aesthetics, 31–36.

71. Bird, "The Hermeneutic Triangle," 33.

72. Shpet uses this metaphor of the actor leaving her real person in the dressing room. Shpet, "Theater as Art," 73.

73. Shpet, "Theater as Art," 79.

74. Shpet, "Theater as Art," 68–69.

75. Shpet, "Theater as Art," 80.

76. Shpet, "Theater as Art," 80.

77. Shpet, "Theater as Art," 78.

78. Shpet, "Theater as Art," 84.

79. Shpet, "Theater as Art," 75.

80. Stanislavsky's relationship to naturalism and realism is complicated, as I discuss briefly in chapter 3; however, he was often referenced in this period as a representative of naturalism. Shpet's allusions to this director are thus less nuanced than is warranted. Such generalizations about Stanislavsky, and also about Meyerhold, were rampant at the time; Tairov, too, makes them.

81. Shpet, "Theater as Art," 87.

82. Matern, "Stanislavski, Shpet, and the Art of Lived Experience," 49. Matern's claim that both Stanislavsky and Shpet feel the actor must draw on "lived, inner experience" seems to be in tension with Shpet's claim that an actor uses expressiveness rather than his own personality to convey a sense of a character.

83. Tihanov remarks that Shpet's argument against the synthesis of the arts critiqued not only the avant-garde but also "obliquely, the religious notion of theater as an extension and modification of the church ritual, an approach made available, before Shpet entered the scene of theater theory, by Pavel Florenskii ('Khramovoe deistvo kak sintez iskusstv,' 1918)." Tihanov, "Gustav Shpet's Literary and Theater Affiliations," 74.

84. Interestingly, Shpet's daughter Lenora Shpet (1905–76) cofounded the Sergei Obraztsov State Academic Central Puppet Theater and, as head of its literary department, shaped its repertoire over many decades.

85. Shpet, "Theater as Art," 85.

86. Shpet, "Theater as Art," 88.

87. Shpet, "Theater as Art," 87.

88. Poole, "Gustav Shpet," 398.

89. See the catalog of Meyerhold's work in Robert Leach, *Vsevolod Meyerhold* (Cambridge: Cambridge University Press, 1989), 194–204.

90. Edward Braun, *Meyerhold: A Revolution in Theatre* (Iowa City: University of Iowa Press, 1995), 274.

91. Katerina Clark, *Moscow, the Fourth Rome: Stalinism, Cosmopolitanism, and the Evolution of Soviet Culture, 1931–1941* (Cambridge, MA: Harvard University Press, 2011), 226–30.

92. Roger J. B. Clark also sees naturalism in Dumas's play, writing: "Characters come and go naturally, they are brought together in realistic contexts for plausible reasons, so that one has little impression of the dramatist pulling strings behind the scene and none of the forced mechanical logic that characterizes the jerky entrances and exits of Scribe's wooden heroes." At the same time, the play seems more interested in the beauty of prostitution than its social conditions. Roger J. B. Clark, introduction to *La Dame aux Camélias* by Alexandre Dumas fils (London: Oxford University Press, 1972), 32. This observation proves an interesting contrast to Meyerhold's love of exaggerated convention and overt theatricality.

93. Vsevolod E. Meierkhol'd, "Spektakl' o sud'be zhenshchiny (1934 g.)," in *Stat'i, pis'ma, rechi, besedy*, ed. A. V. Fevral'skii and B. I. Rostotskii (Moscow: Iskusstvo, 1968), 2:286.

94. Braun discusses the production in detail; see Braun, *Meyerhold*, 273–78.

95. Gustav Shpet, trans., "*Dama s kameliiami.* Kopiia pervogo rabochego rezhisserskogo ekzempliara Z. N. Raikh i M. M. Koreneva. Perevody G. G. Shpeta," f. 963, op. 1, ed. khr. 1058, Russian State Archive of Literature and Art, Moscow.

96. Mitiushin, commentary to "Theater as Art," 89.

97. Liudmila Stepanovna Korzhevich, *Put' aktera: M. I. Tsarev* (Moscow: Vserossiiskoe teatral'noe obshchestvo, 1981), 77.

98. Tsarev expressed amazement at the degree to which Meyerhold stuck with Dumas's play. M. M. Sitkovetskaia, ed., *Meierkhol'd repetiruet*, vol. 2, *Spektakli 30-kh godov* (Moscow: Artist. Rezhisser. Teatr, 1993), 56.

99. A character named Monsieur Kokardo, whose lines consist of ironic recitations of Flaubert aphorisms, was added to the ball scene in the first act. Sitkovetskaia, *Meierkhol'd repetiruet*, 2:55.

100. Meyerhold, "*Lady of the Camellias*," 274.

101. Braun, *Meyerhold*, 276–78.

102. Vsevolod Meyerhold, "On Ideology and Technology in the Theater," lecture, December 1933, in *The Soviet Theater: A Documentary History*, ed. Laurence Senelick and Sergei Ostrovsky (New Haven, CT: Yale University Press, 2014), 396–97 (translation modified).

103. Sitkovetskaia, *Meierkhol'd repetiruet*, 2:55.

104. A. Gvozdev, "*Dama s kameliiami* (K postanovke Vs. Meierkhol'da)," *Rabochii i teatr*, no. 13 (1934), reprinted in *Meierkhol'd v russkoi teatral'noi kritike, 1920–1938*, ed. T. V. Lanina (Moscow: Artist. Rezhisser. Teatr, 2000), 413–14.

105. Dumas, *La Dame aux Camélias*, 210; Shpet, "*Dama s kameliiami*," 121–22.

106. Vsevolod Meyerhold, stenograph of rehearsal (November 11, 1933), in Sitkovetskaia, *Meierkhol'd repetiruet*, 2:75.

107. Vsevolod Meyerhold, stenograph of rehearsal (December 3, 1933), in Sitkovetskaia, *Meierkhol'd repetiruet*, 2:83.

108. Meyerhold, "Vsevolod Meyerhold's Class. Stage Movement Technique," 229.

109. Shpet, "Theater as Art," 77.

110. Konstantin Stanislavsky to Ripsimé Tamantsova, April 18, 1934, in *Stanislavsky: A Life in Letters*, trans. and ed. Laurence Senelick (London: Routledge, 2014), 587.

Chapter 3

1. Gurevich's editorial relationship with Stanislavsky is well known and frequently mentioned though remarkably understudied. More attention has been given to Stanislavsky's editorial relationship with the American Elizabeth Hapgood, who was responsible for introducing a number of translation errors into Stanislavsky's texts that resulted in early misunderstandings of his ideas by American theater artists. See Sharon Marie Carnicke, *Stanislavsky in Focus: An Acting Master for the Twenty-First Century*, 2nd ed. (London: Routledge, 2009), 80–93.

2. Liubov' Gurevich to Konstantin Stanislavskii, Moscow, April 1929, in "V plenu predlagaemykh obstoiatel'stv," ed. V. Dybovskii, in *Minuvshee: Istoricheskii al'manakh*, ed. Vladimir Alloy (Paris: Atheneum, 1990), 10:252–53.

3. V. V. Gudkova, *Teatral'naia sektsiia GAKhN: Istoriia idei i liudei, 1921–1930* (Moscow: Novoe literaturnoe obozrenie, 2019), 285.

4. Vygotsky's lifelong friend Semen Dobkin indicates that Vygotsky ardently attended touring theaters even as an adolescent, publishing reviews in local newspapers there in 1912–16 of companies that visited Gomel, as well. S. F. Dobkin, *L. S. Vygotskii: Nachalo puti; Vospominaniia S.F. Dobkina o L've Vygotskom; Rannie stat'i L.S. Vygotskogo*, ed. I. M. Feigenberg (Jerusalem: Jerusalem Publishing Centre, 1996), 35. These early reviews, if they indeed existed, have not been republished.

5. I capitalize System in this book to refer to Stanislavsky's "sistema" (which he always placed in quotation marks), following tradition in English-language scholarship. See Maria Shevtsova's comment in *Rediscovering Stanislavsky* (Cambridge: Cambridge University Press, 2020), xv–xvi.

6. In fact, Vygotsky's speech on consciousness was published as "Soznanie kak problema psikhologii povedeniia" (Consciousness as a Problem of Behavioral Psychology), with an epigraph from Karl Marx, in the volume *Psikhologiia i Marksizm* (*Psychology and Marxism*, 1925). This volume's primary purpose seems to be the refutation of Chelpanov and assertion of Marxism's central place in Soviet psychology, whether that psychology is reflexological or more "subjective." See K. N. Kornilov, "Psikhologiia i Marksizm Prof. Chelpanova," in *Psikhologiia i Marksizm*, ed. K. N. Kornilov (Leningrad: Gosudarstvennoe izdatel'stvo, 1925), 231–42. Vygotsky's speech is translated as L. S. Vygotsky, "Consciousness as a Problem in the Psychology of Behavior," ed. Michael Cole, trans. Michel Vale, *Soviet Psychology* 17, no. 4 (1979): 5–35.

7. See G. I. Chelpanov, "Rol' podsoznatel'nogo v protsesse tvorchestva," in *Iskusstvo kak iazyk—iazyki iskusstva: Gosudarstvennaia akademiia*

khudozhestvennykh nauk i esteticheskaia teoriia 1920-kh godov, ed. N. S. Plotnikov and N. P. Podzemskaia with Iu. N. Iakimenko (Moscow: Novoe literaturnoe obozrenie, 2017), 2:363–64; G. I. Chelpanov, "Problemy psikhologii khudozhestvennogo tvorchestva," in Plotnikov and Podzemskaia, *Iskusstvo kak iazyk*, 2:368–72; V. M. Ekzempliarskii, "Differentsial'no-psikhologicheskii podkhod k problemam estetiki," in Plotnikov and Podzemskaia, *Iskusstvo kak iazyk*, 2:373–78.

8. Arguably, with the exception of Maria Shevtsova, Stanislavsky's emphasis on the spirit has not been properly appreciated outside of Russia due largely but not exclusively to persistent errors in the translations of his writings, as I discuss later in the chapter. See Shevtsova, *Rediscovering Stanislavsky*, esp. chapter 3.

9. See Hannah Grainger Clemson, "Stanislavsky and Vygotsky: On the Problem of the Actor's and Learner's Work," in *Dramatic Interactions in Education: Vygotskian and Sociocultural Approaches to Drama, Education and Research*, ed. Susan Davis et al. (London: Bloomsbury, 2015), 39–56; Nelson Mok, "On the Concept of Perezhivanie: A Quest for a Critical Review," in *Perezhivanie, Emotions and Subjectivity: Advancing Vygotsky's Legacy*, ed. Marilyn Fleer, Fernando González Rey, and Nikolai Veresov (Singapore: Springer, 2017), 19–45.

10. V. Ia. Briusov, "*Gamlet* v Moskovskom khudozhestvennom teatre," in *Moskovskii khudozhestvennyi teatr v russkoi teatral'noi kritike: 1906–1918*, ed. O. A. Radishcheva and E. A. Shingareva (Moscow: Artist. Rezhisser. Teatr, 2007), 422. In Stanislavsky's lifetime, the Moscow Art Theater would produce one more *Hamlet*: a 1924 production at the Moscow Art Theater II, both directed by and starring Mikhail Chekhov. Stanislavsky also worked closely with Valentina Vyakhireva as she directed student work on *Hamlet* at the Opera-Dramatic Studio in 1937–38. Stanislavsky was particularly involved in coaching the actor Irina Rozanova, whom he cast in the main role.

11. It is not clear that Craig was specifically influenced by Sologub's "The Theater of One Will" or Evreinov's "Introduction to Monodrama"; rather, he likely drew on ideas in the air in Europe at the time.

12. In his memoir Stanislavsky writes that he asked the management of the Moscow Art Theater to invite Craig "so that he would give a jolt to our art and infuse it with new spiritual yeast for fermentation right when it seemed we had succeeded at slightly nudging the theater away from a dead end." Konstantin Stanislavskii, *Moia zhizn' v iskusstve*, in *Sobranie sochinenii v deviati tomakh*, ed. O. N. Efremov (Moscow: Iskusstvo, 1988–89), 1:415. Note that all translations of Stanislavsky's writings here are my own, as the available English translations are unfortunately inadequate. Stanislavsky's emphasis on "spiritual yeast" (*dukhovnye drozhzhi*) here indicates the vitality of *spirit* to his sense of theater's essence and starting point.

13. See discussion in Olga Taxidou, *Modernism and Performance: Jarry to Brecht* (Houndmills, UK: Palgrave Macmillan, 2007), 10–42.

14. L. A. Sulerzhitskii, "Z besedy Krega so Stanislavskim (apr. 1909 g.), zapisannykh L. A. Sulerzhitskim," f. 970, op. 13, ed. khr. 1877, l. 71, Russian State Archive of Literature and Art, Moscow. In his book on the production, Laurence Senelick indicates that some skepticism is warranted in studying these records: "The transcription was standard operating procedure, for the MAT [Moscow Art Theater], with its pervasive sense of history, kept copious records of every production, realized or not. But Craig found the taking down of his every word unsettling; he was used to indulging in extravagant flights of fancy

on café terraces without being called to account for them afterwards. And so he began to 'feed' the stenographers, weaving elaborate and impractical *mises-en-scène*, or adopting outrageously perverse stands, all of which Stanislavsky took seriously and felt obliged to consider or contravene." Laurence Senelick, *Gordon Craig's Moscow "Hamlet": A Reconstruction* (Westport, CT: Greenwood Press, 1982), 44–45.

15. Edward Gordon Craig, "The Actor and the Über-Marionette," *Mask* 1, no. 2 (April 1908): 3, Blue Mountain Project, https://bluemountain.princeton.edu.

16. Stanislavskii, *Moia zhizn' v iskusstve*, 416.

17. Stanislavskii, *Moia zhizn' v iskusstve*, 416.

18. It also must be noted that Stanislavsky does not demonstrate full appreciation of pro-puppet modernist thought when he declares puppets lifeless objects. See Dassia N. Posner, "Life-Death and Disobedient Obedience: Russian Modernist Redefinitions of the Puppet," in *The Routledge Companion to Puppetry and Material Performance*, ed. Dassia N. Posner, Claudia Orenstein, and John Bell (London: Routledge, 2014), 130–43.

19. Sulerzhitskii, "Z besedy Krega so Stanislavskim," l. 49–50. Note that while Laurence Senelick translates many of the stenograms in his volume *Gordon Craig's Moscow "Hamlet,"* this conversation is not among them. Senelick's materials are based on Parisian archives, while mine are from Russian archives.

20. Qtd. in Senelick, *Gordon Craig's Moscow "Hamlet,"* 112, collected in the Edward Gordon Craig papers at the Harry Ransom Humanities Research Center, University of Texas, Austin.

21. Craig told Stanislavsky: "Hamlet is a *spirit*, and everything that surrounds him is *matter*." Sulerzhitskii, "Z besedy Krega so Stanislavskim," l. 20; cf. Senelick, *Gordon Craig's Moscow "Hamlet,"* 67.

22. L. A. Sulerzhitskii, "Kreg-postanovshchik 'Gamleta' v Khudozhestvennom teatre. Iz besedy s L. A. Sulerzhitskim," f. 860, op. 1, ed. khr. 165, l. 3, Russian State Archive of Literature and Art, Moscow; cf. Senelick, *Gordon Craig's Moscow "Hamlet,"* 68.

23. On Stanislavsky's relevance for more abstract, expressionistic, and post-dramatic theaters, see Dennis C. Beck, "The Legacy of Stanislavsky's Ideas in Non-Realistic Theatre," in *The Routledge Companion to Stanislavsky*, ed. R. Andrew White (London: Routledge, 2014), 213–29.

24. N. N. Chushkin, *Gamlet-Kachalov: Iz stsenicheskoi istorii "Gamleta" Shekspira* (Moscow: Iskusstvo, 1966), 37.

25. Sulerzhitskii, "Z besedy Krega so Stanislavskim," l. 13.

26. Elinor Fuchs, *The Death of Character: Perspectives on Theater after Modernism* (Bloomington: Indiana University Press, 1996), 8.

27. A full description of the production is given in Senelick, *Gordon Craig's Moscow "Hamlet,"* 154–73.

28. Konstantin Stanislavskii, *Rabota aktera nad soboi: Chast' 1. Rabota nad soboi v tvorcheskom protsesse perezhivaniia*, in *Sobranie sochinenii v deviati tomakh*, 2:311.

29. Rose Whyman, *The Stanislavsky System of Acting: Legacy and Influence in Modern Performance* (Cambridge: Cambridge University Press, 2008), 1–37.

30. Stanislavskii, *Moia zhizn' v iskusstve*, 371.

31. Stanislavskii, *Moia zhizn' v iskusstve*, 371.

32. Stanislavskii, *Moia zhizn' v iskusstve*, 373.

33. Rhonda Blair, "Reconsidering Stanislavsky: Feeling, Feminism, and the Actor," *Theatre Topics* 12, no. 2 (September 2002): 180.

34. Bruce McConachie, *Theatre & Mind* (Houndmills, UK: Palgrave Macmillan, 2013), 31.

35. Curiously, Craig did not appreciate Stanislavsky's understanding of the spirit: in a 1937 article on Stanislavsky, Craig criticized the System for purporting to teach anyone to act (he felt that actors were *born*), and he also rejected Stanislavsky's realism in hindsight: "It is unnecessary to devote years of a life to teaching would-be actors to be, above all things, 'natural,' since drama at its best is supernatural or 'spiritual.' " Edward Gordon Craig, "Stanislavsky's System," in *Craig on Theatre*, ed. J. Michael Walton (London: Methuen, 1983), 89.

36. Shevtsova, *Rediscovering Stanislavsky*, 87–101.

37. Shevtsova, *Rediscovering Stanislavsky*, 89.

38. Shevtsova, *Rediscovering Stanislavsky*, 95.

39. Stanislavskii, *Rabota aktera nad soboi: Chast' 1*, 2:258.

40. Konstantin Stanislavskii, *Rabota aktera nad soboi: Chast' 2: Rabota nad soboi v tvorcheskom protsesse voploshcheniia*, in *Sobranie sochinenii v deviati tomakh*, 3:20.

41. Whyman, *The Stanislavsky System of Acting*, 45.

42. Shevtsova notes that Stanislavsky's terms *mind*, *will*, and *feeling* correspond to the three "sides" of the soul in the terminology of Orthodox prelate Feofan Zatvornik. Shevtsova, *Rediscovering Stanislavsky*, 95.

43. See Maria Knebel', "Given Circumstances," in *Active Analysis*, ed. Anatoli Vassiliev, trans. Irina Brown (London: Routledge, 2021), 36.

44. Whyman, *The Stanislavsky System of Acting*, 45.

45. Patrick C. Carriere, "Reading for the Soul in Stanislavski's *The Work of the Actor on Him/Herself*: Orthodox Mysticism, Mainstream Occultism, Psychology and the System in the Russian Silver Age" (PhD diss., University of Kansas, 2010), 61.

46. Shevtsova, *Rediscovering Stanislavsky*, 105.

47. Sharon Marie Carnicke chooses to translate *perezhivanie* as "experiencing." Carnicke, *Stanislavsky in Focus*, 132. This nuanced term has been translated and interpreted in many different ways, as Carnicke discusses on pages 129–47. Writing ten years after Carnicke, Shevtsova uses "emotional experiencing." Shevtsova, *Rediscovering Stanislavsky*, 121–24.

48. See Daniel Johnston, "Stanislavskian Acting as Phenomenology in Practice," *Journal of Dramatic Theory and Criticism* 26, no. 1 (Fall 2011): 65–84; Mark Fortier, *Theory/Theatre: An Introduction* (London: Routledge 1997), 32–37; Robert Leach, *Makers of Modern Theatre: An Introduction* (London: Routledge, 2004), 49–51. Another relevant essay, although it does not dwell on phenomenology specifically, is Jerri Daboo, "Stanislavsky and the Psychophysical in Western Acting," in *Acting: Psychophysical Phenomenon and Process: Intercultural and Interdisciplinary Perspectives*, by Phillip B. Zarrilli, Jerri Daboo, and Rebecca Loukes (Houndmills, UK: Palgrave Macmillan, 2013), 158–93.

49. W. B. Worthen, "Of Actors and Automata: Hieroglyphics of Modernism," *Journal of Dramatic Theory and Criticism* 9, no. 1 (Fall 1994): 14.

50. Daniel Johnston, *Theatre and Phenomenology: Manual Philosophy* (London: Palgrave, 2017), 88.

51. Stanislavskii, *Rabota aktera nad soboi: Chast' 2*, 3:400–401.

52. Stanislavskii, *Rabota aktera nad soboi: Chast' 2*, 3:439.

53. Stanislavskii, *Rabota aktera nad soboi: Chast' 2*, 3:440.

54. Shevtsova, *Rediscovering Stanislavsky*, 101.

55. See Bella Merlin, "'Here, Today, Now': Active Analysis for the Twenty-First-Century Actor," in White, *The Routledge Companion to Stanislavsky*, 326. Merlin makes the word order more natural in English. Cf. Shevtsova, *Rediscovering Stanislavsky*, 101–4.

56. Sulerzhitskii, "Z besedy Krega so Stanislavskim," l. 54.

57. Carnicke, *Stanislavsky in Focus*, 102.

58. Whyman, *The Stanislavsky System of Acting*, 62.

59. Ivan Sechenov, *Reflexes of the Brain*, trans. S. Belsky, ed. G. Gibbons (Cambridge: MIT Press, 1965), 3.

60. On Sechenov and Chernyshevsky, see Maya Koretzky, "Sensation(al) Science: Ivan Sechenov's *Reflexes of the Brain* and Revolutionary Physiology, Literature and Politics of the Russian 1860s," *Ezra's Archives* 3, no. 1 (Spring 2013): 75–91. On the Soviet myth of Sechenov and socialism, see David Joravsky, *Russian Psychology: A Critical History* (Oxford: Basil Blackwell, 1989), 53–54.

61. See Robert B. Lawson, Jean E. Graham, and Kristin M. Baker, *A History of Psychology: Globalization, Ideas, and Approaches* (Upper Saddle River, NJ: Pearson Prentice Hall, 2007), 398–412.

62. I. V. Gladkova, *Chelpanov G. I. glazami sovremennikov: Portret na fone epokhi* (Ekaterinburg: UGGU, 2013), 4–5.

63. Vygotsky, "Consciousness as a Problem," 5.

64. M. G. Iaroshevskii, "Kogda L.S. Vygotskii i ego shkola poiavilis' v psikhologii?," *Voprosy psikhologii*, no. 5 (1996): 113. Vygotsky's last spoken words were Hamlet's line, "I am ready." His last written words were Hamlet's dying sentence, "The rest is silence." Ekaterina Zavershneva, "Vygotsky the Unpublished: An Overview of the Personal Archive (1912–1934)," in *Revisionist Revolution in Vygotsky Studies*, ed. Anton Yasnitsky and René van der Veer (London: Routledge, 2016), 125–26. Dobkin even indicates that Vygotsky studied English specifically in order to read *Hamlet*. Dobkin, *L. S. Vygotskii*, 67–68.

65. Lev Semenovich Vygotskii, *Tragediia o Gamlete, printse datskom, V. Shekspira*, in *Polnoe sobranie sochinenii*, vol. 1, *Dramaturgiia i teatr*, ed. V. S. Sobkin (Moscow: Lev', 2015), 165n3.

66. Vygotskii, *Tragediia o Gamlete*, 1:98.

67. Vygotskii, *Tragediia o Gamlete*, 1:79. Vygotsky also cites critic Arkadii Gornfel'd's 1912 essay on literary interpretation as guiding his approach; see Vygotskii, *Tragediia o Gamlete*, 1:82–83.

68. Lev Semenovich Vygotskii, "Teatr i revoliutsiia," in *Polnoe sobranie sochinenii*, 1:324.

69. These two articles are both reprinted in Vygotskii, *Polnoe sobranie sochinenii*, 1:307–25.

70. See Grainger Clemson, "Stanislavsky and Vygotsky"; Michael Michell, "Dramatic Interactions: From Vygotsky's Life of Drama to the Drama of Life,"

in Davis et al., *Dramatic Interactions in Education*, 19–37; L. P. Shchedrovitskii, "L.S. Vygotsky's 'Tragedy of Hamlet Prince of Denmark,'" *Journal of Russian and East European Psychology* 32, no. 2 (1994): 49–65; Peter Smagorinsky, "Vygotsky's Stage Theory: The Psychology of Art and the Actor under the Direction of *Perezhivanie*," *Mind, Culture, and Activity* 18, no. 4 (2011): 319–41.

71. V. S. Sobkin and V. S. Mazanova, "Opyt kommentariev k odnoi teatral'noi retsenzii L.S. Vygotskogo," *Natsional'nyi psikhologicheskii zhurnal* 1, no. 13 (2014): 37.

72. Lev Semenovich Vygotskii, "Ob avtore 'Ne sovsem retsenzii,'" in *Polnoe sobranie sochinenii*, 1:362. In his footnote, Sobkin connects this "partnership" view of Vygotsky's to the latter's concept of the zone of proximal development.

73. V. S. Sobkin, "L. S. Vygotskii i teatr: Abris sotsiokul'turnogo konteksta," introduction to Vygotskii, *Polnoe sobranie sochinenii*, 1:34.

74. Lev Semenovich Vygotskii, "Koroleva i zhenshchina," in *Polnoe sobranie sochinenii*, 1:423.

75. Lev Semenovich Vygotskii, "Kakoi schastliveishii den' vashei zhizni, ili vosklitsatel'nyi znak!," in *Polnoe sobranie sochinenii*, 1:360.

76. Lev Semenovich Vygotskii, "Kogda zagovorit serdtse," in *Polnoe sobranie sochinenii*, 1:427.

77. Lev Semenovich Vygotskii, "Dzhentl'men," in *Polnoe sobranie sochinenii*, 1:416.

78. Lev Semenovich Vygotskii, "Komediia dvora," in *Polnoe sobranie sochinenii*, 1:422.

79. Vygotsky, "Consciousness as a Problem," 8; Lev Vygotskii, "Soznanie kak problema psikhologii povedeniia," in Kornilov, *Psikhologiia i Marksizm*, 178.

80. Vygotsky, "Consciousness as a Problem," 7.

81. Michael Cole, headnote to Vygotsky, "Consciousness as a Problem," 4.

82. Vygotsky, "Consciousness as a Problem," 22.

83. Vygotsky, "Consciousness as a Problem," 31.

84. Smagorinsky, "Vygotsky's Stage Theory," 323.

85. For an excellent overview of the heritage of Vygotsky's concept of *perezhivanie*, see Mok, "On the Concept of Perezhivanie."

86. Lev Vygotskii, "Lektsiia chetvertaia. Problema sredy v pedologii," in *Lektsii po pedologii* (Izhevsk, Russia: Udmurtskii universitet, 2001), 72–73.

87. I am grateful to my colleague Michael Glassman, as well as to Logan Pelfrey and Irina Kuznetcova in the College of Education and Human Ecology at the Ohio State University, for encouraging my work on Vygotsky and Stanislavsky and for sharing the speculation, which I was able to confirm, that Gurevich consulted with Vygotsky on Stanislavsky's drafts.

88. L. S. Vygotsky, "On the Problem of the Psychology of the Actor's Creative Work," in *The Collected Works of L. S. Vygotsky*, vol. 6, *Scientific Legacy*, trans. Marie J. Hall (New York: Kluwer Academic, 1987), 241.

89. Vygotsky, "On the Problem of the Psychology," 6:242.

Chapter 4

1. V. V. Gudkova, "Teatr kak iskusstvo v filosofskoi i teatrovedcheskoi refleksii GAKhN," in *Iskusstvo kak iazyk—iazyki iskusstva: Gosudarstvennaia akademiia khudozhestvennykh nauk i esteticheskaia teoriia 1920-kh godov*, ed. N. S.

Plotnikov and N. P. Podzemskaia with Iu. N. Iakimenko (Moscow: Novoe literaturnoe obozrenie, 2017), 1:266.

2. In fact Sigizmund Krzhizhanovsky uses the term *raznovidnost'* (*varietas*), which comes from botanical taxonomy rather than zoological taxonomy. This is surely an error. Vadim Perel'muter reconstructs this talk in his article "'Akter kak raznovidnost' cheloveka': Popytka rekonstruktsii doklada Sigizmunda Krzhizhanovskogo, prochitannogo na zasedanii Teatral'noi sektsii GAKhN 20 dekabria 1923 goda (po materialam arkhiva S.D. Krzhizhanovskogo)," *Voprosy iskusstvoznaniia* 11, no. 2 (1997): 69–74.

3. Sigizmund Krzhizhanovsky, "A Philosopheme for the Theater," in *That Third Guy: A Comedy from the Stalinist 1930s with Essays on Theater*, trans. and ed. Alisa Ballard Lin (Madison: University of Wisconsin Press, 2018), 37.

4. Krzhizhanovsky, "A Philosopheme for the Theater," 44.

5. Krzhizhanovsky, "A Philosopheme for the Theater," 45.

6. Vadim Perelmuter claims that Krzhizhanovsky had no further involvement with GAKhN; see Perel'muter, "Akter kak raznovidnost' cheloveka," 69. V. V. Gudkova disagrees, though she gives no evidence for her statement that Krzhizhanovsky was an active attendee of Theater Section gatherings in the mid-1920s. See V. V. Gudkova, *Teatral'naia sektsiia GAKhN: Istoriia idei i liudei, 1921–1930* (Moscow: Novoe literaturnoe obozrenie, 2019), 363n144.

7. Sigizmund Krzhizhanovskii, *Zapisnye tetradi*, in *Sobranie sochinenii v shesti tomakh*, ed. Vadim Perel'muter (Saint Petersburg: Symposium, 2001–13), 5:328.

8. Larry D. Bouchard, *Theater and Integrity: Emptying Selves in Drama, Ethics, and Religion* (Evanston, IL: Northwestern University Press, 2011), 23.

9. Michael Goldman, *The Actor's Freedom: Toward a Theory of Drama* (New York: Viking Press, 1975), 119.

10. Karen Link Rosenflanz, *Hunter of Themes: The Interplay of Word and Thing in the Works of Sigizmund Kržižanovskij* (New York: Peter Lang, 2005), 3. Rosenflanz's book contains the most extensive biography of Krzhizhanovsky in English.

11. Vadim Perel'muter, notes to "Stat'i, zametki, retsenzii, opublikovannye v ezhenedel'nike *7 Dnei Moskovskogo Kamernogo teatra*," by Sigizmund Krzhizhanovskii, in *Sobranie sochinenii v shesti tomakh*, 4:819.

12. Vadim Perelmuter has indicated, by personal phone communication with Alexander Spektor on January 1, 2016, that several manuscripts of one-act plays by Krzhizhanovsky have also survived. Perelmuter has not shared information about where the plays have been kept or when they were written.

13. This *Eugene Onegin*, with a score by Sergei Prokofiev, languished in archives until it premiered at Princeton University (in English translation by James E. Falen) in February 2012. The text, in both Russian and English, was subsequently published in *Pushkin Review* 16–17 (2013–14): 36–179. Caryl Emerson discusses the dramatic choices Krzhizhanovsky faced as theatrical adaptor, with a reflection on the Princeton staging, in "Tairov's Theater, Evreinov's Monodramatic Moment, and the Lessons of *Eugene Onegin*, a Drama in Verse," *Pushkin Review* 16–17 (2013–14): 1–23.

14. Sigizmund Krzhizhanovskii, "Fragmenty o Shekspire," in *Sobranie sochinenii v shesti tomakh*, 4:383–84.

15. Valerii V. Petrov, "Platon i ego uchenie u Sigizmunda Krzhizhanovskogo," *Logos* 90, no. 6 (2012): 58.

16. Krzhizhanovsky, "A Philosopheme for the Theater," 26.
17. Krzhizhanovsky, "A Philosopheme for the Theater," 26.
18. Krzhizhanovsky, "A Philosopheme for the Theater," 27.
19. Krzhizhanovsky, "A Philosopheme for the Theater," 28.
20. Krzhizhanovsky, "A Philosopheme for the Theater," 36.
21. Krzhizhanovsky, "A Philosopheme for the Theater," 41.
22. Krzhizhanovsky, "Shakespeare's Comediography," in *That Third Guy*, 168.
23. Krzhizhanovsky, "Shakespeare's Comediography," 169.
24. Krzhizhanovsky, "Shakespeare's Comediography," 182.
25. Krzhizhanovsky, "Shakespeare's Comediography," 181–82. The reference to "theater for oneself" is, of course, a reference to Nikolai Evreinov.
26. Alexander Spektor, "A Timely Discovery: Experimental Realism of Sigizmund Krzhizhanovsky," review article, *Slavic and East European Journal* 59, no. 1 (Spring 2015): 111–12.
27. In the novella, *Hamlet* references are not confined to Rar's tale. The final line of the novella, "Here—I'm giving the words back; all except one: life," alludes to Hamlet's line to Polonius, who has just announced to the prince that he is taking his leave: "You cannot, sir, take from me anything that I will more willingly part withal: except my life, my life, my life." William Shakespeare, *Hamlet*, in *The Norton Shakespeare*, ed. Stephen Greenblatt et al. (New York: Norton, 1997), II.ii.212–13. This final line in Krzhizhanovsky was omitted from the Symposium *Sobranie sochinenii v shesti tomakh*.
28. Sigizmund Krzhizhanovsky, *The Letter Killers Club*, trans. Joanne Turnbull (New York: New York Review Books, 2012), 14.
29. Krzhizhanovsky, "A Philosopheme for the Theater," 27.
30. Cf. Stanislavsky's claim that "for all the work of the actor proceeds not from actual, real, truthful life, but from imaginary, non-existing, unable to exist life. It is for us, actors, the true reality." Konstantin Stanislavskii, *Rabota aktera nad soboi: Chast' 1. Rabota nad soboi v tvorcheskom protsesse perezhivaniia*, in *Sobranie sochinenii v deviati tomakh*, ed. O. N. Efremov (Moscow: Iskusstvo, 1988–89), 2:259–60.
31. Krzhizhanovsky, "A Philosopheme for the Theater," 44–45.
32. Krzhizhanovsky, "A Philosopheme for the Theater," 37.
33. There is a distinct Platonic theme in Krzhizhanovsky's essays and stories, through connections of knowledge to light, allusions to the Cave, and references to the Dialogues. See Petrov, "Platon i ego uchenie." I am also grateful to Alexander Spektor for his insight into this theme.
34. Technically, the more accurate translation of Krzhizhanovsky's "Teatr—sm." would be "Theater—vid.," though the general preference for and greater familiarity with *cf.* over *vid.* in English-language publication (even though *cf.* technically means "compare" rather than "see") motivates my choice of *cf.*
35. Sigizmund Krzhizhanovsky, "The Stage Direction (A Fragment)," in *That Third Guy*, 73.
36. Krzhizhanovsky, *The Letter Killers Club*, 112.
37. Nick Worrall gives a biography of Tairov in *Modernism to Realism on the Soviet Stage: Tairov, Vakhtangov, Okhlopkov* (Cambridge: Cambridge University Press, 1989), 19–22.

38. Tairov discusses Craig extensively, writing in the beginning of *Notes of a Director* that in 1912 "the disappointments of Gordon Craig and his forced glorification of the 'über-marionette' troublesomely kept coming back to me." Aleksandr Ia. Tairov, *Zapiski rezhissera*, in *O teatre*, 2nd ed. (Moscow: Akademicheskii proekt, 2018), 71. The climate of prerevolutionary modernism, which Tairov both rejected and reincarnated in his own ways, decisively shaped his aesthetic.

39. Dassia N. Posner, *The Director's Prism: E. T. A. Hoffmann and the Russian Theatrical Avant-Garde* (Evanston, IL: Northwestern University Press, 2016), 97–98.

40. Posner is an excellent source on Tairov's use of Hoffmann, in *The Director's Prism*, 92–131.

41. See the discussion of the Studio-Workshop and Experimental Theater Workshops by Svetlana Sboeva in "Akter v teatre A. Ia. Tairova," in *Russkoe akterskoe iskusstvo XX veka*, ed. S. K. Bushueva (Saint Petersburg: Rossiiskii institut istorii iskusstv, 1992), 159, 211–12.

42. Sboeva, "Akter v teatre A. Ia. Tairova," 212.

43. Iulii Khmel'nitskii, *Iz zapisok aktera tairovskogo teatra* (Moscow: GITIS, 2004), 17.

44. Sigizmund Krzhizhanovsky, "Man vs. Machine," in *That Third Guy*, 68–69.

45. Sigizmund Krzhizhanovsky, "At a Crossroads," in *That Third Guy*, 69.

46. Sigizmund Krzhizhanovsky, "The Moscow Kamerny Theater and Its Theme," in *That Third Guy*, 62.

47. Aleksandr Ia. Tairov, *Zapiski rezhissera*, in *O teatre*, 2nd ed. (Moscow: Akademicheskii proekt, 2018), 71.

48. Tairov, *Zapiski rezhissera*, 93 (emphasis added). My thanks to Dassia N. Posner for this translation of *stsenicheskii obraz* as "stage figure."

49. Tairov, *Zapiski rezhissera*, 95.

50. Tairov, *Zapiski rezhissera*, 93.

51. Dassia N. Posner, email message to author, March 13, 2024.

52. Tairov, *Zapiski rezhissera*, 96.

53. Sboeva, "Akter v teatre A. Ia. Tairova," 167.

54. Sboeva, "Akter v teatre A. Ia. Tairova," 180.

55. Dassia N. Posner, "An Actor Creates: The Moscow Kamerny Theatre School," paper presented at the annual Association for Slavic, East European, and Eurasian Studies conference, November 22, 2024.

56. Sboeva, "Akter v teatre A. Ia. Tairova," 166.

57. Svetlana Sboeva, "Moskovskii Kamernyi teatr: *Chelovek, kotoryi byl Chetvergom* v nemetskoi i avstriiskoi kritike," in *Mnemozina: Dokumenty i fakty iz istorii otechestvennogo teatra XX veka*, ed. V. V. Ivanov, vol. 5 (Moscow: Indrik, 2014), 179–80.

58. Due to an electrical fire at the Bakhrushin Theatre Museum in the early 1950s, the *Thursday* promptbook with Tairov's notes is charred around the edges, the damage on some pages cutting significantly into the text. The final typescript, which reflects Tairov's corrections from the promptbook, is undamaged, and thus I cite the text from it. To date, this is the only thorough discussion of the script or promptbook in English-language scholarship. Lucas H. Harriman references the script in his article about the production as a fruitful "betrayal" of Chesterton's novel, but he devotes little space to analysis and scant attention to

Tairov's and Krzhizhanovsky's theories as a lens for understanding the nuances of the text. Lucas H. Harriman, "The Russian Betrayal of G. K. Chesterton's *The Man Who Was Thursday*," *Comparative Literature* 62, no. 1 (Winter 2010): esp. 49–53. This weak article is uninformed by Russian scholarship on Tairov and Krzhizhanovsky and by a thorough reading of the *Thursday* script. In Russian scholarship Maria Malikova and Sboeva have discussed the promptbook, and Malikova analyzes its echoes with Krzhizhanovsky's essays on theater. Mariia Malikova, "'Sketch po koshmaru Chestertona' i kul'turnaia situatsiia nepa," *Novoe literaturnoe obozrenie*, no. 78 (2006): esp. 52–53.

59. See Sboeva's excellent study of the German and Austrian reception of the production, accompanied by translations of the foreign reviews, in her "Moskovskii Kamernyi teatr."

60. G. K. Chesterton, "Introduction to *The Man Who Was Thursday*, a Three-Act Play by Cecil Chesterton with Ralph Neale (1926)," in *The Annotated Thursday*, ed. Martin Gardner (San Francisco: Ignatius Press, 1999), 272. This dramatic adaptation by Chesterton's sister-in-law was published with his approval in 1926. Martin Gardner writes: "Chesterton liked to imagine that God has a sense of humor. . . . Nature has its wildly comic side." Martin Gardner, introduction to Gardner, *The Annotated Thursday*, 13, and see 241n4.

61. A. Gvozdev, "O novom teatre," *Zrelishcha*, February 5, 1924, Moskovskii gosudarstvennyi Kamernyi teatr (1914–50), papers, f. 2030, op. 1, ed. khr. 219, Russian State Archive of Literature and Art, Moscow. To compare with European reviews, see the Russian translations in Sboeva, "Moskovskii Kamernyi teatr," 194–210.

62. Malikova, "Sketch po koshmaru Chestertona," 56.

63. Sigizmund Krzhizhanovskii, *Materialy k spektakliu "Chelovek, kotoryi byl Chetvergom": rezhisserskii ekzempliar p'esy S.D. Krzhizhanovskogo s pometkami A. Ia. Tairova, rabochii ekzempliar pomoshchnika rezhissera i spisok butaforii*, Moskovskii gosudarstvennyi Kamernyi teatr, papers, f. 2030, op. 1, ed. khr. 115, l. 37, 40. These prompter's notes list cues for props, lighting, sound effects, and intertitles used in the production.

64. Alisa Koonen, *Stranitsy zhizni* (Moscow: Kukushka, 2003), 381.

65. Koonen, *Stranitsy zhizni*, 381.

66. Posner argues that central to the Kamerny's *Princess Brambilla* (directed by Tairov in 1920) was the idea that the actor is more skilled than the machine. Dassia N. Posner, "Performance as Polemic: Tairov's 1920 *Princess Brambilla* at the Moscow Kamerny Theatre," *Theatre Survey* 51, no. 1 (May 2010): 53. We see a similar dynamic in the contrast between actor and mechanization in *The Man Who Was Thursday*, except that in *Brambilla* the idea is conveyed through a near absence of stage technology, as Posner explains.

67. Tsvibel'fish, "Chelovek, kotoryi byl Chetvergom," undated newspaper clipping (name of newspaper not preserved), Moskovskii gosudarstvennyi Kamernyi teatr, papers, f. 2030, op. 1, ed. khr. 219. For discussion of Glubokovsky and his pseudonym, see Malikova, "Sketch po koshmaru Chestertona," 46n14.

68. Tairov, *Zapiski rezhissera*, 85.

69. See Vesnin's sketches reprinted in A. M. Efros, ed., *Kamernyi teatr i ego khudozhniki, 1914–1934* (Moscow: Vserossiiskoe teatral'noe obshchestvo, 1934), 144–47. Additional images of designs for the production are currently available

in the Gosudarstvennyi tsentral'nyi teatral'nyi muzei imeni A.A. Bakhrushina, Moscow, Kollektsii-online, https://collectiononline.gctm.ru.

70. See, e.g., Krzhizhanovskii, *Materialy k spektakliu*, 1. 34.

71. Sigizmund D. Krzhizhanovskii, *Chelovek, kotoryi byl Chetvergom po D. Chestertonu: Sketch v trekh deistviiakh i 13 situatsiiakh*, Krzhizhanovskii Sigizmund Dominikhovich (1887–1950)—pisatel', papers, f. 2280, op. 1, ed. khr. 19, l. 2. Because Thursday is referred to as the "fourth one" in this opening exchange, it would appear that he is destined to be Thursday (the fourth day of the week). In Russian the words "Thursday" (*chetverg*) and "fourth" (*chetvertyi*) are related.

72. In Chesterton's novel it is Friday who is this character (Professor de Worms, a.k.a. Wilks), and Wednesday is the Marquis de St. Eustache (Friday in the Kamerny version). Why the Kamerny switched the two is not clear, though one meaningful (but perhaps unintended) consequence is that the Russian word for Wednesday (*sreda*) is related to the adjective "middle" (*srednii*) and noun "center" (*seredina*), so the most metatheatrical character is the "center" one. (All the other Days correspond between novel and adaptation.)

73. Krzhizhanovskii, *Chelovek, kotoryi byl Chetvergom*, 34–35.

74. In Chesterton's novel, the naming of the seats in the Council of Anarchists by the days of the week is connected to the biblical seven days of Creation, as emphasized in the costume ball, in which they dress in robes designated with imagery of what God created on their associated day. The novel uses the Christian symbology of days to connect the characters to a spiritual realm beyond human reality. In the production, even though Chesterton's religious allegory has been diminished, it is hard not to think of Sunday as God—in control of his subjects—and Gregory, the anarchist assassin, as Satan. Chesterton outlines this parallel in the novel in an interview from 1926: "there is one character, the real anarchist, Lucien [Lucifer] Gregory, who does stand for the forces of evil and despair," and, "You ask me who Sunday is? Well, you may call him Nature, if you like. But you will note that I hold that when the mask of Nature is lifted, you find God behind." G. K. Chesterton, interview in *The Illustrated Sunday Herald* (January 24, 1926), reprinted in *The Annotated Thursday*, 276, 277–78. Krzhizhanovsky, raised Catholic in Ukraine, a country with rich traditions of folk theater, was well versed in mystery and miracle plays, in which the seven deadly sins are associated with the seven days of Creation.

75. Krzhizhanovskii, *Chelovek, kotoryi byl Chetvergom*, 63.

76. Krzhizhanovskii, *Chelovek, kotoryi byl Chetvergom*, 3.

77. Krzhizhanovskii, *Chelovek, kotoryi byl Chetvergom*, 31.

78. Krzhizhanovskii, *Chelovek, kotoryi byl Chetvergom*, 32.

79. Krzhizhanovskii, *Chelovek, kotoryi byl Chetvergom*, 54.

80. Krzhizhanovskii, *Chelovek, kotoryi byl Chetvergom*, 54. This prefigures Krzhizhanovsky's discussions of the velocity of images in the theater in his "Shakespeare's Comediography" (1934).

81. Tairov, *Zapiski rezhissera*, 141.

82. Krzhizhanovskii, *Chelovek, kotoryi byl Chetvergom*, 65.

83. See Robert Russell's discussion of the genre in "Red Pinkertonism: An Aspect of Soviet Literature of the 1920s," *Slavonic and East European Review* 60, no. 3 (July 1982): esp. 392–94.

84. Krzhizhanovskii, *Chelovek, kotoryi byl Chetvergom*, 63.

Coda

1. Nicholas Rzhevsky, *The Modern Russian Theater: A Literary and Cultural History* (Armonk, NY: M. E. Sharpe, 2009), 99.

2. See V. V. Gudkova, *Teatral'naia sektsiia GAKhN: Istoriia idei i liudei, 1921–1930* (Moscow: Novoe literaturnoe obozrenie, 2019), 120–40.

3. Pavel M. Iakobson, "Aktery o svoem tvorchestve," in *Teatral'nyi al'manakh: Sbornik statei i materialov* (Moscow: Vserossiiskoe teatral'noe obshchestvo, 1948), 7:114–17.

4. Pavel M. Iakobson, *Psikhologiia stsenicheskikh chuvstv aktera: Etiud po psikhologii tvorchestva*, ed. V. Kolbanovskii (Moscow: Khudozhestvennaia literatura, 1936), 172.

5. Iakobson, *Psikhologiia stsenicheskikh chuvstv aktera*, 173.

BIBLIOGRAPHY

Aikhenval'd, Iulii. "Otritsanie teatra." In *V sporakh o teatre: Sbornik statei*, by Iu. Aikhenval'd, S. Glagol', V. I. Nemirovich-Danchenko, F. Komissarzhevskii, Vas. Sakhnovskii, M. Bonch-Tomashevskii, A. Iuzhin-Sumbatov, and D. Ovsianiko-Kulikovskii, 5–23. 1914. Reprint, Moscow: RATI-GITIS, 2008.

Aquilina, Stefan. *Modern Theatre in Russia: Tradition Building and Transmission Processes*. London: Methuen Drama, 2020.

Aristov, V. V. "G. G. Shpet i proekt sozdaniia im Akademii Moskovskogo khudozhestvennogo teatra." *Voprosy psikhologii* 3 (2009): 108–15.

Armstrong, Tim. *Modernism, Technology, and the Body: A Cultural Study*. Cambridge: Cambridge University Press, 1998.

Beck, Dennis C. "The Legacy of Stanislavsky's Ideas in Non-Realistic Theatre." In White, *The Routledge Companion to Stanislavsky*, 213–29.

Bird, Robert. "The Hermeneutic Triangle: Gustav Shpet's Aesthetics in Context." In Tihanov, *Gustav Shpet's Contribution to Philosophy and Cultural Theory*, 28–44.

Blair, Rhonda. *The Actor, Image, and Action: Acting and Cognitive Neuroscience*. London: Routledge, 2008.

———. "Reconsidering Stanislavsky: Feeling, Feminism, and the Actor." *Theatre Topics* 12, no. 2 (September 2002): 177–90.

Bleeker, Maaike, Jon Foley Sherman, and Eirini Nedelkopoulou. Introduction to Bleeker, Sherman, and Nedelkopoulou, *Performance and Phenomenology*, 1–19.

———, eds. *Performance and Phenomenology: Traditions and Transformations*. New York: Routledge, 2015.

Blok, Aleksandr. "The Puppet Show." In Green, *The Russian Symbolist Theatre*, 42–53.

Bouchard, Larry D. *Theater and Integrity: Emptying Selves in Drama, Ethics, and Religion*. Evanston, IL: Northwestern University Press, 2011.

Bowlt, John E. "RAKhN on Trial: The Purge of Gustav Shpet." *Experiment* 3 (1997): 295–305.

Braun, Edward. *Meyerhold: A Revolution in Theatre*. Iowa City: University of Iowa Press, 1995.

Brintlinger, Angela. "Writing about Madness: Russian Attitudes toward Psyche and Psychiatry, 1887–1907." In *Madness and the Mad in Russian Culture*, edited by Angela Brintlinger and Ilya Vinitsky, 173–91. Toronto: University of Toronto Press, 2007.

Briusov, V. Ia. "*Gamlet* v Moskovskom khudozhestvennom teatre." In *Moskovskii khudozhestvennyi teatr v russkoi teatral'noi kritike: 1906–1918*, edited by O. A. Radishcheva and E. A. Shingareva, 422–32. Moscow: Artist. Rezhisser. Teatr, 2007.

———. "Nenuzhnaia pravda (po povodu Moskovskogo khudozhestvennogo teatra)." In *Sochineniia v dvukh tomakh*, edited by A. A. Kozlovskii, vol. 2, 56–67. Moscow: Khudozhestvennaia literatura, 1987.

Bushueva, S. K., ed. *Russkoe akterskoe iskusstvo XX veka*. Saint Petersburg: Rossiiskii institut istorii iskusstv, 1992.

Camp, Pannill. "The Stage Struck Out of the World: Theatricality and Husserl's Phenomenology of Theatre, 1905–1918." In Bleeker, Sherman, and Nedelkopoulou, *Performance and Phenomenology*, 20–34.

Caplan, Eric. *Mind Games: American Culture and the Birth of Psychotherapy*. Berkeley: University of California Press, 1998.

Carlson, Marvin. *Shattering Hamlet's Mirror: Theatre and Reality*. Ann Arbor: University of Michigan Press, 2016.

Carnicke, Sharon Marie. *Stanislavsky in Focus: An Acting Master for the Twenty-First Century*. 2nd ed. London: Routledge, 2009.

———. *The Theatrical Instinct: Nikolai Evreinov and the Russian Theatre of the Early Twentieth Century*. New York: Peter Lang, 1989.

Carriere, Patrick C. "Reading for the Soul in Stanislavski's *The Work of the Actor on Him/Herself*: Orthodox Mysticism, Mainstream Occultism, Psychology and the System in the Russian Silver Age." PhD diss., University of Kansas, 2010.

Chelpanov, G. I. "Problemy psikhologii khudozhestvennogo tvorchestva." In Plotnikov and Podzemskaia, *Iskusstvo kak iazyk*, vol. 2, 368–72.

———. "Rol' podsoznatel'nogo v protsesse tvorchestva." In Plotnikov and Podzemskaia, *Iskusstvo kak iazyk*, vol. 2, 363–64.

Chesterton, G. K. "Introduction to *The Man Who Was Thursday*, a Three-Act Play by Cecil Chesterton with Ralph Neale (1926)." In Gardner, *The Annotated Thursday*, 271–75.

Chushkin, N. N. *Gamlet-Kachalov: Iz stsenicheskoi istorii "Gamleta" Shekspira*. Moscow: Iskusstvo, 1966.

Clark, Katerina. *Moscow, the Fourth Rome: Stalinism, Cosmopolitanism, and the Evolution of Soviet Culture, 1931–1941*. Cambridge, MA: Harvard University Press, 2011.

Clark, Roger J. B. Introduction to Dumas, *La Dame aux Camélias*, 7–48.

Cole, Michael. Headnote to "Consciousness as a Problem in the Psychology of Behavior" by L. S. Vygotsky. *Soviet Psychology* 17, no. 4 (1979): 3–4.

Craig, Edward Gordon. "The Actor and the Über-Marionette." *Mask* 1, no. 2 (April 1908): 3–15. Blue Mountain Project. https://bluemountain.princeton.edu.

———. "Stanislavsky's System." In *Craig on Theatre*, edited by J. Michael Walton, 88–92. London: Methuen, 1983.

Daboo, Jerri. "Stanislavsky and the Psychophysical in Western Acting." In *Acting: Psychophysical Phenomenon and Process: Intercultural and Interdisciplinary Perspectives*, by Phillip B. Zarrilli, Jerri Daboo, and Rebecca Loukes, 158–93. Houndmills, UK: Palgrave Macmillan, 2013.

Davis, Susan, Hannah Grainger Clemson, Beth Ferholt, Satu-Mari Jansson, and Ana Marjanovic-Shane, eds. *Dramatic Interactions in Education: Vygotskian and Sociocultural Approaches to Drama, Education and Research*. London: Bloomsbury, 2015.

Dobkin, S. F. *L. S. Vygotskii: Nachalo puti; Vospominaniia S.F. Dobkina o L've Vygotskom; Rannie stat'i L.S. Vygotskogo*. Edited by I. M. Feigenberg. Jerusalem: Jerusalem Publishing Centre, 1996.

Dumas, Alexandre, fils. *La Dame aux Camélias*. London: Oxford University Press, 1972.

Dybovskii, V., ed. "V plenu predlagaemykh obstoiatel'stv." In *Minuvshee: Istoricheskii al'manakh*, edited by Vladimir Alloy, vol. 10, 243–329. Paris: Atheneum, 1990.

Dzhurova, Tat'iana [T. S.], ed. *Nikolai Evreinov: K 130-letiiu so dnia rozhdeniia (materialy nauchnoi konferentsii, sostoiavsheisia 16 fevralia 2009 goda)*. Saint Petersburg: Rossiiskii institut istorii iskusstv, 2012.

———. "'Salomeia' v Teatre na Ofitserskoi: Triumf formy." in Dzhurova, *Nikolai Evreinov*, 23–32.

Efros, A. M., ed. *Kamernyi teatr i ego khudozhniki, 1914–1934*. Moscow: Vserossiiskoe teatral'noe obshchestvo, 1934.

Ekzempliarskii, V. M. "Differentsial'no-psikhologicheskii podkhod k problemam estetiki." In Plotnikov and Podzemskaia, *Iskusstvo kak iazyk*, vol. 2, 373–78.

Emerson, Caryl. "The Actor's Task as Philosophical Quest in the Russian 1920s: Two Case Studies." In *Russian Performances: Word, Object, Action*, edited by Julie A. Buckler, Julie A. Cassiday, and Boris Wolfson, 227–34. Madison: University of Wisconsin Press, 2018.

———. "Tairov's Theater, Evreinov's Monodramatic Moment, and the Lessons of *Eugene Onegin*, a Drama in Verse." *Pushkin Review* 16–17 (2013–14): 1–23.

Etkind, Alexander. *Eros of the Impossible: The History of Psychoanalysis in Russia*. Translated by Noah Rubins and Maria Rubins. Boulder, CO: Westview Press, 1997.

Evreinov [Evreinoff], Nikolai [Nicholas, Nicholay] N. *Chto takoe teatr: Knizhka dlia detei*. Saint Petersburg: Svetozar, 1921.

———. *Demon teatral'nosti*. Edited by A. Zubkov and V. Maksimov. Moscow: Letnii sad, 2002.

———. "Introduction to Monodrama." In *Russian Dramatic Theory from Pushkin to the Symbolists: An Anthology*, edited and translated by Laurence Senelick, 183–99. Austin: University of Texas Press, 1981.

———. *Istoriia russkogo teatra: S drevneishikh vremen do 1917 goda*. New York: Chekhov, 1955.

———. *Original o portretistakh*. Edited by T. S. Dzhurova, A. Iu. Zubkov, and V. I. Maksimov. Moscow: Sovpadenie, 2005.

———. *Predstavlenie liubvi*. In Dzhurova, *Nikolai Evreinov*, 68–159.

———. *Theater as Life: Five Modern Plays*. Translated and edited by Christopher Collins. New York: Ardis, 2012.

———. *The Theatre in Life*. Edited and translated by Alexander I. Nazaroff. New York: Brentano's, 1927.

Evreinov, V. N. *"Moia zhizn'—teatr": Vospominaniia o Nikolae Evreinove*. Saint Petersburg: Zhurnal "Zvezda," 2018.

Féral, Josette. "Theatricality: The Specificity of Theatrical Language." Translated by Ronald P. Bermingham. *SubStance* 31, no. 2/3 (2002): 94–108.

Fortier, Mark. *Theory/Theatre: An Introduction*. London, Routledge, 1997.

Fuchs, Elinor. *The Death of Character: Perspectives on Theater after Modernism*. Bloomington: Indiana University Press, 1996.

Gardner, Martin, ed. *The Annotated Thursday*. By G. K. Chesterton. San Francisco: Ignatius Press, 1999.

———. Introduction to Gardner, *The Annotated Thursday*, 9–21.

Garner, Stanton B., Jr. *Bodied Spaces: Phenomenology and Performance in Contemporary Drama*. Ithaca, NY: Cornell University Press, 1994.

Gerould, Daniel. "Introduction: The Politics of Theatre Theory." In *Theatre/Theory/Theatre: The Major Critical Texts from Aristotle and Zeami to Soyinka and Havel*, edited by Daniel Gerould, 11–42. New York: Applause, 2000.

Gladkova, I. V. *Chelpanov G. I. glazami sovremennikov: Portret na fone epokhi*. Ekaterinburg: UGGU, 2013.

Goldman, Michael. *The Actor's Freedom: Toward a Theory of Drama*. New York: Viking Press, 1975.

Golub, Spencer. *Evreinov: The Theatre of Paradox and Transformation*. Ann Arbor, MI: UMI Research Press, 1984.

Gordon, Robert. *The Purpose of Playing: Modern Acting Theories in Perspective*. Ann Arbor: University of Michigan Press, 2006.

Gosudarstvennyi tsentral'nyi teatral'nyi muzei imeni A. A. Bakhrushina, Moscow. Kollektsii-online. https://collectiononline.gctm.ru.

Grainger Clemson, Hannah. "Stanislavski and Vygotsky: On the Problem of the Actor's and Learner's Work." In Davis et al., *Dramatic Interactions in Education*, 39–56.

Green, Michael, trans. and ed. *The Russian Symbolist Theatre: An Anthology of Plays and Critical Texts*. New York: Ardis, 2013.

Gudkova, V. V. *Teatral'naia sektsiia GAKhN: Istoriia idei i liudei, 1921–1930*. Moscow: Novoe literaturnoe obozrenie, 2019.

———. "Teatr kak iskusstvo v filosofskoi i teatrovedcheskoi refleksii GAKhN." In Plotnikov and Podzemskaia, *Iskusstvo kak iazyk*, vol. 1, 264–88.

Gurevich, Liubov' Ia. *Tvorchestvo aktera: O prirode khudozhestvennykh perezhivanii aktera na stsene*. 2nd ed. Moscow: Knizhnyi dom "Librokom," 2012.

Gvozdev, A. "*Dama s kameliiami* (K postanovke Vs. Meierkhol'da)." *Rabochii i teatr*, no. 13 (1934). Reprinted in *Meierkhol'd v russkoi teatral'noi kritike, 1920–1938*, edited by T. V. Lanina, 410–16. Moscow: Artist. Rezhisser. Teatr, 2000.

Harriman, Lucas H. "The Russian Betrayal of G. K. Chesterton's *The Man Who Was Thursday*." *Comparative Literature* 62, no. 1 (Winter 2010): 41–54.

Hickey, Wakoh Shannon. *Mind Cure: How Meditation Became Medicine*. New York: Oxford University Press, 2019.

Iakobson, Pavel M. "Aktery o svoem tvorchestve." In *Teatral'nyi al'manakh: Sbornik statei i materialov*, edited by M. S. Grigor'ev, vol. 7, 114–40. Moscow: Vserossiiskoe teatral'noe obshchestvo, 1948.

———. *Psikhologiia stsenicheskikh chuvstv aktera: Etiud po psikhologii tvorchestva*. Edited by V. Kolbanovskii. Moscow: Khudozhestvennaia literatura, 1936.

Iakovich, Elena. *Doch' filosofa Shpeta v fil'me Eleny Iakovich: Polnaia versiia vospominanii Mariny Gustavovny Shtorkh*. Moscow: ACT, 2014.

Iaroshevskii, M. G. "Kogda L.S. Vygotskii i ego shkola poiavilis' v psikhologii?" *Voprosy psikhologii*, no. 5 (1996): 110–21.

Ignatieva, Maria. *Stanislavsky and Female Actors: Women in Stanislavsky's Life and Art*. Lanham, MD: University Press of America, 2008.

Ivanov, Viacheslav. "The Need for a Dionysian Theatre." In Green, *The Russian Symbolist Theatre*, 113–20.

James, William. *The Varieties of Religious Experience: A Study in Human Nature*. Mineola, NY: Dover, 2002.

Jesterovic, Silvija. "Theatricality as Estrangement of Art and Life in the Russian Avant-Garde." *SubStance* 31, no. 2/3 (2002): 42–56.

Johnston, Daniel. "Stanislavskian Acting as Phenomenology in Practice." *Journal of Dramatic Theory and Criticism* 26, no. 1 (Fall 2011): 65–84.

———. *Theatre and Phenomenology: Manual Philosophy*. London: Palgrave, 2017.

Jones, Phil. *Drama as Therapy: Theory, Practice and Research*. 2nd ed. London: Routledge, 2007.

Joravsky, David. *Russian Psychology: A Critical History*. Oxford: Basil Blackwell, 1989.

Kachalov, V. I. "Anketa Gosudarstvennoi akademii khudozhestvennykh nauk po psikhologii akterskogo tvorchestva." In *Sbornik statei, vospominanii, pisem*, edited by V. Vilenkin, 637–48. Moscow: Iskusstvo, 1954.

Kashina-Evreinova, Anna. *N. N. Evreinov v mirovom teatre XX veka*. Paris: Les Editeurs Réunis, 1964.

Kazanskii, B. V. *Metod teatra: Analiz sistemy N. N. Evreinova*. Leningrad: Academia, 1925.

Kemp, Rick. *Embodied Acting: What Neuroscience Tells Us about Performance*. London: Routledge, 2012.

Khmel'nitskii, Iulii. *Iz zapisok aktera tairovskogo teatra*. Moscow: GITIS, 2004.

Knebel', Maria. *Active Analysis*. Edited by Anatoli Vassiliev. Translated by Irina Brown. London: Routledge, 2021.

Koonen, Alisa. "Anketa po psikhologii akterskogo tvorchestva." Edited by Nina Panfilova and Oleg Fel'dman. *Voprosy teatra*, 2014, 232–40.

———. *Stranitsy zhizni*. Moscow: Kukushka, 2003.

Koretzky, Maya. "Sensation(al) Science: Ivan Sechenov's *Reflexes of the Brain* and Revolutionary Physiology, Literature and Politics of the Russian 1860s." *Ezra's Archives* 3, no. 1 (Spring 2013): 75–91.

Kornilov, K. N., ed. *Psikhologiia i Marksizm*. Leningrad: Gosudarstvennoe izdatel'stvo, 1925.

———. "Psikhologiia i Marksizm Prof. Chelpanova." In Kornilov, *Psikhologiia i Marksizm*, 231–42.

Korzhevich, Liudmila Stepanovna. *Put' aktera: M. I. Tsarev*. Moscow: Vserossiiskoe teatral'noe obshchestvo, 1981.

Krzhizhanovskii [Krzhizhanovsky], Sigizmund D. *Chelovek, kotoryi byl Chetvergom po D. Chestertonu: Sketch v trekh deistviiakh i 13 situatsiiakh*. Krzhizhanovskii Sigizmund Dominikovich (1887–1950)—pisatel'. Papers. f. 2280, op. 1, ed. khr. 19. Russian State Archive of Literature and Art, Moscow.

———. *Eugene Onegin*. Translated by James E. Falen with Caryl Emerson. *Pushkin Review* 16–17 (2013–14): 36–179.

———. *The Letter Killers Club*. Translated by Joanne Turnbull. New York: New York Review Books, 2012.

———. *Sobranie sochinenii v shesti tomakh*. 6 vols. Edited by Vadim Perel'muter. Saint Petersburg: Symposium, 2001–13.

———. *That Third Guy: A Comedy from the Stalinist 1930s with Essays on Theater*. Translated and edited by Alisa Ballard Lin. Madison: University of Wisconsin Press, 2018.

Kugel', Aleksandr. *Utverzhdenie teatra*. Moscow: Teatr i iskusstvo, 1922.

Law, Alma, and Mel Gordon. *Meyerhold, Eisenstein and Biomechanics: Actor Training in Revolutionary Russia*. Jefferson, NC: McFarland, 1996.

Lawson, Robert B., Jean E. Graham, and Kristin M. Baker. *A History of Psychology: Globalization, Ideas, and Approaches*. Upper Saddle River, NJ: Pearson Prentice Hall, 2007.

Leach, Robert. *Makers of Modern Theatre: An Introduction*. London: Routledge, 2004.

———. *Revolutionary Theatre*. London: Routledge, 1994.

———. *Stanislavsky and Meyerhold*. Bern: Peter Lang, 2003.

———. *Vsevolod Meyerhold*. Cambridge: Cambridge University Press, 1989.

Lisakova, Iu. B. "Rol' traditsii Starinnogo teatra v sozdanii teatral'noi teorii N.N. Evreinova." *Vestnik Novogorodskogo gosudarstvennogo universiteta im. Iaroslava Mudrogo*, no. 27 (2004): 87–92.

Livak, Leonid. *In Search of Russian Modernism*. Baltimore, MD: Johns Hopkins University Press, 2018.

Maksimov, V. "Filosofiia teatra Nikolaia Evreinova." Introduction to Evreinov, *Demon teatral'nosti*, 5–28.

Malikova, Mariia. "'Sketch po koshmaru Chestertona' i kul'turnaia situatsiia nepa." *Novoe literaturnoe obozrenie*, no. 78 (2006): 32–59.

Matern, Frederick. "Stanislavski, Shpet, and the Art of Lived Experience." *Stanislavski Studies* 2, no. 1 (2013): 44–63.

McCaw, Dick. *Rethinking the Actor's Body: Dialogues with Neuroscience*. London: Methuen Drama, 2020.

McConachie, Bruce. *Evolution, Cognition, and Performance*. Cambridge: Cambridge University Press, 2015.

———. *Theatre & Mind*. Houndmills, UK: Palgrave Macmillan, 2013.

McReynolds, Louise. *Russia at Play: Leisure Activities at the End of the Tsarist Era*. Ithaca, NY: Cornell University Press, 2002.

Meierkhol'd [Meyerhold], Vsevolod E. *Meyerhold on Theatre*. Translated and edited by Edward Braun. Rev. ed. London: Methuen Drama, 1998.

———. "On Ideology and Technology in the Theater." Lecture, December 1933. In *The Soviet Theater: A Documentary History*, edited by Laurence Senelick and Sergei Ostrovsky, 396–97. New Haven, CT: Yale University Press, 2014.

———. *Stat'i, pis'ma, rechi, besedy*. Edited by A. V. Fevral'skii and B. I. Rostotskii. 2 vols. Moscow: Iskusstvo, 1968.

Merlin, Bella. "'Here, Today, Now': Active Analysis for the Twenty-First-Century Actor." In White, *The Routledge Companion to Stanislavsky*, 325–40.

Michell, Michael. "Dramatic Interactions: From Vygotsky's Life of Drama to the Drama of Life." In Davis et al., *Dramatic Interactions in Education*, 19–37.

Mitiushin, A. A. Commentary to "Theater as Art" by Gustav Shpet. *Soviet Studies in Philosophy* 28, no. 3 (Winter 1989–90): 89–91.

Mok, Nelson. "On the Concept of Perezhivanie: A Quest for a Critical Review." In *Perezhivanie, Emotions and Subjectivity: Advancing Vygotsky's Legacy*, edited by Marilyn Fleer, Fernando González Rey, and Nikolai Veresov, 19–45. Singapore: Springer, 2017.

Moskovskii gosudarstvennyi Kamernyi teatr (1914–50). Papers. f. 2030, op. 1. Russian State Archive of Literature and Art, Moscow.

Mulford, Prentice. "The Doctor Within." In *The White Cross Library: Your Forces, and How to Use Them*, by Prentice Mulford, vol. 2, 1–11. 1888. New York: F. J. Needham, 1910.

Olenina, Ana Hedberg. *Psychomotor Aesthetics: Movement and Affect in Modern Literature and Film*. New York: Oxford University Press, 2020.

Perel'muter, Vadim. "'Akter kak raznovidnost' cheloveka': Popytka rekonstruktsii doklada Sigizmunda Krzhizhanovskogo, prochitannogo na zasedanii Teatral'noi sektsii GAKhN 20 dekabria 1923 goda (po materialam arkhiva S.D. Krzhizhanovskogo)." *Voprosy iskusstvoznaniia* 11, no. 2 (1997): 69–74.

Pesochinskii, N. V. "Akter v teatre Meierkhol'da." In Bushueva, *Russkoe akterskoe iskusstvo XX veka*, 63–152.

Petrov, Valerii V. "Platon i ego uchenie u Sigizmunda Krzhizhanovskogo." *Logos* 90, no. 6 (2012): 58–84.

Petzold, Hilarion G. *Gestalttherapie und Psychodrama*. Kassel, West Germany: Nicol, 1973.

Pitches, Jonathan. *Science and the Stanislavsky Tradition of Acting*. London: Routledge, 2006.

———. "Tracing/Training Rebellion: Object Work in Meyerhold's Biomechanics." *Performance Research* 12, no. 4 (2007): 97–103.

———. *Vsevolod Meyerhold*. London: Routledge, 2018.

Plotnikov, N. S., and N. P. Podzemskaia, with Iu. N. Iakimenko, eds. *Iskusstvo kak iazyk—iazyki iskusstva: Gosudarstvennaia akademiia khudozhestvennykh nauk i esteticheskaia teoriia 1920-kh godov*. 2 vols. Moscow: Novoe literaturnoe obozrenie, 2017.

Poole, Randall A. "Gustav Shpet: Russian Philosopher of the Human Level of Being." *Kritika: Explorations in Russian and Eurasian History* 14, no. 2 (Spring 2013): 395–410.

Posner, Dassia N. "The Commedia Dell'arte Origins of Biomechanics." In *The Routledge Companion to Vsevolod Meyerhold*, edited by Jonathan Pitches and Stefan Aquilina, 211–50. London: Routledge, 2023.

———. *The Director's Prism: E. T. A. Hoffmann and the Russian Theatrical Avant-Garde*. Evanston, IL: Northwestern University Press, 2016.

———. "Life-Death and Disobedient Obedience: Russian Modernist Redefinitions of the Puppet." In *The Routledge Companion to Puppetry and Material Performance*, edited by Dassia N. Posner, Claudia Orenstein, and John Bell, 130–43. London: Routledge, 2014.

———. "Performance as Polemic: Tairov's 1920 *Princess Brambilla* at the Moscow Kamerny Theatre." *Theatre Survey* 51, no. 1 (May 2010): 33–64.

Postlewait, Thomas, and Tracy C. Davis. "Theatricality: An Introduction." In *Theatricality*, edited by Tracy C. Davis and Thomas Postlewait, 1–39. Cambridge: Cambridge University Press, 2003.

Puchner, Martin. *Stage Fright: Modernism, Anti-Theatricality, and Drama*. Baltimore, MD: Johns Hopkins University Press, 2002.

Rayner, Alice. *To Act, to Do, to Perform: Drama and the Phenomenology of Action*. Ann Arbor: University of Michigan Press, 1994.

Roach, Joseph R. *The Player's Passion: Studies in the Science of Acting*. Ann Arbor: University of Michigan Press, 1993.

Rosenflanz, Karen Link. *Hunter of Themes: The Interplay of Word and Thing in the Works of Sigizmund Kržižanovskij*. New York: Peter Lang, 2005.

Rudnitsky, Konstantin. *Russian and Soviet Theatre: Tradition and the Avant-Garde*. Translated by Roxane Permar. Edited by Lesley Milne. London: Thames and Hudson, 1988.

Russell, Robert. "Red Pinkertonism: An Aspect of Soviet Literature of the 1920s." *Slavonic and East European Review* 60, no. 3 (July 1982): 390–412.

Rzhevsky, Nicholas. *The Modern Russian Theater: A Literary and Cultural History*. Armonk, NY: M. E. Sharpe, 2009.

Sayler, Oliver M. *The Russian Theatre*. Rev. ed. New York: Brentano's, 1922.

Sboeva, Svetlana. "Akter v teatre A. Ia. Tairova." In Bushueva, *Russkoe akterskoe iskusstvo XX veka*, 153–256.

———. "Moskovskii Kamernyi teatr: *Chelovek kotoryi byl Chetvergom* v nemetskoi i avstriiskoi kritike." In *Mnemozina: Dokumenty i fakty iz istorii otechestvennogo teatra XX veka*, edited by V. V. Ivanov, vol. 5, 176–240. Moscow: Indrik, 2014.

Schechner, Richard. *Performance Studies: An Introduction*. 3rd ed. New York: Routledge, 2013.

Schuler, Catherine. *Women in Russian Theatre: The Actress in the Silver Age*. London: Routledge, 1996.

Sechenov, Ivan. *Reflexes of the Brain*. Translated by S. Belsky. Edited by G. Gibbons. Cambridge: MIT Press, 1965.

Segel, Harold B. *Pinocchio's Progeny: Puppets, Marionettes, Automatons, and Robots in Modernist and Avant-Garde Drama*. Baltimore, MD: Johns Hopkins University Press, 1995.

Senelick, Laurence, ed. and trans. *The Crooked Mirror: Plays from a Modernist Russian Cabaret*. Evanston, IL: Northwestern University Press, 2023.

———. *Gordon Craig's Moscow "Hamlet": A Reconstruction*. Westport, CT: Greenwood Press, 1982.

———, trans. and ed. *Stanislavsky: A Life in Letters*. London: Routledge, 2014.

Serebrennikov, N. V., ed. *Shpet v Sibiri: Ssylka i gibel'*. Tomsk: Vodolei, 1995.

Shakespeare, William. *Hamlet*. In *The Norton Shakespeare*, edited by Stephen Greenblatt, Walter Cohen, Jean E. Howard, and Katherine Eisaman Maus, 1668–756. New York: Norton, 1997.

Shchedrina, T. G. *"Ia pishu kak ekho drugogo . . .": Ocherki intellektual'noi biografii Gustava Shpeta*. Moscow: Progress-Traditsiia, 2004.

Shchedrovitskii, L. P. "L.S. Vygotsky's 'Tragedy of Hamlet Prince of Denmark.' " *Journal of Russian and East European Psychology* 32, no. 2 (1994): 49–65.

Shcherbakov, Vadim. "Meyerhold and the Russian Commedia Dell'arte Myth." Translated by Dassia N. Posner and Kevin Bartig. In *Three Loves for Three Oranges: Gozzi, Meyerhold, Prokofiev*, edited by Dassia N. Posner and Kevin Bartig with Maria De Simone, 207–34. Bloomington: Indiana University Press, 2021.

Shevelenko, Irina. "A Centennial Perspective on Modernist Studies." Introduction to *Reframing Russian Modernism*, edited by Irina Shevelenko, 3–19. Madison: University of Wisconsin Press, 2018.

Shevtsova, Maria. *Rediscovering Stanislavsky*. Cambridge: Cambridge University Press, 2020.

Shpet, Gustav, trans. "*Dama s kameliiami*. Kopiia pervogo rabochego rezhisserskogo ekzempliara Z. N. Raikh i M. M. Koreneva. Perevody G. G. Shpeta." f. 963, op. 1, ed. khr. 1058. Russian State Archive of Literature and Art, Moscow.

———. *Iskusstvo kak vid znaniia: Izbrannye trudy po filosofii kul'tury*. Edited by Tat'iana Shchedrina. Moscow: ROSSPEN, 2007.

———. "Theater as Art." *Soviet Studies in Philosophy* 28, no. 3 (Winter 1989–90): 61–88.

Sirotkina, Irina. *Diagnosing Literary Genius: A Cultural History of Psychiatry in Russia, 1880–1930*. Baltimore, MD: Johns Hopkins University Press, 2002.

Sirotkina, Irina, and Roger Smith. *The Sixth Sense of the Avant-Garde: Dance, Kinaesthesia, and the Arts in Revolutionary Russia*. London: Methuen Drama, 2017.

Sitkovetskaia, M. M., ed. *Meierkhol'd repetiruet*. Vol. 2, *Spektakli 30-kh godov*. Moscow: Artist. Rezhisser. Teatr, 1993.

Skinner, Amy, ed. *Russian Theatre in Practice: The Director's Guide*. London: Methuen Drama, 2019.

Smagorinsky, Peter. "Vygotsky's Stage Theory: The Psychology of Art and the Actor under the Direction of *Perezhivanie*." *Mind, Culture, and Activity* 18, no. 4 (2011): 319–41.

Smith, Matthew Wilson. *The Nervous Stage: Nineteenth-Century Neuroscience and the Birth of Modern Theater*. New York: Oxford University Press, 2018.

Sobkin, V. S. "L. S. Vygotskii i teatr: Abris sotsiokul'turnogo konteksta." Introduction to Vygotskii, *Polnoe sobranie sochinenii*, vol. 1, 10–75.

Sobkin, V. S., and V. S. Mazanova. "Opyt kommentariev k odnoi teatral'noi retsenzii L.S. Vygotskogo." *Natsional'nyi psikhologicheskii zhurnal* 1, no. 13 (2014): 35–46.

Sologub, Fyodor. "The Theatre of the Single Will." In Green, *The Russian Symbolist Theatre*, 147–62.

Spektor, Alexander. "A Timely Discovery: Experimental Realism of Sigizmund Krzhizhanovsky." Review article. *Slavic and East European Journal* 59, no. 1 (Spring 2015): 110–15.

Stanislavskii, Konstantin. *Sobranie sochinenii v deviati tomakh*. 9 vols. Edited by O. N. Efremov. Moscow: Iskusstvo, 1988–89.

States, Bert O. *Great Reckonings in Little Rooms: On the Phenomenology of Theater*. Berkeley: University of California Press, 1985.

———. "The Phenomenological Attitude." In *Critical Theory and Performance*, edited by Janelle G. Reinelt and Joseph R. Roach, rev. and enlarged ed., 26–36. Ann Arbor: University of Michigan Press, 2010.

Stone, Jonathan. *The Institutions of Russian Modernism: Conceptualizing, Publishing, and Reading Symbolism*. Evanston, IL: Northwestern University Press, 2017.

Strutinskaia, Elena. "Legenda o 'Salomee.'" *Russkoe iskusstvo*, no. 1 (2004): 140–49.

Sulerzhitskii, L. A. "Kreg-postanovshchik 'Gamleta' v Khudozhestvennom teatre. Iz besedy s L. A. Sulerzhitskim." f. 860, op. 1, ed. khr. 165. Russian State Archive of Literature and Art, Moscow.

———. "Z besedy Krega so Stanislavskim (apr. 1909 g.), zapissannykh L. A. Sulerzhitskim." f. 970, op. 13, ed. khr. 1877. Russian State Archive of Literature and Art, Moscow.

Tairov, Aleksandr [Alexander, A.] Ia. "Fokusnichestvo v nauke teatral'nogo iskusstva." *Masterstvo teatra: Vremennik Kamernogo teatra*, no. 1 (December 1922): 25–30. Sankt-Peterburgskaia gosudarstvennaia teatral'naia biblioteka. https://sptl.spb.ru.

———. *Notes of a Director*. Translated by William Kuhlke. Coral Gables, FL: University of Miami Press, 1969.

———. *O teatre*. 2nd ed. Moscow: Akademicheskii proekt, 2018.

Taxidou, Olga. *Modernism and Performance: Jarry to Brecht*. Houndmills, UK: Palgrave Macmillan, 2007.

Tihanov, Galin. *The Birth and Death of Literary Theory: Regimes of Relevance in Russia and Beyond*. Stanford, CA: Stanford University Press, 2019.

———, ed. *Gustav Shpet's Contribution to Philosophy and Cultural Theory*. West Lafayette, IN: Purdue University Press, 2009.

———. "Gustav Shpet's Literary and Theater Affiliations." In Tihanov, *Gustav Shpet's Contribution to Philosophy and Cultural Theory*, 56–80.

Tikhvinskaia, L. *Kabare i teatry miniatiur v Rossii, 1908–1917*. Moscow: RIK "Kul'tura," 1995.

Toropova, Anna. *Feeling Revolution: Cinema, Genre, and the Politics of Affect under Stalin*. New York: Oxford University Press, 2020.

Vaingurt, Julia. *Wonderlands of the Avant-Garde: Technology and the Arts in Russia of the 1920s*. Evanston, IL: Northwestern University Press, 2013.

Volkonskii, S. M. *Chelovek na stsene*. 5th ed. Saint Petersburg: Lan' / Planeta muziki, 2019.

Vygotskii [Vygotsky], Lev S. [Semenovich]. "Consciousness as a Problem in the Psychology of Behavior." Edited by Michael Cole. Translated by Michel Vale. *Soviet Psychology* 17, no. 4 (1979): 5–35.

———. *Lektsii po pedologii*. Izhevsk, Russia: Udmurtskii universitet, 2001.

———. "On the Problem of the Psychology of the Actor's Creative Work." In *The Collected Works of L. S. Vygotsky*, vol. 6, *Scientific Legacy*, translated by Marie J. Hall, 237–44. New York: Kluwer Academic, 1987.

———. *Polnoe sobranie sochinenii*. Vol. 1, *Dramaturgiia i teatr*. Edited by V. S. Sobkin. Moscow: Lev', 2015.

———. "Soznanie kak problema psikhologii povedeniia." In Kornilov, *Psikhologiia i Marksizm*, 175–98.

Wachtel, Michael. *Russian Symbolism and Literary Tradition: Goethe, Novalis, and the Poetics of Vyacheslav Ivanov*. Madison: University of Wisconsin Press, 1994.

Walsh, Fintan. *Theatre & Therapy*. New York: Palgrave Macmillan, 2013.

White, R. Andrew, ed. *The Routledge Companion to Stanislavsky*. London: Routledge, 2014.

Whyman, Rose. *The Stanislavsky System of Acting: Legacy and Influence in Modern Performance*. Cambridge: Cambridge University Press, 2008.

Wilshire, Bruce. *Role Playing and Identity: The Limits of Theatre as Metaphor*. Bloomington: Indiana University Press, 1982.

Worrall, Nick. *Modernism to Realism on the Soviet Stage: Tairov, Vakhtangov, Okhlopkov*. Cambridge: Cambridge University Press, 1989.

Worthen, W. B. "Of Actors and Automata: Hieroglyphics of Modernism." *Journal of Dramatic Theory and Criticism* 9, no. 1 (Fall 1994): 3–19.

Zarrilli, Phillip B. *(Toward) a Phenomenology of Acting*. London: Routledge, 2020.

Zasse, Sil'viia. "'Mnimyi zdorovyi': Teatroterapiia Nikolaia Evreinova v kontekste teatral'noi estetiki vozdeistviia." Translated by Elena Novak. In *Russkaia literatura i meditsina: Telo, predpisaniia, sotsial'naia praktika; Sbornik statei*, edited by K. A. Bogdanov, Iurii Murashov, and Rikkardo Nikolozi, 209–19. Moscow: Novoe izdatel'stvo, 2006.

Zavershneva, Ekaterina. "Vygotsky the Unpublished: An Overview of the Personal Archive (1912–1934)." In *Revisionist Revolution in Vygotsky Studies*, edited by Anton Yasnitsky and René van der Veer, 94–126. London: Routledge, 2016.

Zinchenko, Vladimir. "Thought and Word: The Approaches of L. S. Vygotsky and G. G. Shpet." In *The Cambridge Companion to Vygotsky*, edited by Harry Daniels, Michael Cole, and James V. Wertsch, 212–45. Cambridge: Cambridge University Press, 2007.

Zinchenko, Vladimir, and James V. Wertsch. "Gustav Shpet's Influence on Psychology." In Tihanov, *Gustav Shpet's Contribution to Philosophy and Cultural Theory*, 45–55.

INDEX

Page locators in *italics* indicate illustrations.